CHEROKEE STORIES OF THE TURTLE ISLAND LIARS' CLUB

CHEROKEE STORIES OF THE TURTLE ISLAND LIARS' CLUB

Dakasi Elohi Anigagoga Junilawisdii
(Turtle, Earth, the Liars, Meeting Place)

Written by Christopher B. Teuton
Noya Uwowelanv

Told by Hastings Shade, Sammy Still,
Sequoyah Guess, and Woody Hansen
*Ulasgvhi, Siquotsi, Sigwoya, ale
Digowelisgi Uninohetlanv*

Illustrations by America Meredith

THE UNIVERSITY OF NORTH CAROLINA PRESS
CHAPEL HILL

© 2012 Christopher B. Teuton
Illustrations © 2012 America Meredith
All rights reserved
Manufactured in the United States of America
Designed by Kimberly Bryant and set in Miller and
Aller types by Tseng Information Systems, Inc.

The paper in this book meets the guidelines for permanence
and durability of the Committee on Production Guidelines
for Book Longevity of the Council on Library Resources. The
University of North Carolina Press has been a member of the
Green Press Initiative since 2003.

Library of Congress Cataloging-in-Publication Data
Teuton, Christopher B.
Cherokee stories of the Turtle Island liars' club : Dakasi
elohi anigagoga junilawisdii (turtle, earth, the liars, meeting
place) / written by Christopher B. Teuton (Noya Uwowelanv) ;
told by Hastings Shade, Sammy Still, Sequoyah Guess, and
Woody Hansen (Ulasgvhi, Siquotsi, Sigwoya, ale Digowelisgi
Uninohetlanv) ; illustrations by America Meredith.
p. cm.
Includes bibliographical references.
ISBN 978-0-8078-3584-5 (cloth : alk. paper) 1. Cherokee
Indians—Folklore. 2. Tales—Oklahoma. 3. Oral tradition—
Oklahoma. I. Title.
E99.C5T35 2012
398.209766—dc23   2012014163

16 15 14 13 12   5 4 3 2 1

for Hastings Shade
(1941–2010)

Contents

Note on Pronunciation of Cherokee ix

Introduction: Opening the Door 1

Sagwu (One): *Alenihv* (Beginnings) 17

Tali (Two): *Adanvsgvi* (Movements) 81

Joi (Three): *Dideyohvsdi* (Teachings) 133

Nvgi (Four): *Ulvsgedi* (The Wondrous) 203

Afterword: Standing in the Middle 249

Acknowledgments 251

Works Cited 253

Note on Pronunciation of Cherokee

A is not A as in day but A as in father.

E is not E as in Easter but E as in feather.

I is not I as in idea but I as in police.

O is the exception to the rule. However, it has a throaty tone.

U is not U as in unit but U as in butte.

The V is sounded as uh.

Cherokee Heritage Center Memorial Chapel, Park Hill, Oklahoma: "Dedicated to the Memory of All Those Cherokees Who Failed to Complete Their Journey over the 'Trail Where They Cried,' 1838–39." Erected in 1976, the chapel is a memorial bequest by Jimalee "Ho Chee Nee" Burton, 1913–77.

Introduction

Opening the Door

On a chilly autumn evening we gather at the Cherokee Heritage Center in Park Hill, just outside of Tahlequah in northeastern Oklahoma. I am meeting with Hastings Shade, Sammy Still, Sequoyah Guess, and Woody Hansen, a group of Cherokee storytellers who call themselves the Turtle Island Liars' Club. The Turtle Island Liars' Club is an institution—its members have performed together for nearly twenty years and are known throughout Cherokee country and nationally for their mastery of Cherokee oral performance and traditional teachings. The club and I are collaborating on the first collection of Western Cherokee storytelling published in over forty years. The core of the book is the stories themselves, traditional and contemporary Cherokee narratives rarely if ever seen in print. Not simply a compilation, *Cherokee Stories of the Turtle Island Liars' Club* represents an evolving conversation with the Liars' Club concerning their understanding of Cherokee storytelling, or *gagoga* (literally "he/she is lying"; pronounced gah-gōh-gá), as it is known in the Cherokee language. It explores how the members of the club conceive the power and purposes of Cherokee storytelling and how stories articulate Cherokee tradition, the "teachings" that, say the storytellers, are fundamental to a construction of Cherokee selfhood and cultural belonging.

Cherokee Stories of the Turtle Island Liars' Club presents the stories and teachings of the four core members of the Liars' Club. Before his passing in February 2010, Hastings Shade was the senior elder of the group. The former deputy chief of the Cherokee Nation, Shade was an honored elder, cultural traditionalist, and storyteller who brought the Liars' Club together and led it with his knowledge and wisdom. In 1991, Chief Wilma Mankiller of the Cherokee Nation declared Shade a Cherokee National Treasure for his traditional knowledge. Sammy Still is a well-known traditional craftsman, noted photographer, and journalist. He is a citizen of the United Keetoowah Band of Cherokee Indians and is editor of the *Keetoowah News* tribal newspaper. Sequoyah Guess, also a member of the United Keetoowah Band, is a renowned storyteller, novelist, filmmaker, and Cherokee language teacher. Like Shade and Still, he speaks, reads, and writes Cherokee. In 2002 and 2005 Guess was nominated as a Living Treasure by the Cherokee Heritage Museum and the Cherokee Nation. Woody Hansen has worked for many years as a community health and wellness advocate for the Cherokee Nation, of which he is a citizen. Hansen is a sought-after storyteller, snake handler, and reptile-safety educator.

I am both a citizen of the Cherokee Nation and a Native American literary and cultural studies scholar. Over the past several years I have worked with the Cherokee Nation on research projects, including a study of Cherokee Nation reading practices and the development of a Cherokee K-12 education curriculum for use in northeastern Oklahoma public schools. For me, *Cherokee Stories of the Turtle Island Liars' Club* represents a coming together of the concerns of my published work as a scholar and my personal journey home to learn from my elders.

The Turtle Island Liars' Club has no by-laws, constitution, or organizational leadership. No badges. No certificates. You cannot send away to become a member. In fact, their use of the word "club" to describe themselves is a fine example of Cherokee dry humor—razor sharp and subtle, a way for this group of a dozen or so Cherokee traditionalists, storytellers, and craftspeople, kin and friends alike, to thumb their noses at a mainstream society that has to bureaucratize in order to create community. At the same time, there is something sincere in the use of "club" as it reflects a need to actively engage like-minded folks interested in furthering Cherokee community, celebrating traditional culture and passing it along to future generations.

A better term for the Turtle Island Liars' Club would be a *sgadug*. As Hastings Shade explained to me, "*Sgadug* is a county, state, or community. That's what that means. *Sgadug* is when they—*sgadudv duhdatlesuh*—that's when the whole, as a community, come together." It is a traditional practice of Cherokee community to come together to help one another and especially those in need. In Shade's words, "Our teachings have always been, if you see somebody that needs something, help 'em." Like any *sgadug*, the Liars' Club has its own ideas of membership and belonging, but at first I did not understand that.

Initially I thought the club revolved around its stories and teachings; I did not see it was really about people. But during my years of recording and learning the stories I was taught that the Turtle Island Liars' Club, as a *sgadug*, depends on relationships: those between families, between generations, between friends, and between Cherokee communities and other cultures. The stories, teachings, and crafts are a means of keeping the *sgadug* strong and of sharing Cherokee culture with others in the hope that the knowledge will continue. Hastings Shade explained that a core Cherokee value that the Liars' Club embraces is the idea of sharing knowledge, and Sequoyah Guess agreed: "It's not about us, the storytellers. It's about everybody else. We're here to share what we've got." The club in its deepest sense includes listeners as well as speakers, younger folks as well as elders, traditional craftspeople alongside traditional storytellers. This book focuses on four male storytellers, but club members are quick to point out the crucial and continuing influence of female elders, storytellers, and members of the Liars' Club. All members have something to teach and something to learn; this is the Cherokee way.

Across Cherokee country there are traditionalists who share stories, crafts, and teachings within their families and communities; the four members of the Liars' Club represented in this book are no different and make no pretense to being better or more authoritative than others. Within the fourteen-county Cherokee territory of northeastern Oklahoma there are dozens of small towns, each with its unique history, character, and families. Each town has its elders and traditionalists, and some share their stories and teachings with those beyond their families. Shade, Still, Guess, and Hansen have visited Cherokee communities all over Cherokee country and the places where Cherokee people have settled, from North Carolina and Tennessee to Texas, New Mexico, and California. They have shared their stories and knowledge. And in return, they have listened to others and learned their stories and teachings.

Sharing knowledge is a part of Cherokee traditional culture, but that does not mean that all Cherokee knowledge is open to all Cherokee people, much less the general public. Sacred knowledge—of spiritual matters, family matters, and knowledge of medicine, among other kinds—are only shared with those who need to know these things. Many Cherokees do not want to share their knowledge with those outside their families and communities. The Liars' Club (hereafter referring to Shade, Still, Guess, and Hansen, unless otherwise stated) embraces the process of sharing Cherokee culture, but they are also respectful of Cherokee cultural boundaries. In order to honor both traditions they have come up with a novel solution: when they tell stories publicly, they change them slightly, often through omission, leaving out certain parts that should only be shared with particular Cherokee audiences. The stories you will read in this book are appropriate to share and have been told publicly for many years. Many of them, however, are written down here for the first time. There is some anxiety about writing stories down because in written form they may take on an air of authority. But Cherokee oral tradition is fluid; "loose" is how Sequoyah Guess describes it. The stories may change slightly, but the nucleus of their message remains. The stories shared in this book change a little bit with each storyteller, each telling. By the time you have read them here, they have already changed; they are living things.

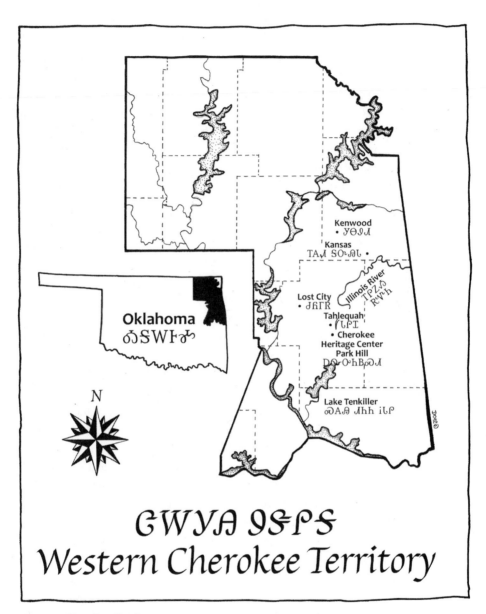

Kenwood
• ᏴᎾᎥᎯ

Kansas
ᎢᎠᎯ ᏍᎣ·ᎠᏞ •

Lost City
• ᏚᏟᎡᎡ

Illinois River
ᎢᏢᏃᎭᏦ
ᎡᏫᏂ

Tahlequah
• ᏆᏞᏆ

• Cherokee
Heritage Center
Park Hill
ᎠᎾ ᎤᏂᎻᏮᎦᎯ

Lake Tenkiller
ᎣᎠᎮ ᏞᎻᎻ ᎢᏞᎮ

Oklahoma
ᎤᏍᏬᎻᎻᏋ

N

ᏣᏪᏯᎮ ᎩᏍᏢᎬ
Western Cherokee Territory

Western Cherokee Territory

The members of the Turtle Island Liars' Club have been telling stories together since the early 1990s, but, like the teachings and stories, their histories go back much further. Hastings Shade and Sequoyah Guess were cousins and knew each other their whole lives. Shade, Guess, and Woody Hansen knew each other for decades. In 1993, when all four worked for the Cherokee Nation developing language and culture programs, they began to work together giving presentations to visiting college students. Shade would present on history and government. Sammy Still would present on crafts. Guess would tell stories. And Hansen would speak about snakes and the natural world. They gave presentations at the Cherokee Heritage Center, in local schools, and out of state and began meeting informally but regularly to tell stories as the Liars' Club.

The Liars' Club and I gathered at several locations in Cherokee country. We recorded stories along the banks of Spring Creek near Kenwood, under the roof of Hastings Shade's open workshop at his home in Lost City, in motel rooms in Tahlequah, and while driving the back roads of northeastern Oklahoma. But more often than not we met at the chapel on the Cherokee Heritage Center grounds in Park Hill, Oklahoma. The Heritage Center was a central location for us, and the chapel provided a natural setting to record Cherokee traditional stories and teachings. Densely covered with venerable oaks, pecans, sycamores, and bois d'arc, the Heritage Center grounds were once the site of the Cherokee Female Seminary, a place of great meaning to Cherokees. Destroyed by fire in 1887, the Female Seminary was one of the first institutions of higher education west of the Mississippi. All that is left of the building are the majestic columns that stood at its entrance. But since the construction of the Cherokee Heritage Center in the late 1960s, the spirit of Cherokee education and cultural perpetuation has carried forward at this site of knowledge sharing. For decades now, visitors have come to the Heritage Center to learn about the Cherokee. Each year, the Cherokee Nation holds our National Holiday on the Heritage Center grounds. Cherokees from all over the world gather and celebrate Cherokee history, culture, and art. During the holiday we rekindle our ability to adapt and grow while remaining a unique people.

Tonight, we make our way inside the small, circular, stone chapel. There are no pews, no altar. We sit in plastic chairs around plastic tables on the plush, red carpet. I press record on my digital recorder, and, as on other nights together, the Liars' Club members begin to talk, laugh, and share stories with me and with one another, allowing the stories and their commentary to elucidate the meaning of "lying." What it means to be a *gagoga*, a storyteller, is a topic to which the members of the club frequently return. There is no exact word for "storyteller" in the Cherokee language; the term *gagoga* arises out of a tradition of punning and wordplay within Cherokee. What first may appear as a derogatory name for bearers of tribal oral tradition has its roots in the grammar of the Cherokee language. Cherokee puns allow for a sometimes necessary slippage of meaning in language, and the club relishes the rich irony of speaking "lies" and being called "liars," knowing full well that stories are the foundation of Cherokee culture.

Whether of ancient origin or recent occurrence, the stories and narratives in *Cherokee Stories of the Turtle Island Liars' Club* are traditional, though not in the static, unchanging sense that word might imply. They are traditional because they are told by storytellers who were raised within a Cherokee storytelling tradition and have come to see themselves and be accepted by the Cherokee community as storytellers. They were taught stories by their grandparents, relatives, friends, and other elders, and they have learned how to tell these stories and their own through living in Cherokee community. Cherokee storytelling has its own aesthetic, with, for example, repeating patterns of formal and thematic elements. But neither Cherokee storytelling nor culture is monolithic, and so the Liars' Club and I represent the diversity of Cherokee perspectives through story, a diversity that reflects generational, educational, familial, and spiritual differences among the storytellers. *Cherokee Stories of the Turtle Island Liars' Club* presents traditional stories in multiple and varied formats: myths, legends, animal stories, family stories, and those about beliefs, medicine, and the spirit world. Many of these stories and teachings trace back to ancient times, such as the story of the Cherokee migration and the origin of fire. Other stories vary in age and make up the fabric of contemporary Cherokee folklore in the Cherokee territory of northeastern Oklahoma. Much of the conversation in *Cherokee Stories* provides oral history and personal-experience narratives. These narratives of the life and times of the members of the Liars' Club are told with an audience in mind and, as such, differ in form and content from everyday conversation; they are remembrances shared for the purpose of education.

As an open-ended term for a culturally central Cherokee art, "lying" has multiple meanings that change with particular cultural contexts. Among Cherokees, telling "lies" refers to storytelling generally, but in particular to telling stories that stretch the imagination and belief. As Hastings Shade says, when people hear the stories of a *gagoga* they often say, "That can't be true." Stories of the ancient time when animals could talk and when monsters roamed the earth may be believed by Cherokee listeners, but their veracity depends upon an element of faith in the teachings of the elders, which ultimately must be validated through personal experience. Whether stories are truth or lies, Shade points out, depends upon how they are interpreted and what they come to mean to the listener. The most venerable form of "lying" is sharing stories of the elders of the past, tribal myths and legends. But in addition to the sharing of traditional stories, lying invokes a Cherokee cultural process of interpreting contemporary experience in relation to the cultural truths traditional stories express. Sharing contemporary "lies" and talking about them is an integrative process. These stories are told in relation to the context of traditional tales and knowledge, and the connections and disconnections found between the teachings of oral traditional stories and contemporary stories are a deep source of wisdom, humor, and irony. In constantly relating contemporary stories and experiences to the teachings of oral tradition, the Liars' Club reasserts the continuing power of stories as a source of cultural tradition and critical knowledge.

The purpose of *Cherokee Stories of the Turtle Island Liars' Club* is to spread this power by sharing Cherokee stories of the past and present with interested readers, both non-Cherokee and Cherokee living in their homelands or in the far-ranging Cherokee diaspora. As a product of that diaspora, I did not spend my early years within northeastern Oklahoma hearing *gagoga* stories from a community of elders. Although I grew up with the stories of my grandmother and grandfather, whom I lived with, I did not experience storytelling within a broad Cherokee communal context. But mine is not an atypical experience. Of the more than 300,000 citizens of the Cherokee Nation, the largest Native American nation by population, only 110,000 live within the state of Oklahoma. Fewer live within the territorial boundaries of the Cherokee Nation, which are comprised of the fourteen counties of northeastern Oklahoma. As a young man, I went home to the Cherokee Nation, where my mother's family has resided near Honey Creek in Delaware County since the time we were forcibly removed from our Appalachian homelands during the 1838–39 Trail of Tears. Like many Cherokees, I now return to the Cherokee Nation several times a year for extended visits with kin and friends, to attend events at my ceremonial grounds, and to reconnect with Cherokee community.

The Liars' Club and I came to an understanding of how to write this book and what we hoped it would accomplish. *Cherokee Stories of the Turtle Island Liars' Club* documents and perpetuates contemporary Cherokee oral traditional stories and practices, presents Cherokee oral traditional knowledge within a historical and contemporary context, supports Cherokee literary arts, and perpetuates the Cherokee language. The great majority of stories in this work and all of the conversation were shared orally and in an unscripted manner. We would gather for a storytelling, I would push record on my digital recorder, and the event would take on a life of its own. I present these stories and conversations as they were recorded in order to showcase the artistry of Cherokee storytelling and teachings, with its specific aesthetic and thematic concerns. Readers will recognize, for example, how Cherokee storytelling is rhythmic, with particular important ideas and phrases repeated in a story for emphasis.

Although they are known for their oral performance craft, the Liars' Club emphasizes the importance of the teachings found in Cherokee oral tradition. And while these teachings illustrate Cherokee cultural traditions, in the end they serve one central goal: they teach a person about Cherokee values through the process of storytelling. Hastings Shade speaks of what he understands as the cultural confusion some younger Cherokees experience today. Seeing two paths before them, one mainstream American, the other Cherokee, people must decide how they wish to live their lives. Stories provide critical models for making sense of one's cultural belonging; they teach one how to "stand in the middle," or know how to negotiate the influences of Western culture while remaining Cherokee. Cherokee oral tradition provides the lessons and critical framework through which the middle way may be achieved. This goal of helping people "stand in the middle" is an additional inspiration for writing *Cherokee Stories of the Turtle Island Liars' Club*.

My method of working with the Liars' Club and recording their stories and teachings arises out of my complex position as a participant-observer in relation to the group. *Cherokee Stories of the Turtle Island Liars' Club* is shaped by the fact that I am a member of the culture I am studying. Rather than attempt a pose of false objectivity, I foreground my presence as a friend, kinsman, researcher, listener, and student of the club. Indeed, as one of the club's central goals for the book is to share knowledge of the "middle way" with readers who have a similar background to myself—a Cherokee who grew up outside of traditional culture but seeking a greater understanding of Cherokee lifeways—I became a stand-in for the interested reader. And often I asked the questions I imagined such a reader might present to the group, even though I may have already known the answers.

When drafting *Cherokee Stories of the Turtle Island Liars' Club* I sought out the best work of folklorists, cultural anthropologists, ethnographers, and literary scholars who have recorded and written on oral tradition. I found compelling models in works such as Zora Neale Hurston's *Mules and Men* (1935); N. Scott Momaday's *The Way to Rainy Mountain* (University of New Mexico Press, 1969); Larry Evers and Felipe S. Molina's *Yaqui Deer Songs, Maso Bwikam: A Native American Poetry* (University of Arizona Press, 1987); Keith H. Basso's *Wisdom Sits in Places: Landscape and Language Among the Western Apache* (University of New Mexico Press, 1996); and Barbara R. Duncan's edited collection, *Living Stories of the Cherokee* (University of North Carolina Press, 1998). Jack F. and Anna G. Kilpatrick's *Friends of Thunder: Folktales of the Oklahoma Cherokees* (University of Oklahoma Press, 1964) was particularly important to me. Their publications of the 1960s are the most recent texts that have resulted from an ethnographic engagement with Cherokee storytellers.

Throughout this process I saw my role as that of a student, not a teacher, a relationship I hope is clear in the text. Each chapter of *Cherokee Stories of the Turtle Island Liars' Club* is presented in the form of juxtaposed vignettes because this, in fact, is how Cherokee stories work: they nudge up against one another and share meaning across apparent gaps of understanding or connection. In inviting the reader to venture across the vignettes of conversation and story that shape each chapter, the Liars' Club and I are asking readers to actively interpret the stories and recognize patterns of Cherokee thought.

Members of the club are bilingual, but they often tell their stories in English. They chose to record their stories in English in order to reach the largest audience. However, four stories are written in the Cherokee syllabary, the eighty-five symbols of the Cherokee writing system, and accompanied with a phonetic translation and literal translation. Some stories are presented using an oral poetic method of transcription developed by Dennis Tedlock and Dell Hymes. This transcription method is designed to approximate the sound of hearing the stories just as they were spoken, requiring that one write them down word for word with appropriate line breaks in close accordance with the natural cadences, emphases, and pauses of oral recordings. Some storytellers, such as Sequoyah Guess, have an oral performative style that lends itself to this form of transcription. Others, such as Hastings Shade, did not tell stories in a way that depended as much on evocative pauses and cadences in order to heighten the experience of his listeners. In any case, Hastings Shade and the other members of the club preferred that some stories be recorded in prose. "I mean, I'm not a storyteller as far as having a plot and taking it through, you know, to the end. But the stories like this, that tell something real quick. Then move on to the next," Hastings said and snapped his fingers.

The Liars' Club and I agreed to focus the collection to reflect a commitment to both the tradition of Cherokee storytelling as well as to the lived reality of Cherokee storytelling in the twenty-first century. As such, *Cherokee Stories of the Turtle Island Liars' Club* offers little context in terms of Cherokee history. In part, the club members came to this decision because they wanted to avoid the perception that Cherokee storytelling is an art of the past. Instead, they wanted to express how a vital Cherokee worldview continues to be expressed through the art of storytelling. And so it was left up to me to offer readers some explanation of Cherokee history.

Like many Cherokees who grew up outside of a predominantly Cherokee community, I had known Cherokee history mostly through books. I had learned that since time immemorial, the Cherokees have claimed the mountains and valleys of Southern Appalachia as their homeland. Archaeology tells us indigenous peoples have lived in the Smoky Mountains for over 11,000 years, and linguists estimate the Cherokee language broke away from other Iroquoian languages some 3,500 years ago. While it remains unclear precisely how far Cherokee prehistory traces back in this area, it is known the Cherokee were the largest and most powerful indigenous nation of the Southeast before and after European contact. Cherokee territory once comprised over 81 million acres of mountains, valleys, and rich agricultural fields circling from what is now northern South Carolina, through western North Carolina and Virginia, to east Tennessee and northern Alabama and Georgia. The nation consisted of autonomous towns of 200 or more people, each with their own White (Peace) Chief and Red (War) Chief as well as a council made up of representatives from each of the seven prominent clans: Deer, Wolf, Paint, Bird, Long Hairs, Blue, and Wild Potato. A common language, kinship system, and culture united the Cherokee people across this vast territory.

Beginning in the late sixteenth century, Cherokees suffered wave after wave of epidemics and warfare. In one twenty-year stretch in the late seventeenth century the Cherokee population dropped from approximately 35,000 to 11,000. In the mid-eighteenth century the Cherokee population dipped to approximately 7,000. By the end of the Revolutionary War, in which Cherokees allied with the British, the Cherokee were seeking peaceful coexistence with the United States. Dozens of treaties with both Britain and the United States resulted in land cessions that reduced Cherokee territory to a fraction of its original size, confining it to an area made up of present-day northern Georgia, western North Carolina, and northeastern Alabama.

As a means of preserving themselves the Cherokee adopted a general policy of acculturation. The Cherokee Nation gave up clan governance and became a constitutional government modeled on the United States. Cherokees built schools and embraced education. They created a bilingual newspaper, the *Cherokee Phoenix*, the first among Native American nations. Many Cherokee were Christians and sent their children to mission schools and for further education in the East. They maintained stores, inns, and farms, and some owned larger plantations. By the 1830s, the Cherokee were a prosperous people by any standards of the day. Slavery was a part of Cherokee society, and the Cherokee Nation's wealth, like that of its southern white neighbors, was buoyed by slave labor. Generations of intermarriage between Cherokees and English and Scottish soldiers and traders had created a class of Cherokees who were often more embracing of acculturation than their culturally traditional kin, and much of the Cherokee Nation's wealth was consolidated in their hands. Cherokee society and culture were complex and diverse; there were those who lived lives nearly indistinguishable from Euro-Americans, and there were those who lived much as their ancestors had.

In the early nineteenth century the federal government sought land for expansion in the Southeast. The federal government's Indian Removal Act was passed in 1830 and ethnic cleansing became its policy. Cherokee, Creek, Choctaw, Seminole, and Chickasaw people were taken from their homes, held in stockades, and forcibly marched west to Indian Territory. Before the removal the Cherokee Nation had a population of more than 20,000. Over 4,000 Cherokees—mostly children and elders—died during the forced relocation of 1838–39, now known as the Trail of Tears. Disease, deprivation, and despair also took their toll on those who did reach Indian Territory. Some estimate that as many as 8,000 people died during the Trail of Tears period.

As they had many times before, the Cherokee renewed themselves. They rebuilt their nation in Indian Territory, and it prospered until the Civil War, when the people's allegiance was divided between North and South. All suffered. After the war, the Cherokee Nation's territory was reduced by a victorious United States; a postwar treaty had demanded a railroad right-of-way through Cherokee country, thus opening the door to non-Native settlement of Indian Territory. Many years in the making, the Curtis Act was passed by the United States in 1898, and lands Cherokees once held in common were allotted to individuals and heads of families. By 1906, the government of the Cherokee Nation was essentially dissolved. In 1907 Indian Territory and Oklahoma Territory consolidated to become the state of Oklahoma. Cherokee citizens were now subject to Oklahoma law, and their government buildings and schools belonged to the United States. The Cherokee Nation, however, never ceded its inherent sovereignty. And though for many years it only existed on paper, by the 1960s, after decades of work by many Cherokees, a rebirth of the Cherokee Nation was on the horizon. In 1970 the U.S. Congress passed an act that allowed for Cherokee Nation elections, which were held in 1971. Parcels of land were returned to the Cherokee Nation, and it began to govern its people once again.

Today, the Cherokee people are represented by three national governments recognized by the federal government. These include the Cherokee Nation, with a population of approximately 300,000 citizens; the United Keetoowah Band of Cherokee Indians, with 15,000 citizens; and the Eastern Band of Cherokee Indians, with 13,000 citizens. The Cherokee Nation and United Keetoowah Band are both located in northeastern Oklahoma. The Eastern Band of Cherokee Indians is comprised of descendants of those Cherokee who remained in the East or returned there after the Trail of Tears and is located on the Qualla Boundary, a 57,000-acre tract of land in the mountains of western North Carolina.

The above traces only key moments in Cherokee history. It provides but the barest of details for one to begin to understand the journey of a people, but even in this short sketch cultural patterns emerge: the will to survive; the strength to regenerate; the courage to adapt; and the respect to honor our ancestors, kin, and best selves through remaining Cherokee. I experienced firsthand the meaning of these lessons in my regular visits to Cherokee country to learn from the Liars' Club. When I was gone, the club members and I continued to talk often about our book. Information was shared via email and telephone conversations. When Hastings or Sammy mentioned a story I wanted to record, I sometimes would ask them to write it down or share a copy with me if they had already written it. Hastings, in particular, shared written stories with me to incorporate into the book. These stories differ from those Hastings told out loud, and you will recognize that in his choice of words and in the pacing of the stories. I include them in this book because the important thing for Hastings was that the stories be shared with future generations of Cherokee people and those interested in Cherokee culture and history. Whether the stories were recorded orally or written down and passed along later was not such a concern for him. At our last meeting together, Hastings handed me the remaining collections of his writings and said, "Use any of 'em you want." Stories that were recorded orally I present as "told by" the story-teller, while those that were written, and which I edited, I present as "by" the author.

In addition to this introduction and an afterword, *Cherokee Stories of the Turtle Island Liars' Club* consists of four chapters, each of which circles around a particular aspect of the Cherokee tradition as it evolves in a changing world. "*Sagwu* (One): *Alenihv* (Beginnings)," recounts origin stories of earth, fire, the Cherokee people, and the Liars' Club. Both Hastings Shade and Sequoyah Guess tell versions of the rarely told Cherokee migration story. "*Tali* (Two): *Adanvsgvi* (Movements)," explores the ways Cherokees have moved, physically and metaphorically, and how stories may lead one "home" to either a literal place or a cultural space. The members of the club tell of growing up Cherokee in the 1950s and 1960s, and I tell of my journey back home. "*Joi* (Three): *Dideyohvsdi* (Teachings)" presents stories and conversation about "teachings." Deceptively complex, animal stories such as those shared in this chapter are not just for children, as they express important points regarding knowledge, social relations, and communal responsibility. "*Nvgi* (Four): *Ulvsgedi* (The Wondrous)" shares stories of how the spirit and world interconnect within a Cherokee worldview. The Liars' Club members tell stories of ghosts, medicine people, and mysterious phenomenon.

Each chapter of this book begins with an illustration by award-winning Cherokee Nation artist America Meredith. These illustrations create an important link to Cherokee visual art and, with their range of emotions and meanings, enable us to see and understand the stories in new ways.

As the Liars' Club and I gathered on that chilly autumn evening at the Cherokee Heritage Center chapel and pored over our work together, hundreds of pages of stories and conversation, it became clear to us that we were not telling our individual stories, nor simply those of the elders who had imparted us with knowledge. We were telling stories of our people-hood. In doing so, we would be sharing processes that forge relationships. With humility, Hastings embraced this responsibility on behalf of the Liars' Club, explaining that "sharing is probably the main thing as far as a *value* that we have. To me, sharing what we know, just like we're sitting here, getting ready to do this book, we're sharing with the other part of the world or the other people that says, 'What is a Cherokee?' What's their *belief*? What do they *do*? What do they *know*? I mean, then you get down to the nitty gritty, 'What are they good for?'" he said and laughed, leaning back in his chair. And with that as our impulse, we offer this book.

Alenihv (Beginnings)

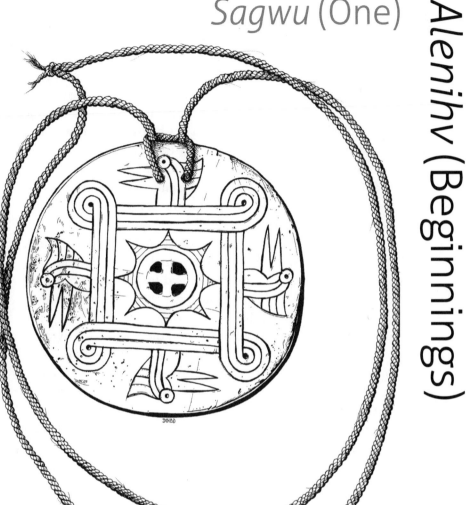

Cox Mound gorget

I'm sitting in my rental car with Hastings Shade outside of the chapel at the Cherokee Heritage Center in Park Hill, Oklahoma. It's early December, and late autumn seems to place us both in a contemplative mood. Autumn is my favorite time of year, and especially autumn in northeastern Oklahoma. The deep heart-heat of the Oklahoma summer slowly gives way to brisk fall winds that shake the leaves from the trees. The copperheads seek their burrows; the blue of the sky lightens; and the air on the Ozark Plateau loses some of its moisture. The Cherokee New Year arrives with the first new moon in October, when the Earth, moon, and sun align so that the moon is directly between the Earth and sun. Cherokee life realigns in autumn. Crops are harvested and families ready themselves for the coming winter. At this time when nature turns inward it is fitting we reflect on Cherokee life by telling stories.

This Sunday morning is cold, gray, and quiet on the Heritage Center's acres of level, forested grounds. For three years I've been working with Hastings and three other Cherokee elders and traditionalists to gather the stories of the Turtle Island Liars' Club. Today will be our last recording session. This afternoon I'll head back home to begin writing a book, partly mine and partly theirs, that will weave together the stories, teachings, experiences, and memories they shared with me. As we wait for Sequoyah Guess and Woody Hansen to meet us after services at Tiyo Baptist Church, Hastings talks me through a collection of teachings and writings he has given me to incorporate into the book.

Hastings Shade expresses a gentle strength beyond his physical presence. In his late sixties, he is of medium height and build, with straight black hair parted on the side, a moustache and goatee. There is an urgency in Hastings's manner today. His dark eyes flash under his amber-colored glasses as he reflects upon the meaning of one particular Cherokee symbol, the looped square. I've seen this symbol in books and read what archaeologists and anthropologists think it means. They say it symbolizes the four cords that suspend the earth from Galvladi—the Sky World—the Cherokee name for the world above the sky. The symbol is a square with corners that loop, never coming to ninety-degree angles, flowing from one side to the next.

"See, they never fully come together," Hastings says as he points to the corners.

"That's a symbol of Elohi?" I say, using the Cherokee word for Earth.

"Mmhm, yeah."

"And that's the cords?" I say, pointing to the corners.

"That's the cords, yeah."

"But it also symbolizes a kind of movement? Towards maturity?"

"Yeah, well, it symbolizes your life cycle," Hastings says. "You're born. You mature. You age. And then you die."

"And where does it start?"

"There's no starting and there's no beginning," Hastings says quickly, emphatically. "Just like conception. You know, there's no set time for conception. It's just when it happens. There's no set time for death. Just when it happens."

"The Cherokee conception of death," I think out loud. "You just keep on going."

"Yeah. Yeah," Hastings agrees. "There's no . . . it don't end, you know? It just one more step in who we are. It just like, an old man gave me a good example one time. He said, 'In your life, your daily life, you should walk, you should take each step just like the next step you take you're going to be standing in front of the Creator.' Just like my next step, I'm going to be standing in front of him. Our life should be to a point where we shouldn't dread that next step. If our life is pure or good as we can live it, then the next step is just another step in life."

"Is there an end?"

"There's no end. This is the journey that the Cherokees followed as a tribe and as individuals," he said pointing to the looped square. "As a tribe, north, *tsuyvtlv*, from their ancestral homeland. East, *dikalvgv*, to a land that was only temporary. South, *tsuganawv*, to warmth that lasted fourteen generations, about 700 years, until contact with Europeans. Then west, *wudeligv*, to suffering and death."

The bird images on each of the four sides represent the Bird Warriors, those who the Cherokee culture hero Solegeh, the Winged One, gathered to kill the priest clan that governed the Dinikani, the Red Eye People, the name the elders gave those the scholars call the mound builders. The direction of the birds' movement has meaning, Hastings explained: "As the Cherokees danced in the counterclockwise direction, the smoke from the fire, as a gift from the Creator, rises upward, carrying the songs and the prayers from the people to the Creator, along with the aroma from the seven sacred woods that the Creator told us we must use. The center of the symbol is the four directions, *nvgi widuyugatvi*. They are represented by four logs that meet at the center as a cross. This cross of logs represents *atsila*, fire."

Hastings's words played over in my mind when, two months later, he passed on. Although I had known him only a few years, the time we'd spent together was in intense discussions of things he valued deeply: Cherokee culture, stories, language, history, crafts, and teachings. He had spent his life passing on these traditions to generations of Cherokees. Our book would be an extension of that work. Sammy Still, Sequoyah Guess, and Woody Hansen, the other core members of the Liars' Club, honored Hastings as their elder, the glue that held the club together. They had known each other most of their lives, were kin as well as friends. Speaking with Sammy and Sequoyah in the days after Hastings's passing, I offered the condolences I thought most appropriate: Hastings's own teachings and the teachings of the Liars' Club. There is no end. Life continues. We will see each other again. Life is a mix; the key is finding a balance. Laugh and celebrate each other. Value Cherokee culture and one another.

As the former deputy chief of the Cherokee Nation and an honored elder, teacher, husband, father, kinsman, and friend, Hastings was many things to many people. His memorial at the Sequoyah High School gym reflected his value to the community. Sammy, Sequoyah, and Woody visited his grave a few days after he was laid to rest in Mother Earth. They wanted to reflect on their time together, the laughter, stories, and teachings they had shared. I was honored when Sequoyah called me and asked if there was something I wanted to say to Hastings when they visited. I asked him to tell Hastings *wado* for sharing the stories and teachings with me and for honoring me with the responsibility of this book. I asked him to say that I would do my best to write in a way that reflected the wisdom of the teachings of the elders that had been passed on to the Liars' Club. My greatest hope was that it would be a book future generations of Cherokees could read and reflect upon. Sequoyah would relay my message. I reminded him to tell some jokes and have a good laugh.

They went out to Hastings's grave and paid their respects, secure in the knowledge they would see each other again. Driving back from the cemetery they witnessed an unusual sight. Three birds flew around each other in the sky: an eagle, which, for Cherokees, represents the spirit; a hawk, which represents the warrior; and a turkey buzzard, which represents traditional medicine. Sequoyah told me they thought Hastings was telling them to carry on the traditions.

Standing in the Doorway

When I came home to Cherokee country fresh out of high school, I began a quest for knowledge and meaning. I wanted to better understand my connection with the Cherokee culture and history that shaped the life of my mother and her Cherokee family. It was also a quest to find my place within that history as a Cherokee citizen who grew up away from the Cherokee Nation. This journey has continued for nearly twenty years now. It started with stories learned at my grandmother's feet as she rocked in her rocking chair, reminiscing about her girlhood in Miami, Oklahoma, and Honey Creek. It continued as I grew to manhood and began to understand myself in relation to my Cherokee heritage. It matured as I went back to the Cherokee Nation as a graduate student and, later, professor of Native American literature to find my place and contribution within Cherokee community.

Not until I was well into working with the Liars' Club did I realize I was on another journey, the one that would lead to this book. The journey began with new friendships, chance meetings, and periodic discussions with the members of the Liars' Club. We gathered together and I became their student, the one who was going to write these stories down.

This chapter of *Cherokee Stories* is about beginnings. It is about the beginnings of the Cherokee people and their worldview, about the beginnings of the Liars' Club, and about the beginning of the story this book tells. But as the looped square, the symbol of the Journey of Four Directions, indicates, one cannot ever truly separate beginnings and endings. The journey never ends; it only changes through interconnected cycles of experience.

Hastings once told me how balance and interconnection were fundamental to Cherokee cosmology. The Cherokee cosmos, he explained, is divided into three levels: the Sky World, the Middle World, and the Under World. The Sky World, Galunlati, is a place of order and stability, an unchanging place from which the original life forms came to populate Turtle Island. Below the earth is the Under World, Elohi Hawinaditla, a place of water, chaos, and mystery where things mix, but also a source of creative power and change. The Middle World, Elohi, is the earth on which humans, animals, and plants live. Living between the opposing natures of the Sky World and the Under World, the creatures of the Middle World must negotiate both sky and water energies. Human beings in particular have the responsibility to create dynamic balances between the Sky World and the Under World through our application of knowledge. If we do not maintain these balances, it is said, Elohi will sink into the waters. Cherokees are still balancing the forces of above and below, still trying to keep this world above water for another generation. Just as an unwavering balance will never be achieved once and for all, the Journey of Four Directions describes a process of becoming.

Woody Hansen once said that each of us, in our spirits, is a council house. The traditional Cherokee council house was located at the center of a village atop an earthen mound. It was a meeting place where people sat around the sacred fire and discussed politics or took part in ceremonies. Our individual spirits compose a similar space: a place of memory where we gather our thoughts and the teachings of our elders to deliberate on how we should act, what we should believe. In its own humble way, Woody said, this book is a council house of the Turtle Island Liars' Club. He told me, "You know, you're being used by the Creator to help open the door to the council house. Unfortunately, we won't be around forever, but the book will. And the words. So that's the opening of the door." I write from my experience as a Cherokee who journeyed home. As you stand in the doorway of the council house, at the beginning of this journey, the Liars' Club and I welcome you in.

Hastings Shade

One rainy afternoon in early July, Hastings, Sequoyah, Woody and his daughter Jade Hansen, and I sat out under the roof of Hastings's outdoor workshop at his home in Lost City, Oklahoma. Tables were covered with half-carved blocks of wood, pieces of iron used for gig making, and wood and iron forging tools. It was a muggy day and the rain had brought the bugs out. We gathered around and talked as Sequoyah and Woody whittled on a couple staves. The crickets, cicadas, and coop full of chicks filled the air with a low hum.

It was on a day like this that I had first met Hastings Shade. I'd known him as my deputy principal chief but had never met him in person. Once, while visiting the Eastern Band of Cherokee Indians reservation on the Qualla Boundary, I'd seen Hastings walking quietly by himself along the Oconaluftee River. I'd considered introducing myself, but I thought it better to leave him to his thoughts. When I did finally meet him years later at his home and we began speaking about Cherokee tradition, I was nervous and forgot my manners. He'd said, "Used to be you'd need to offer someone tobacco when you'd ask about these matters." I went to the car and brought him back two packs of cigarettes. Seeing that I was sufficiently chastened, Hastings offered a cigarette to all of us and added, "Don't tell my wife about this." He'd had to give up smoking because of his heart condition.

Today, we'd been sitting around telling lies all afternoon, and as we began to wrap it up so we could all head out and get something to eat, I asked Hastings how he'd like to be introduced in the book.

"Full blood," he said and grinned.

"Me, too," Woody joined in.

"Say, '*Heeere's*, Hastings!'" Sequoyah offered. We laughed lightly. Then, after a few moments of quiet, Hastings spoke again: "Traditional. I was raised traditionally. Everything we ever did had to do with tradition. I was born in 1941. I had one of my grandfathers thirty-nine years, the other one I had fifteen. The one I had the longest taught me a lot. I do all the traditional Cherokee arts, all the arts. I can do anything the older people used to do. Anything that they made I can make. Some of the things I didn't learn at all. I wish now I had paid more attention to them.

"I just listened to the elders. Learned from the elders what I know. Always, the elders used to tell me a long time ago, you know, 'Why would I lie to you? Because when I ain't here anymore it won't make any difference. So, why would I lie to you?' I always remembered that, and when they tell me something I take it as the truth. There's no reason to lie to you. When they ain't going to live any longer it won't make any difference.

"So, these sayings are traditional. My children are traditional. I tell them things traditionally. And I haven't lost that part of it. My boys, my family still do things we were taught to do. You know, most of the wild things to eat we still gather. We live modern, also. You know, we have to live in the modern world. We can't ignore our ancient roots but we still have to live modern. Society dictates it. It's *dictated*; it's not something you can get away from.

"That's how I'd like to be known, as traditional. English is my second language. That's why I make a lot of mistakes when I speak English and when I write I can't spell nothing. That's something I never did learn to do. In my spelling I want to spell it like it sounds, not the way it's spelled. That puts me at a disadvantage. And I can read and write Cherokee anything you want. When it comes to English I have to check my spelling. Punctuation. When you write Cherokee you don't punctuate. There's no punctuation. So, as a traditional . . ."

The Dark One and the Seven Sisters

When gathered with the Liars' Club, I let myself ask questions that I'd always wondered about. "Where did the Cherokee people come from?" I asked Hastings once. He knew I wasn't asking what anthropologists or historians thought about our origins. I was asking about what Cherokee tradition tells about our beginnings as a people. After a moment, Hastings said: "The elders say we came from the stars somewhere around what is now known as the Pleiades system. The elders called it Galaquogi Dinadalv, or the Seven Sisters.

"The legend that the elders tell says one of the sisters, the one that was called the Dark One, Ulisigi, felt sorry for how the brown-skinned people were being treated, so she gathered up the Indians and she brought them to Earth. Elohi. At that time Elohi was known as the Turtle's Back, Dalasgugag Gasohi. Snapping Turtle. Siligu. The legend says Star Woman fell from the stars and landed on Elohi. When she landed she broke open and man stepped forth. This is how we came to be on Earth.

"Star Woman, or the Dark One, was punished when she returned to the stars. Her six other sisters punished her and hid her behind a cloak. To this day you can look at the Pleiades star system and you can see six of the stars with the naked eye. You have to use a telescope to see the seventh one. She's hidden behind a space cloud, and that's why she's known as the Dark One.

"The elders also say there is another star located farther beyond the Pleiades star system known as the seven-pointed star, Galaquogi Digosdayi Noquisi. This is where the sons of the Creator came from to live with the women of Elohi. They created the sons and daughters who could control the elements. As we came to earth and learned the things as told to us by our ancestors, we became who we are today. The Bible says that only God and his sons were masters over the elements. As the sons of the Creator came and took the women of Elohi, their sons and daughters became the medicine people that are here among the Indian people. Some were good, some were mean. As we come into modern times we are losing these medicine people. They cannot see us as learning the old ways, or the things that they know. We, as Indian people, are getting away from our culture. And taking to one that is foreign to us. Will we lose all that we know or will we retain some of it?

"So, who are we? Where did we really come from? Is this really the place we came from? The seven-pointed star is where we got our symbol. Also the seven clans. The seven important things on earth. The seven directions. The seven herbs for the black drink. The number seven is an important number to the Cherokee."

Sammy Still

I met Sammy Still several years ago when for two weeks he and Sequoyah Guess tutored me daily in the Cherokee language. We gathered each afternoon at his house north of Tahlequah, the capital of the Cherokee Nation. Under the shade of a big sycamore, we sat in lawn chairs around a small fire that my nephew Matt tended to keep the bugs away. Sammy kept a cooler full of cold drinks on hand.

In his fifties, Sammy is a powerfully built man—all chest, neck, and arms. He walks with a limp. He keeps his hair short and his face shaved. His ready smile reveals his good-natured self. Sequoyah once told me that Sam cares about what people think of him, and I gather that's because he cares about people. He likes to laugh, and he's beloved by the other members of the club for, among other things, his uncanny ability to get himself in humorous fixes, of which he has many stories. As Woody says, "If it's going to happen to someone, it's going to happen to Sammy."

As the book was coming together, I asked Sammy how he'd like to be introduced.

"Gol, I don't know!" he said and laughed.

"Now you're just starting like everyone else said!" I protested.

"Here, let *me* tell you how to introduce him . . . ," Sequoyah interrupted, joking.

"I think I can do it!" Sammy said and waved Sequoyah off. "I don't know. I'd just say it like this," he said, turning serious. "I consider myself a very traditional Cherokee person. And in a lot of ways I still live like our ancestors did. I do a lot of craft making. I do a lot of traditional basket making, stone marble making. But I've learned all this from my elders. I give all the credit that I know—the stories, everything I've heard, everything I've said—I give credit to the elders. 'Cause that's who I've learned from. That's who I was taught from. For example, let me give you this little story."

THE BOY WITH THE CAMERA BAG
Told by Sammy Still

And, uh, I used to take photographs.
For eighteen years,
even longer for the CNO, for the tribe.

You know, I went to school.
Well let me go back, let me go back.

Left to right: Hastings Shade and Sammy Still

I used to speak Cherokee fluently.
Up to the age of six years old.
And then when I went to school
I lost it; I was taught English,
so I lost that.
But I didn't lose my
      understanding of the language.
I understood it fluently.
But I think it was to the point where I was
afraid to speak my language
after I got into school because,
like everything else,
people made fun of you, your language and all this.

So, I went to school, I did what everybody said.
You go to school, get your education, and then you get a job or
      whatever.
So I did that.
And, when I did do that, my job took me out into the rural
      communities.
Going back to the Cherokee people.

And, I didn't realize that.
I didn't realize that until after I left,
after I had gone and stopped doing that
and gone into, like, language and culture and history.
That later on in life, that this is what God was preparing me for,
was to go back to my rural . . . to my roots.

I may not be saying this right and you may not even want to record
      this part, but . . .
My job took me out in the rural areas where I was to take a
      photograph
and do an interview with this elder Cherokee man.

"Mmhm," I said. After a pause, Sammy continued.

I go to his house, knock on his door.
He's the only one there.
No TV, no nothing.
He's just there sitting at the window looking out.

Nobody else there.
I knock on the door.
He comes and opens the door and invites me in.
I sit down there and I say he's a recipient of one of the health
      programs.
He's getting help or aid through one of the home health
providers or whatever.
I'm there to do a story about him and how he likes
the healthcare he's receiving and all this.
I sit down.
I get my camera bag.
And I always carried a big old camera bag.
It was black and had a camera.
And so, I said, "Can I take a photograph of you?
I'm here to interview you and take a photograph."

And, of course, him not being that fluent in English
but he understood what I was saying.
He sits down there and he says,
    "Yeah, I guess so."
You know, just like we're doing here.
We sit down.
I'm the interviewer . . .
just say I'm the elder here and you're who I was.
So I get my notepad out,
I get my camera and set it out here 'cause I want to take a
      photograph of him.
I get ready to write the story, to interview him.

Well, while in the interview,
I see he's real uncomfortable.
He don't know why I'm there.
He don't know why I'm there invading his home, his own privacy.
"What is this for?"
He didn't ask that question but you can see it in his eyes.
You can see it by his movements.

I know he's uncomfortable with me.
And if I ask a question it's,
    "Well, yeah."

He's real cautious about answering.
So, I see that.
I understand what's happening so I put my camera in the bag,
I put my notepad down,
    and we sit down.
    And, just like you and me,
    we sit and talk.

And he noticed that.
I guess he understood that I knew that he was uncomfortable.
So I put everything away.
We sit there.
And he looks at me and he knows I'm Cherokee.
He says,
    "You speak Cherokee?"
    I said, "Yeah. I understand it."
I said, "I speak a little bit. I don't speak much but I understand it."
So, he starts speaking to me in Cherokee.
What *he's* comfortable with.
In his home he speaks his own Native tongue.
And I understand him.
We laugh and we talk.
Pretty soon, he gets comfortable and says,
"Hey, I got some coffee. Let's go and drink some coffee.
And I made some biscuits this morning for breakfast.
You want a biscuit?"
I said, "Yeah."
We go in there and all this time he's talking to me in Cherokee.
We go there, get coffee, sit down and drink.
Eat biscuits.
And he gets to talking about his grandkids,
how proud he is of his grandkids.
Talks about his garden. I just let him talk.
I just let him talk.
And we start laughing and
I tell him a story or two about who I am,
my family and things that happened to us.
Just like when we tell stories.
And he feels real comfortable about it.

So I stayed there maybe an hour or so with him.
Maybe longer.
And drank coffee and ate biscuit and stuff and had a good ole time.
Then I get ready to leave.
And he said, "Oh, aren't you going to take a picture of me?"
I said, "Yeah. Yeah."
Get my camera out.
Oh, he poses for me and I take a picture of him.
And I said, "Well, can I ask you about your healthcare?"
"Oh yeah!"
He tells me everything. He doesn't hold anything back.

When I get ready to leave he says,
"You come back now. Come back and see me."
I said, "I will. I will."
And I did.
I went back several times and saw him.
But I leave there,
    and it made me feel good in my heart
    because I know as I left there . . .
    I was there to share his day there.
Because he was by himself;
there was nobody there.
He was there by himself and lonely.
And so, I start doing this.

I started going back and my job
took me back into the rural areas again, visiting Cherokees.
And the elders.
I would visit elders out there.
And I would sit down with them and visit with 'em.
And I got to realize that they weren't asking for anything.
    They're out there now in the rural areas.
    They're not *asking* for anything.
All they ask for is someone just to sit and listen to them.
I sit there and listen to their stories, listen to them.
And they always invite me,
    "Hey, I got some beans on the table.
    I got some food on the table.
    Eat, eat before you go.

Eat before you go."
So I did.
And, from that I earned their trust.
And so, I would go out there in the communities and stop and visit
    them,
sit on the porch.
They start *teaching* me things.

They start teaching me about *crafts*.
They start teaching me about *medicine*.
They start telling me about their families,
their trip to town.
How fun it was and what happened.
We sit there and we talk.

We laughed,
we cried together,
we shared stories and had a good ole time, you know?
And they got to know me as
the boy who carried the black bag.
That's how they knew me in the community.
"Well, come back and visit us. Come back and visit us."

Well, after a while,
I changed jobs and went to doing language and history and all
    that.
And then working with Sequoyah and them with the language
    and stuff.
I put my camera down
and I didn't take photographs anymore.
But every now and then I see 'em and it's,
"Well where you been? Where you been?
Where's your camera bag?
Come back and visit us. Come back and visit us."
And so, I always think back.
I said, "One of these days I'm going to get that camera bag
and I'm going to dust it off.
I'm going to put it back on my shoulder
and I'm going to go back out in the community.
And I'm going to sit and visit with 'em."

Because these elders weren't my elders,
they became my *family*.

"Mm," I said and nodded.

They became my *grandparents*.
And so, one of these days I'm going to go back there
and go visit my grandparents.
And sit back and listen to them.
Listen to what they have to teach,
what they have to say and what they can teach me.
'Cause they put that trust in me
knowing that I would share what they taught me.
Share it with other people.
And there's many of 'em already gone.
There's a lot of 'em that's already gone,
but they're still up *here*.

We all nodded as Sammy touched his head.

And I remember them.
Their smiles.
Their eyes.
And, even today, sometimes they'll say,
"Well where's your camera bag? Where's your black bag?
Why don't you come out and say hi?
Come back and visit."
So one of these days I guess I will, you know?
But I really enjoyed them.

"I know I got away from me introducing who I am," Sammy said.
"Nah, this is it," I said.
"But that's who I am. To me, that's who I am. I mean, I hold my tradition, culture, and my people close to my heart. And I guess, in a way,
maybe that's a way if someone wants to remember who I am, maybe that's
just the way it is. I love my people. I really do. And that's why being with
Hastings and Sequoyah and sharing these stories and stuff, it's . . . our
life. It's what we do. It's not what we go out and try to accomplish. It's
not going out there and doing things for *ourselves*. It's for everybody. And

that's what I like about this book. It's something that can show my family, 'Hey, this is what we shared with people. This is what we *did* with people.' Not to just say, *I, I, I,* but for *everybody.*"

"Mmhm."

"And even today . . . even today, now that I'm with the United Keetoowah Band, and I'm back in the newspaper business again, I got my camera again. And my camera bag. And I talk to these people when they come in, and I'm going out and visiting people. Even today, now. I'm going back out there and talking to them again. And they're teaching me things. So that's just me, but as far as explaining who I am or whatever it is, *I* can't do that. *I* can't say, 'Well this is who I am,' or, 'I do this . . .' That's not me. What's me is out there in the communities. Out there with the elders. And the ones that's passed. So. That's the best way I can explain it."

Is It a Lie, or Is It Truth?

Since the beginning of our work together on the book, the Liars' Club and I had a running discussion of the purpose and meaning of Cherokee oral storytelling. Imagining questions readers of the book might have, I asked, "Why has storytelling been so important to Cherokee culture? What was it about the process of getting together with friends and sharing 'lies' that is so crucial to Cherokee tradition?"

Sitting at plastic tables in the chapel one late fall afternoon, Hastings explained how stories have a way of helping people find a balance when they are wavering between different ways of being.

"See, we're still dependent on a lot of things that people take as stories," Hastings said. I nodded.

"To us, we still depend on 'em. Hearing stories, that's part of it. If you're Native American, whether you know them or not, they're still a part of you. If you keep hearing them, pretty soon, you'll say, 'Hey, that's me!' That's what they say. 'I'm Indian, you know. But how much am I? Do I want to be a real Indian, or do I want to go just back and forth?'

"And to me, with our children, we need to say, 'Okay, this is who you are.' Once we teach them, then they'll decide which way they want to go. But you got to get that teaching in them first. You got to get 'em lined up, you know? 'This is who you are. You're not this, you're here,'" Hastings said, gesturing with both hands to either side.

"And *they* decide. 'Ah, this ain't no good for me,'" Hastings gestured to the left. "'This *sure* ain't no good for me,'" he said, gesturing to the right. "'I need to be here,'" he said, pointing both his hands to the middle. "'Because everything I know, everything I attribute to my being here is right here. It's not over here, it's not over here, not over there. But it's right *here.*' So if our book reaches one person . . . One out of how many? . . . Then we'll have accomplished something."

I nodded.

"Yeah. And if we reach a million, then, oh man, that's something!"

"Well, they're craving direction," I said, thinking about some of my students over the years.

"Yeah. Yeah."

"And I think that's what stories can do, can offer that direction."

"Yeah. And these stories are not . . . there's no false to 'em," Hastings said. "Even though they call us 'liars.' Storytellers. There's nothing false about 'em. They're all true. The thing about it is you've got to prove it. It's left up to you to prove it if they're true or not. That's what I always tell my students: 'Don't believe me. Come try it, then you'll believe it yourself.' That's what happens with these stories. They're all true. It's, how much do we want to *prove* that they are true?"

"Yeah. And that's a kind of play on that word. . . . Is it a lie or is it truth?" I said, laughing at the paradox.

"Yeah. Is it lie or is it truth? But the only reason we use that 'liar' name is because in Cherokee there's no real word for storyteller. We don't have a word for, you know . . . all we can say is *kanohesg* and that's just 'talk about it.' It's not really 'storyteller.' *Gahigogesgi*, now that's 'a liar.' *Gagogesgi* means 'that liar's going to be speaking or telling it,' and that's usually a storyteller. That's what they call it because a lot of people look at you and say, 'That can't be true.' Because they've never tried it. And we *know*. I know for a fact that a lot of these stories that we tell are true. There's no deviation in 'em; they're all true. There's no such thing as you're going to be on this side or this side," Hastings said, gesturing to the right and left, "you're going to be right in the middle."

"Mmhm."

"You're always in that middle. And they always say, 'Stand right in the middle.' *Ayetli hidogesdi*. 'Don't stand this side or stand on that side.' *Ayetli hidogesdi*. 'Stand right in the middle.'"

"Mmhm."

"That's our teaching. Whether it's something we like to do or don't like to do, we still take on that responsibility. I've done a lot of things. I've worked a lot of places I didn't want to work, but I had to raise a family. My boys live right around me. I pray to the Lord every day for that, because I get to see 'em, pretty much all of 'em at least once a week. We all sit down at the table and eat."

Sequoyah Guess

One afternoon I was browsing through a bookstore in Tahlequah when I came across several self-published books by a local United Keetoowah Band author named Sequoyah Guess. From the blurbs on the backs of the dust jackets, Sequoyah Guess's books looked to be Cherokee horror novels. I bought a copy of each one. They were well written—action packed and deeply aware of Cherokee cultural beliefs regarding the spirit world. They were all set in the Cherokee territory of northeastern Oklahoma, and virtually all the characters were everyday Cherokees. The books' plots were shaped by tensions between traditional Cherokee beliefs and modern American values, a distinctively Cherokee refashioning of the horror genre. In Guess's novels, characters are not frightened of death or pain, but an evil that corrupts community.

I interviewed Sequoyah and over the next few years he became my Cherokee language teacher and friend. We share a mutual love of literature, storytelling, and Cherokee culture. When I head back to the Cherokee Nation every few months, I always look forward to spending time with Sequoyah. Whether it's talking about Cherokee history and culture, playing the slots, or simply driving the roads between Kansas, Oklahoma, and Tahlequah, we always seem to have a good time with each other.

Sequoyah's physical presence is unassuming: he's in his fifties, of medium height and slight build, with mid-length black hair and a mustache. He walks with an upright posture, the effect of a back injury years ago. He's gone by the nickname of Rabbit, and I've sometimes thought he shares some resemblances with that trickster, most notably with his intelligence. But what's most striking about Sequoyah is his eloquence. I have listened to hours of recorded storytelling sessions of the Liars' Club, and it's remarkable that no matter how much I speed up or slow down the recordings of Sequoyah talking or telling stories, his voice comes through in measured, articulate sentences. Others, like myself, often find difficulty in connecting thought to speech; Sequoyah's fluency appears effortless, although I know it's not.

Like his namesake and ancestor, the famed nineteenth-century Cherokee linguist and patriot, Sequoyah, who was also known by his English

Sequoyah Guess

name, George Guess, Sequoyah Guess is a man of many talents. In addition to being a fine novelist, he's an amateur filmmaker, a screenwriter, and a master storyteller. For his storytelling skills, Sequoyah gives all the credit to his grandmother, Maggie Turtle: "My gramma died in 1981 when she was ninety-eight years old. And all my life she would tell me these stories, even when she was on her sickbed. At the house, she would always call me over and tell me these stories. And I never realized that I was the only one that she was doing that to. My brothers, my stepsister and -brothers, she wouldn't do that to. And finally, I asked my mom after Gramma died. I told her 'I remember all these stories from Gramma.' And she told me that Gramma had picked me to carry on her stories even before I was born. Mom told me that one day while she was still carrying me in her belly Gramma came up to her and said, 'This is the one that's going to take my place.' And that's why she told me all these stories over and over and over. And I probably know, all together, forty-five or fifty stories that she told me. And that's including funny stories, scary stories, histories, family stories. And that's including the one that we just call 'Grandpa,' which is the original Sequoyah, of whom I'm a sixth-generation descendant. Hastings Shade is a fifth-generation descendant. All these stories are in me, and I try to honor Gramma by doing just about the same thing that she did all her life in telling me these stories. So, in storytelling everything I do is an effort to honor her. These people in Austin asked me to come down there to tell stories about two years ago. And, after I got through, some of the people, they enjoyed it so much they presented me with different gifts. Each time I would tell them, 'I can't really accept your gift, but on behalf of Gramma, who I learned the stories from and who I honor, I accept it in her behalf.' Because it wasn't me, it was Gramma that did the stories, and I'm just repeating what she said" (Guess 160–61).

Sequoyah explained, "When I tell stories, I do it like Gramma used to. I start my stories just the way she used to, except, of course, she gave all hers in Cherokee. So, I translated her introductions and everything else into English. And I explain that before I start telling the stories. When Gramma finished her stories she would always say in Cherokee, 'That's what the elders used to say.' And, since I learned my stories from Gramma, I always end my stories, 'At least that's what Gramma said.' One of Gramma's storytelling tricks was to use different little voices for different characters, so I do that, too, because that's what she did. Like, Rabbit has a high voice and Wolf has a low voice and sounds kind of dumb.

Gramma used to change her voice, and so I do the same. And the kids love it . . . not only the kids but the grownups, too" (Guess 160–61).

Although there are both male and female storytellers, it is customary for a boy to be taught stories and teachings by his grandfathers or uncles. But Cherokee tradition is flexible and accommodating. Sequoyah's reverence for his grandmother shows in his gratitude for the way she rose to the occasion and taught him when circumstance demanded. He explained how Gramma became his teacher: "My dad died when I was eleven years old. My uncle, who would've been the one to teach me—should have been the one to teach me, anyway—he died when I was nine years old. And so I really had no male figure to teach me. Me and my brother. And that's where Gramma came in. She took over all the teachings. And, my brother, who was older than me, even though Gramma talked with him and told him some stuff, too, he never really totally latched onto it. He was in the . . . what would you call it? That age where there was rock and roll? Woodstock era. All that. That's the age he was in. But, when Gramma started teaching me, even though I didn't latch on too tightly to the medicine part that she was trying to teach me, the stories are what caught in my heart. And so I guess she noticed that. And so she told me over and over all these different stories. And, again, just like Hastings said, she wasn't really Gramma. Blood wise. Family wise. She was our great aunt. But, we called her Gramma. She's the only grandma I ever knew. So, she's the one that taught me all these things. I'm sure mom knew quite a bit, you know. But Gramma's the one that taught me. So."

"So it became her role?" I asked.

"Yeah."

Turtle Island

When I began to work on this book with the Liars' Club, I found there were some stories that everyone knew and often referred to, but rarely told. Many of them were the stories that anchored the Cherokee worldview. One such story is the story of Turtle Island. I asked Sequoyah if he could tell the story he knew of Turtle Island. "Well, mine's just really short," he said. He told me that if I wanted a fuller version that I should ask Hastings if he would tell it. I never got the chance.

"All I remember is . . . ," Sequoyah began . . .

A STORY OF TURTLE ISLAND

Told by Sequoyah Guess

A long time ago
the earth was covered with water.
And over this water
this giant turtle
flew.
And on the back of the turtle was us,
the people.
And, the people kept getting more and more,
until there was so many that they started falling off the sides.
Well, Unetlvnv, the Creator,
saw that happening and so he told
the water beetle to dive down
and bring up a speck of mud.
And so the water beetle dove down to the bottom,
brought up this little speck of mud.
But as soon as it hit air,
that speck of mud started spreading out.
And, the people, they sent out
the giant buzzard.
Suli.
To fly and find a dry spot.
And Suli flew all over the world.
And he started getting tired.
And, as he started getting tired,
he kept getting lower and lower to the earth.
And, when he'd flap his wings whenever he'd go down,
that's where the valleys were formed.
Whenever they'd come up,
that's where the mountains were formed.
And so finally, Suli got back to the turtle.
And he told 'em there was no dry land yet.
So the people waited a while again
and finally they sent out a raven.
And it went out and it stayed out for a long time.
Finally, it came back and it had a
    branch in its mouth.

And that told the people that the mud was dry enough to step on
now, so.
So the turtle landed and the people walked off.
So that's how we got . . .

"And I know that kind of sounds a bit like . . . Noah? With the birds and stuff," Sequoyah said. "But, that's a story that Gramma told me. But, like I said, it's not much. I'm sure Hastings has an expanded version of it. That's what I remember of it."

Names

There are many opinions and some debate regarding our names for ourselves. Are we the Cherokee? The Keetoowah? The Anitsalagi? The Anitsila? The Anigidui? The Aniyunwiya? Are we some of these? All of them? I asked the club about the process of naming.

"Hastings, I've heard differing accounts about the original name for the Cherokee people. Today we often call ourselves the Aniyunwiya, or Real People. The Choctaws called us the people of the caves, and I know that some suspect our name comes from the Creek *chilokee*, which means 'people of a different speech.' But I also know that we are said to come from Kituwah, one of the mother towns near Qualla Boundary in North Carolina."

"We have a documented history of the name or some form of it since 1540 when De Soto wrote it down as Che-La-Que," Hastings said. "The name Cherokee has been spelled about sixty different ways since it was first written by different tribes and nationalities. So, the Cherokee people have a written, documented name of over 470 years.

"The original name for the Cherokee was the Anigidui, or the Coming to the Top or Coming Out people. This is where we get the name Keetoowah. In all the stories, the Creator says, 'From this point in time, you're going to be Keetoowahs.' Gaidwu Desadoesti. That's going to be your name. This was way . . . I mean, this happened right after the time we come out of the ground. We come up on the surface. 'From this day forward, you'll be known as Keetoowah.'"

"And what is that word again you said? The name for coming up out of the ground?" I asked.

"*Giduninugo*—that means, like, this come out," Hastings said, making a motion with his fingers reaching up, like the stems of a plant stretching toward the sun. "See, at one time we were gatherers. We gathered, we hunted, and then we established villages. We began to farm. We began to be growers. Then we began to establish villages.

"The Cherokees were the first to get the fire. This is where we get part of our name: Anitsalagi or Anitsila. The Fire People. Hernando De Soto called us 'Che-La-Que.' The Choctaws called us 'Chu-lok.' From these two names came Cherokee.

"Another original name for the people was Aniugatena, or Dragon Clan. Winged Serpent Clan. They were part of the mound-builder society that the ancient Cherokee called the Red Eye or Fierce People. The Red Eye people ruled the Cherokee and the people were getting tired of this, so there was an uprising and the mean priests, as they were called, were killed."

Sequoyah and Sammy agreed with Hastings. "We're all Keetoowahs," Sequoyah said. "That's our real name. Cherokee is a name given to us by another nation. We call ourselves Keetoowahs."

Sammy added, "Yeah, see. The saying goes that we were given the name Cherokee by the Choctaws. Which meant 'cave dwellers.' Well, the original homeland, it's called the Keetoowah mounds. That's where we all came from. And so this is where we came about. But then, everybody started calling us Cherokees. But we specify today, when we say Keetoowah, we say Keetoowah Cherokees, because that's who we are, Keetoowahs. But people more or less understand that we're Cherokee people."

"Yeah," Sequoyah said, "they've heard the name Cherokee more."

The Liars' Club and I talked about how some folks think they are not Cherokee unless they somehow acquire a Cherokee name, even if it is from a dubious source. Names, they explained, are associated with a person's destiny. They are given to a person, usually in ceremony. But one does not need to have a Cherokee name in order to be Cherokee; in fact, changing one's name without cause may create turmoil in a person's life, a confused destiny.

Driving home that evening, I thought about how the names of the people changed through time with our changing destinies. The Cherokee culture hero, Solegeh, the Winged One, was said to have the head of a snake and wings of a bird. The people took their name from him and became the Aniugatena, or People of the Winged Serpent. We've gained other names in our journey as a people, and we still remember them: Anigidui, Anitsalagi, Anitsila, Keetoowah, Cherokee. There are stories about these names, and they chart the destinies of the people as they changed through time—Anigidui, Anitsila, Aniugatena, Cherokee, Keetoowah, Anitsalagi, Aniyunwiya, Anigiduwagi.

Woody Hansen

"Hey, Woody, do you want to give a little bit of bio that I can put down for the book?" I said. Woody looked up and flashed a wide grin. Since he'd told me a story about a yellow trickster rattlesnake he'd seen in a vision, I'd always seen in him the features of that creature. Bright-eyed, friendly, and contemplative, Woody speaks and moves with an openness of spirit rooted in his Christian faith, values, and a belief in brotherhood and sisterhood across differences. I'd known him before he was hit by a car and had his lower leg shattered. He walks with a limp now and uses a cane, but that nearly fatal encounter between a man, snake, and car seems to have only strengthened his spirituality.

"Why, I'm not much," he said. "I'm just nothing but a carbon unit. Water, mostly. Mostly water, little bit of carbon. Well, you know, I really don't know. I don't know how to describe myself, you know?"

"Me neither," Hastings said.

"I think people that know me could describe me better than I can describe myself."

After a moment, Woody continued: "I am a fellow of the woods. I'm a product of them, just like a lot of Cherokees. My biggest (and this is a personal observation), my biggest drawback about me is I'm not able to speak the language. I understand it.

"When my mom and dad divorced I was young and had the option of living with my mother, who was going to move away. And my mother was a very traditional woman who could do a lot of things that women did in her era, which was cook, sew, can, grow a garden, beadwork. In her early years she was a deaf-mute. She was sent away to school for the deaf and so she could do sign language. Very creative; she loved the arts. Loved songs. And poor dad was just a man of the woods. Planted a garden. Cut railroad ties. He had less than a third-grade education. Spoke perfect Cherokee. He didn't know English very well. He couldn't read English. Or write English. Didn't drive a car. But he could read and write Cherokee and sing in Cherokee. He could grow a heck of a garden.

"But I chose to live with my dad when I was about eight years old during the divorce time. And he told me, he goes, 'Son, I'm not going to teach you Cherokee. Because, look at me. I can't survive in a white world. And

Woody Hansen

today's world is changing so quickly.' This was in the 60s. And he goes, 'I can't keep up.' He goes, 'You're goin' to have to learn English.' Of course, I'd already had first and second grade in English, but I was also bilingual then.

"After second grade I wasn't. Number one, the advent of television came into our house. That became my babysitter because I was the youngest of the family. The next to me was four years older. And they had the benefit of having both parents in the house, of the more traditional Cherokee upbringing with the language, and herbs and roots and stuff. So I was caught in an era where modernism came in, you know? Inside toilet. The television set. Plus, my second-grade teacher scolded me a lot for speaking Cherokee and that scared me. And, to this day, I kind of attribute a lot of that to those two factors. The advent of television being my primary companion and my dad saying, you know, 'I'm not going to teach you Cherokee. The only way you're gonna survive is to learn their ways.' I still remember that.

"I've survived. I've learned their ways. In every other sense I'm Cherokee, Keetoowah, whatever, so. Storytelling? I don't know. I do have stories. But my story, I guess, is just of survival—like a lot of people. I've had this traumatic, broken leg busted real bad. I've been buried alive in 1986 in Arizona in construction. Survived that. I was thrown out of a car and landed on my side where the car spun me around a time and a half without running over me or crushing me. I got spun right up like I was sliding to third base.

"And I'm still looking for me, you know? These three events in my life I could have been killed. Or taken. You know, people say you have a destiny. And each time, they say, 'Well, it wasn't your time.' And I think, 'Well, what do I do in the meantime? How can I contribute?' I don't know. I'm just me. I'm raising kids. I'm there for friends. I don't really see myself being one thing, or two things."

"Yeah. Yeah," I said.

"I'm still looking," Woody said and laughed gently. "I am a snake handler and educator. I have a lot of respect for the reptiles but I don't fear them. But I've never always been that way. I used to do like everyone else, leery and afraid of snakes. Until I had that dream. Is that my goal in life, to be a snake handler and educator? A nonschooled person, just a layman? And that's what I tell a lot of the audience: 'I didn't go to university and get trained.' I'm not a student, per se, or didn't go to college, otherwise I would have been. I know I'm Cherokee and I know I'm Indian and I'm proud of it. But, professionally, as for having a title or label? No, I'm just like that rock there, one of many."

"Mmhm."

"Or that tree," he said and smiled. "Or that star. Like a star I may shine for somebody, and hopefully for my family. And my friends."

"Not everybody 'sees' you, right?" Hastings asked, joking.

"Yeah. Just one of many and sometimes I fall. So, it's hard to say. You might ask Sequoyah here, he'll tell you who I am. Or Hastings . . ."

A Vision Dream

The Creator had given Woody a spiritual gift, a kind of second sight that came to him in vision dreams. When we got together the topic would often turn to Woody's stories about his dreams and the insights their interpretations offered him.

"Well, you know, let me tell you a little quick story that just happened this past week," Woody said. "But, however, the forecasting of it or the vision of it happened two weeks ago. About four or five days before Thanksgiving I had a little vision dream.

"They usually happen in the morning after Joyce gets up and goes to work. And I get up about forty-five minutes later. But usually I've noticed in my life, between that time period, initial waking up, and I'm in that little transition to trying to wake up, I always get a dream vision. And it's . . .

"But this latest one was, my two daughters, Jade and Lani, they were in a golf cart. And, in an unfamiliar place. And I was there, but I wasn't there physically, as I analyzed it. Because I was watching them in this golf cart going rather fast, you know. And going down a grassy path, and I saw a limb in the road and I knew they were going to hit it—there was nothing I could do. I was just watching 'em. Jade was driving. They hit that limb and Lani goes flying out the back, and Jade goes tumbling forward. And Lani bounces up. And Jade was laying there. I said, 'Get up, Jade! Get up, Jade!' She was just kind of sprawled out. I thought, 'Oh man!' And I couldn't get to her. And so, finally, just in a flash I was able to start moving. And two people come out and say, 'No. Stop. She's alright. She'll be okay.' And I say, 'I want to see her!' And they say, 'No, it's alright. She just got a little cut on her head.' So I say, 'Okay.' And I wake up.

"Well, December 1st, which was Tuesday, we get a call. She had donated some blood and in recovery they have you drink some juice and chips. Well, she falls forward, blacks out. And hits her head! And just lays there. You know? I didn't know about this till about two hours after the fact. And Joyce called me, and I said, 'Why didn't you tell me two hours ago, when you learned of it?! We could've been there!' She said, 'No, that's okay. She'll be alright.'"

"Hunh," Sammy said.

"And so, last night, we was watching TV, and all of a sudden I said, 'Hey, you remember that dream I had I told you about Jade?' I said, 'I wonder if this was all connected?' Her falling, lying there. And today she came back from school and she was telling me. She said, 'I was out for quite a bit!' She said, 'All of a sudden, I just pitched forward and hit my head on the carpeted floor.' It wasn't a cut, per se, but it was some scrapes and a goose egg."

"Hunh."

"I knew, maybe, something would happen to Jade. But that was two weeks ago and I kind of put it aside. But I did tell my wife about a day or so later. Well, you're always supposed to wait seven days or even seven weeks before something like that . . . seven, anyway, to tell. I didn't. But it was just like, 'Hmm.'

"And, the two people in the dream that said, 'Wait' turned out to be my wife. Somebody who I thought would be wanting to rush down there. Totally out of her character. So, I got to thinking today when Jade was telling me when we was driving back to Tahlequah to the house. And, I was telling her, 'Jade, this is what I dreamed about you. And this is what you were telling me what happened.'

"It sounds fairly reasonable that it was a message dream. A vision dream. And I said, 'I was upset at your mom for not wanting to go and I was wanting to because a head injury to me' . . . I'm EMS, first responder. That part of me kicked in outside of being a parent. And, plus the dream. Then I remembered, you know, Joyce said everything's going to be alright, like she said in the dream. But then I got to thinking a little bit further into that and said, 'Well, maybe by Joyce not telling me, thinking that I would want to jump in the car and go blazing, I might have had a blowout or an auto accident, or anything.'"

"Yeah," Sammy said.

"According to that dream. So, I had to take those steps," Woody said. "I was telling my daughter, 'You know, to me I always make something big out of what's perceived to be nothing to other people.' I said, 'I don't know why.'"

"Hmm," Sammy said.

"I don't worry," Woody continued. "But that was just something that was like, 'Wow!' It's been a couple of years since I had a vision dream like that. Kind of felt good. But I was telling Jade, 'Those kind of gifts are from above.' Said, 'You have to accept them whether you want them or not. Sometimes it could be a burden because you *know* something's gonna happen, and you've *seen* it, but there's nothing you can do.'" Woody laughed. "So, there it is."

"I saw something like that, and I can still see it in my mind," I said. "It's a place I'm going to try to avoid."

"Mmhm. Yeah. Yeah," Woody nodded.

"I know what it looks like, too. When I see that place . . . ," I said.

"Yep."

"Yeah, I see that place, too," Sammy said as he started to get up. "If I don't get *home* my wife's going to make something happen!" Everyone started laughing. "I want to avoid it! I'll see you guys tomorrow."

Our Hands in the Weave

Hastings, Sequoyah, Woody, and I were discussing how Cherokee stories, like Woody's dreams, require analysis and interpretation. "See, all of our animals, everything that we see was at one time white, *pure*," Hastings said. "And they got their color by getting the fire for the Indians. It wasn't actually given, like we see here. We had to figure out a way to get it. And man, in his infancy, didn't have that concept, but the birds knew and all the animals knew that some point in time man was going to need that fire. So, they devised a way. Crow got black. Mole turned grey. Owl got big eyes. Everything tried, and the spider was the only thing that could get it. And to me that shows how it doesn't matter how small you are, you can accomplish big things."

"Is that why the spider's so . . . ," I said.

"That's why she's so revered," Hastings continued. "The water spider is actually the one that got the fire for us."

"What's the name of the water spider?"

"Doyunisi. Beaver's grandma. And they weren't little back then. Back then they were huge. They weren't small as we see them today. We think, 'That little thing?' But back a long time ago they were big. The water spider is the one that Creator, he seen she done all this for the Indians, he give her that ability to live underwater. Because that's how she got away from the people that guarded the fire. Like I said, it was there, it was a gift, but we had to get it . . ."

"We had to work for it," Woody said slowly, deliberately.

"We had to work for it," Hastings repeated.

"It's the key," Woody said.

"The key is the work," Hastings agreed.

"And we're losing that," Woody continued. "Kids these days don't seem to want to work for it. Or put much effort into it."

"And working together," I said. "These stories always seem to be about people helping each other out."

"Yeah. Yeah," Hastings nodded.

"Animals working together . . . ," Woody said.

"See, each one of them tried, all the animals tried and . . . ," Hastings began.

"And there was no shame in not making it," Woody continued.

"Yeah, yeah," Hastings continued. "And they kept looking at spider and she kept saying 'Let me try.' And they said, 'No, you're too little.' You know how we look at a little person, we think they can't do it. But finally she was the only one left and they said, 'Now it's your turn. You do it.' And so she did. And she was the one that showed us how to make the pottery and how to fire it. And how to weave a basket. We didn't actually make that up; we watched her. And we learned to manipulate our hands in the weave. We learned a lot of things from spider, just by looking. She's a teacher. She's not just a spider to us. She's a *teacher*. The kids, when they're little, like early in the morning, when there's dew on the web, they used to take the web and wash their hands with it and put it on their face. It made them able to use their hands. Made them nimble so they could do things. She's a teacher. That's how come we revere her so much. She's the one that lays her eggs underwater."

"She can go back and forth between the water and land. Is there some power in that?" I asked.

"Yeah. Some creatures can go up and down, in and out. That's power. Anything that can come up and bore down is more powerful than the ones that actually have to stay on top of the earth because they have the abilities to go into Mother Earth and come back out. There's a lot more power to them than we give them credit for. Anything that bores down into something solid is powerful. Like the mole. A long time ago they tied mole paws around their necks to give them a real strong grip, real strong hands."

"That underwater place. I've heard it's a place of creative power," I said.

"Any time you see water, any time you see a spring where it bubbles, that's where the power is," Hastings said. "The power is in that bubbling. And if you can, you need to get the water from that bubbling. Because that's coming right out of Mother Earth. There's not that many springs where they do that around here. They flow out. But very seldom do you see one that actually is bubbling out of the ground."

"That reminds me of when a medicine person blows into the medicine and creates those bubbles," I said.

"Yeah. That's Mother Earth breathing, the bubbles that come back up. That's her breath. There's a lot of things that modern medicine, if they would use it . . . Well, they would *try* to use it but the belief wouldn't be there. They might say, 'I'm going to try it.' But if you say *that* there's no use in even trying it because you have that doubt. There's a difference between *doing* something and *trying* it. Trying it, if you fail, then, well . . . But if you *do* something you set your mind to it." Hastings looked over at Sequoyah carving on a stick. "It's like Sequoyah saying, 'I'm going to try to carve this stick into something.' He started on it, but will he do it?" Sequoyah looked up, and we all started laughing.

The Gift of Fire

When I first met Hastings and we began to talk about the stories, he took me to his storage shed and showed me his craftwork of carved deer horn and handmade bows, arrows, and gigs. From one of his shelves cluttered with papers and carving tools he pulled down a dog-eared copy of the collection of stories, teachings, and Cherokee cultural knowledge he had written down over the years and handed it to me.

Years later, as *Cherokee Stories* began to take shape, Hastings had run into a problem. He and Sequoyah had been using an old Cherokee language-writing program that would only run on an outdated Macintosh computer. I went to work looking for one in Denver and finally found one at a middle school rummage sale. I sent it to Hastings, and he and Sequoyah used that computer to create lesson materials for their Cherokee language courses and write down their stories in Cherokee. At our last meeting together, Hastings handed me the remaining collections of his writings and said, "Use any of 'em you want."

THE WATER SPIDER AND THE FIRE
By Hastings Shade

Many years ago, when Mother Earth was still young, it was dark and cold where the Indians lived. All the creatures that the Creator had put here on Mother Earth were white, except Man. They

Doyunisi

all communicated with each other because their language was the same. And they cared about one another.

The creatures knew that the Indians needed something to keep them warm. They knew that the Creator had told Thunder to put fire into a sycamore tree on an island where he knew that only the ones that could figure out how to get the fire would be the ones he would give the fire to. They could do what they wanted to with it after they got it.

All the animals, birds, insects, and reptiles called a council meeting, and it was decided one of them would have to get the fire. The Bear, being the largest and strongest said, "Let me go first." So with his white coat on he took off towards the island. This is where bear learned how to swim. As he got to where the fire was, he began to walk around trying to figure out how he would carry the fire. Every now and then he would get close to the fire and it began to scorch his fur, at first just enough to turn it a yellow shade. As time went on while he was around the fire it got darker until he realized his fur had turned black. He failed to get the fire, but this is where we get the different shades of colors in bears today.

All the others tried, and they lost their white color. The black snake fell into the fire and it turned him black. The blue racer, it scorched his skin. The black racer burnt his skin and scorched his eyes. This is why all snakes shed their skin to this day.

The raven, crow, and the black birds all turned black. The buzzard burnt the feathers off his head and lost his ability to smell.

The screech owl landed on a limb and looked down into the tree where the fire was and it flamed up and burnt his eyes. They are still red today and he can't see good in the daytime, so he comes out at night. The bigger owl looked into the tree and the fire burnt rings around his eyes. You can still see the stripes in the rings where he rubbed his feathers putting out the fire.

All the creatures got the colors that they have today trying to get the fire. Each one has a story of his own.

When all had failed, the little water spider was given the chance. All this time she had asked them to let her try. They said she was too small.

She lived near the water and had watched the dirt dauber fashion the little balls of mud to carry back to where he was building his nest. She took one of these balls he had dropped and made a small clay pot with a lid and put it on her back and used her web to tie it on with, and she took off.

At this time, she couldn't go under water, but she could glide over it, her being so little.

When she got to where the fire was, she found Thunder had sent a race of giant people, the Fire People, down to watch over the fire. The Creator thought someone who hadn't earned the fire might try to steal it. The Fire People guarded the fire jealously and knew instantly when a small part of it was missing.

She seen the Fire People watching the fire. Her being so small she thought they might step on her. So she would run a little ways, and hide. Run a little ways, and hide. Just as you see spiders do today.

When she reached the fire she took out a small ember of fire. She put it in her clay pot, put it back on her back, and started towards the water. About this time the Fire People decided to go around the fire. She seen them coming and she took off.

She would run a little ways, and hide. Run a little ways, and hide. Until she got to the edge of the water. When the Fire People got close to her, she went under the water, thinking they might take the fire away from her. She hid under the water, and the Fire People could not follow her there. They thought the fire was surely out. But the ember inside the pot had baked the clay and made the pot waterproof. And she brought the fire to the Cherokee people and gave them fire.

The Cherokees took the fire and buried it in the ground to keep it safe. Whenever the Cherokees want to thank the Creator they dance around the fire. This is the eternal fire that we have today that is at the stomp grounds.

The water spider taught us how to make pottery and fire it. The dirt dauber showed us how to work the clay so when it dries it will last a long time. We used this method when we built our homes. We would wet the mud before we daubed it on the walls, just like the dirt dauber does.

We still honor the water spider to this day. We use her designs on our pottery. You can see her image and geometric designs she uses to weave her web on our pendants and gorgets.

The Creator gave her the ability to live under water, which is where she hides her egg sac to this day. She is still revered by the

Cherokee people. See, you don't have to be big to accomplish great things in your life.

The Language and the Fire

"There is a legend," Hastings said, "that as long as we speak to the fire in Cherokee it will not go out, and as long as the terrapins sing around the fire we will have the fire for our use. When the language is gone, the fire will be gone. And so will the Cherokees. That is why the terrapin shells are used for the shackles the women wear while they are stomp dancing; this is how the terrapin sings."

The flame that Doyunisi gave us as a gift of the Creator has burned continuously since ancient times. Called the eternal flame, the fire was brought over from the Cherokee homelands in the east when we were removed to Indian Territory. It is a sacred fire, a living embodiment of Creator. It is watched over and maintained to this day.

The Cherokee language that we speak is another gift of the Creator. It is said that the ancient language Cherokees spoke transformed through the course of the long migration from the south to where we are today. The language we speak today is the fourth language we've spoken.

Hastings, Sequoyah, Woody, and I talked about the connections between the fire and the language, and about the perpetuation of Cherokee peoplehood:

"The focal point, rightly, is the *language*," Hastings said emphatically. "Because, we lose the language we lose the fire. The Jews have already lost their fire. There was only two entities, and that was the Native people or indigenous people and the Jews that had fire at one time. They have done something that put their fire out; I don't know what it was."

"And to me that fire was the Ark of the Covenant," Woody offered.

"Yeah. It was a direct gift from the Creator. It wasn't something that we thought of, it wasn't something . . ."

"Or a gift from somebody else. But, from above!" Woody said.

"The Creator. And it took a, it took a little spider to get it for us; it didn't take the biggest animal. It took the smallest," Hastings said.

"And just like the story of David slaying the lion," Woody said.

"I've seen that fire," I said. "I've seen it rain and the fire would not go out."

"Mmhm. Yeah," Hastings said and smiled. "Yeah, once you start the fire at the stomp grounds . . . I don't care how much rain, it won't go out. People don't realize that."

"That's the prayer, you know," Woody offered.

"I've seen the water go right around it. Flood right around it," I said.

"Yeah."

After a moment, Hastings said, "But if you start a fire at the grounds . . . I don't care if it rains, it won't go out. Because it's been called up. I mean, somebody's, 'Where's the fire at?' It's there, I mean, it's *there*." He laughed. "You can't see it, I can't see it, but when you call it up it's there."

"The fire is *alive*. It's an entity in itself," Sequoyah said.

"If you could see it. It's just like them four directions. It's burning this way," Hastings said, and made a weaving gesture with his hand. "If we could actually see it with these eyes. But they have certain ones—the fire starters—that they've doctored. They can go out there and, just like you and I sitting here, next thing you know they got a fire. You don't see 'em doing this or that with it. Pretty soon that fire's burning."

"They don't have to fan it," Sequoyah added. "They don't have to keep feeding it wood and stuff. But that fire, like I said, it's alive and it knows what it's doing. I mean, it has a mind of its own. At the grounds, of course you know this, you're not supposed to be drinking or using drugs when you're at the grounds. But if there's somebody there doing that the fire will tell, will point him out. That this person isn't supposed to be there. And, it knows what it's doing and I say it's got a mind of its own. Was that last weekend when we was at the lake?" Sequoyah asked Woody.

"Mmhm."

"We couldn't get the fire going. I mean, this was just a regular campfire. We had a bunch of coals, but the fire just wouldn't start, you know?"

"And, finally it kind of started just enough. Just a little bit. And, there was a couple little boys there. It kept them busy all night long. So that fire knew what it was doing. If those boys didn't have that fire to keep on feeding and trying to get it going, they would have got bored right away. 'Cause there was just a bunch of grownups there."

"Who knows what they would have gotten into," I said.

"Hmm," Woody nodded, then laughed.

"So that fire *knew* what it was doing," Sequoyah said.

"Well, they might have burned themselves if it was a flaming fire," Woody added.

"Yeah, a big flaming fire. 'Cause it was kind of windy," Sequoyah said.

"A long time ago they would evaluate you by what kind of fire you started," Hastings said. "If you were smart, not lazy, and you build a fire it'd happen quick. If you were lazy it takes that fire a little while to . . ."

"You know, I was lazy that night 'cause I'm the usual fire starter in our family at gatherings like that," Woody said. "And I just attributed it to being lazy, because I broke my first rule of thumb. Which is to start small. Well, to pray about it and walk around it first. And I didn't! I had my former wife there and my present wife there and my kids and other people, you know, and it's just like, 'Let's hurry up. It's getting dark.' And I broke my rule. Didn't pray, didn't walk around it. And didn't start small," he said and laughed. "And boy it bothered me for three or four days. I kept telling Joyce, 'I can't believe I did that.' But then again, you know, the fact of those little boys."

"Yeah," Sequoyah agreed.

"And I said as we were sitting around, fanning it, I said, 'I'm glad we have young men to help at least keep this going.' So it did have a good thing about it."

"There's people that can build fire that tall," Hastings put his hand waist high, "that fire will be cold."

"Mmhm," Sequoyah agreed.

"There's people that can build fire, be like that," Hastings placed his hand shin high, "and you can have all the heat you want."

"Yeah, even at the house, if there's just a couple of coals in my wood stove I can get it going without paper," Woody said. "And I've always been that way."

The Journey of the Four Directions and the Winged One

In my work with the Cherokee Nation government and within Cherokee community, I'd often heard people speak of the need to revitalize and perpetuate our language, culture, and history. Early in our work on this book, the members of the Liars' Club and I discussed the most well-known source on Cherokee worldview, stories, and medicine, the American ethnologist James Mooney's *Myths of the Cherokee* (1890). While they recognized the importance of Mooney's work, Hastings and the others were quick to point out that Mooney's texts provided, at best, a glimpse of Cherokee culture and beliefs.

In *Myths of the Cherokee*, Mooney wrote this of the Cherokee migration story: "Owing to the Cherokee predilection for new gods, contrasting strongly with the conservatism of the Iroquois, their ritual forms and national epics had fallen into decay before the [American] Revolution, as we learn from Adair. Some vestiges of their migration legend still existed in Haywood's time [1823], but it is now completely forgotten both in the

East and in the West" (20). Not surprisingly, due to his lack of information, Mooney was incorrect about this facet of Cherokee mythic history.

On a cool afternoon at Hastings's home in Lost City, I asked him if he would share with me the story of the Cherokee migration from our ancient homeland to our beginnings in the Smoky Mountains. He told this version of the migration story that Mooney believed did not exist:

THE JOURNEY OF THE FOUR DIRECTIONS
Told by Hastings Shade

Well, a long time ago they talk about an island that was surrounded by water that was undrinkable. That's where all the Cherokee lived at one time.

And one day the island began to shake. And the mountains opened up with fire. *Atsila unegojv.* This is told in Cherokee and it's been translated into English, so. Because we use English, I'll kind of have to describe what happened.

The mountains opened up and fire issued forth. Fire come out. The island began to sink. And that's when they sent the warrior groups, the first ones out. And that's the one we know today as the Wolf Clan. But they wasn't clans at the time, they was warriors. And the runners, which were Deer Clan, were the second group. They left in seven groups. The last one to leave the island was the Wild Potato group, which was the keepers of Mother Earth.

And it says that they had to, the story goes they had to get to the main island. *Elo egwa* in Cherokee they called it, the "main island." The way they talked it was, you know, quite a ways.

It took them a while to get there, but the fourth day's journey out the last group to leave the island, as they topped a big mountain they looked back, they seen their homeland go under water— *uhnequoje* they say. That's what that means, you know: "sunk under water."

And that's when the journey to the cold started. They didn't say "north," they says "cold." And they say they journeyed north, you know, this group. Some of them stayed, some came on, and they found a place, you know, of barren lands and fertile lands. Some stayed, some came on. That's the way this migration happened as they headed toward the cold.

And they seen big animals, you know, on their way. Some were

Solegeh

killed for food, shelter, and clothing. These were the huge animals, not the ones we typically see nowadays.

As that journey come north, which took many, many years, at that time the languages begin to change—*unedliyvse* they say. As they come north, they come to the place where the white mountain moved—they say *janadisgo*, and that's what that means in English: "where the white mountain that moves." Anohilinese. Anohilinese.

And they stayed there two nights. And the elders that could see the future said, "This is not a good place to be. It's not a good place." So they started forward to the place where the sun comes up. And as they started towards where the sun come up on their journey they crossed this big *kanogeni*, which is river. A big river— *egwa kanogeni* they called it. Could have been the Mississippi.

And they said *nadehidwa*, that's where they found the mound builders. They were already there, you know? Cherokees found them. They encountered the mound builders. They stayed there for a long time till they became one—*saqwu unastvne*—that's what that means: "they became one" with the mound build-ers. And that's how come the Cherokees now are associated with mound builders. They weren't mound builders at the time, but they were associated. And that was when the priest clan and all them came in.

But the journey says they continued toward the east, toward where the sun come up. They didn't say "east" either, they said toward where the sun come up, which we know today as "east." And as they continue on they come to the place that kind of favored their homeland, the mountains and some of the materials that they were used to in their homeland was there. And that's where they stayed. And that's where they were when the Europeans found 'em. Today it's known as the Smoky Mountains.

So, that's the origin. One origin.

The other origin told us of the priest clan and how the, the Winged One came to be, came to earth.

It says, *unohilole*: he who flew down. A lot of them seen him. This is the one that had the serpent head and the human body. And as the priest clan began to kill the Cherokee people, sacrifice them, the Cherokees told them to quit and they quit for a little while. Just like people do, you tell people something and sometimes they stop.

But later they started killing again, so that's when he got the bird warriors together.

They called them the "bird warriors." That's where they got that mask—the lightning whelk mask. That was the actual protection. And he gave these warriors the ability to fly. That's how come the Cherokees still to this day know how to get around, other than the typical transportation. So . . .

And they were killed. Most of the priest clan was killed, but some of the blood survived, you know. Later on, as the blood appeared the elders knew what to look for and they was also killed. That's where all these other things come in, like the priest clan, whether you've heard about it or not, that's where the priest clan come in. They were mean. And they were not . . . they were not of this world, the elders used to say—*tla elo unadehnv yigese*. And that's what that means: "they were not born of the earth." They were from somewheres else.

And as we continued on to North Carolina, that's where we built some of the mounds. We didn't build a whole lot of the mounds. A lot of the mounds was already there when we got there. The star mound that they talk about in North Carolina is where we got our information. It's either in North Carolina or Georgia, somewhere like that. Tennessee. It's something we really need to find. That's where they got their information. Whenever they wanted something they went to this Star Mound and that's where the information was and they got it. And that's all they would get is what they went after.

And one day they went and they found holes in the mound that somebody dug into it. And they had turned all this stuff loose in the world. That's how come we have all this stuff going on. The wind, the fire and all that stuff is, is turned loose. At one time it was kind of contained, to be used as needed. So that's part of the migration story.

"Mmhm," I murmured. I asked Hastings, "When the Cherokees got together with the mound builders—are there stories about how that relationship fell apart?"

"They just, after the priest clan were killed they kind of turned them loose. I guess they were kind of held captive for a while," Hastings said.

"But they just says they 'became one.' Married into it." Hastings paused a moment, then shifted the conversation to the present. "That's where we get some of our medicine people. The blood that was mixed between the ones not of this earth and some of the Cherokees. That's how that blood mingled. And that's how we got our teachers, you know, our medicine people. The people that taught things, you know. So."

"What did those otherworldly people, those priests, what did they want from the Cherokee?" I asked.

"They was wanting domination," Hastings said. "They wanted to dominate 'em. Slaves, I guess, if you wanted to call it that. See, slavery is not something that just happened with the blacks. It was way back. Way before Europeans ever thought about coming over."

"Mmhm."

"So, that was their goal. The ones that the elders rebelled against. And that's when the Winged One, Solegeh they call him—there's no known meaning for the word or the name—that's when he come down. So elders, you know, they talk about seeing him. And that's how you describe him, *unohilole*, and to me it says "he flew down." *Diiyutlawidohe*, that says, "he landed here on earth." Flew down and landed here on earth. They say he came from where we did. The sky. And that's when he began to tell this priest clan what they were doing was wrong. And that's when they started doing it again and he got some of the warriors together—*dinatli*. This time the Winged One gathered up warriors and gave them the ability to fly and protection against the ones they were to kill. He gave 'em that ability to fly and that mask was their protection from the priest clan. That's the lightning whelk mask. And that's what they used. And all they used it for was protection. And that's the only mask that we ever used that meant anything to us. It was more like a shield, I guess."

"And he looked like a bird?" I asked.

"That's what they said. He had bird wings, a human body, and a serpent head. That's the way he's described. *Jisqua kanogeni, yvwuh uyelia, inadvhn asgoli*. That's what that means: he had bird wings, human body, and a serpent head."

"So he had a serpent head just like the priests did," I said. "The chief of the priests did, too."

"Probably. He may have been one of 'em. And he could of told 'em what they were doing was wrong." After a pause, Hastings said, "That's a story, you know, and you kind of have to look into it. 'What was he? Why did he come?'"

"Mmhm."

"He may have been *their* leader, from where we come from. We don't know. That's just a story that says *unohilole*; it don't say where he come from. Well, it does say *galunlati diyulose*."

"Heaven," Woody said.

"He come from the heavens," Hastings continued.

"Mm," I murmured, wondering how that piece of information might change my understanding of the story.

After a pause, Woody said slowly, "And it's kind of . . . it may not line up chronologically, you know, but if you read in the Bible, it tells of Methelem, the fallen angel that came and intermarried with earthly women and that was forbidden. And a lot of them were destroyed and things of that nature, too."

"Mmhm," I agreed.

"So . . . it's possible!" Woody said.

"There's a lot of parallels with the modern Bible and some of our old stories," Hastings added.

The Liars' Club and I would often return to the topic of the Winged One and his battle with the mound builders, who the Cherokee know as the Dinikani, the Red Eye People, or the Aninayegi, or Fierce People. When looking for parallels for Keetoowah myths and legends, Woody would point to stories from the Bible. When the Winged One came and liberated the Keetoowah people by training the men to fly as Bird Warriors, he was like Moses liberating the Israelites. When little Doyunisi stole the fire from its guardians, it was like David slaying Goliath. Christians as well as traditionalists, Hastings, Sequoyah, and Woody frequently switched back and forth between biblical and Cherokee traditions. We often talked about the differences between Christian doctrine and Cherokee religious beliefs, such as the fact that there is no concept of hell in Cherokee thought, but the members of the club would return to the unifying idea of faith to find common ground between these different religious systems. Christianity is based in faith in the Bible as the word of God; Cherokee beliefs are based in faith in the stories and teachings of the elders.

The war with the Dinikani was a traumatic event for the Cherokee. They had joined the Dinikani and were part of them in every way; the Cherokee had married into their society and were governed by their priests. But as Hastings explained, over time the governing priest clan became more and more power hungry and abusive. "These were the ones that sacrificed people and were cannibals," Hastings said. "Not that they craved the human flesh. If they captured or killed someone that was brave or strong they believed that if they ate their flesh they would get the strength and courage the individual had." At first they gained symbolic power by sacrificing captives from other tribes. But Hastings said, "As time went on they became meaner and meaner and began sacrificing some of their own people, the Cherokees. These people were so mean that when they buried their dead into Mother Earth she would reject them. The elders say when they would bury the mean ones into the ground as we do our people that have died, the next day they would be lying on top of the ground. So in order to bury their dead they built mounds. This is how they became known as the mound builders. This way they would be buried above the ground and not into Mother Earth." Hastings believed that when the mounds were excavated and tampered with by archaeologists, the spirits of those Red Eye people were let loose in the world.

"The priest clan were killed out, but the blood remains," Hastings said, referring to the blood of the Cherokee people. "There is always going to be blood somewhere. It don't go away. The elders that knew, every now and then the priest clan blood came out and they would get rid of it. But after they left and nobody watched anymore, you know, there's no telling what's there, what kind of blood is left. The ones that know how to look for the blood no longer try to find it and are not willing to teach the younger generation because they say they are not interested in learning it anyway. You have to know the language to do this and people now days wouldn't believe you any way."

"Did Solegeh stay with the people?" I asked.

"After they defeated the priest clan Solegeh went back to where he came from. But he left some of his blood to remind us of his being here on earth," Hastings added. The elders say the Winged One left a species of smaller flying snake, and those are his descendants. This snake had leathery wings like the *siniqua*, or pterodactyl. "They say you could hear it coming," Hastings said. "When it was flying it sounded like someone was swinging a rope, like a swishing sound." On some of the effigies, pendants, and other materials you can see the image of the Winged One. "Before the Winged One left he taught us how to doctor the bites of poisonous snakes," Hastings said.

ᎤᎩ ᎠᏗᎵ ᏧᏂᏟᎣᏒᎯ
NVGI ADITLA TSUNILOSVHI
FOUR, DIRECTIONS, WHERE THEY JOURNEYED FROM

Ꮒ'ᏪᏲᎯᎡᎦ Ꮂ'ᏃᏢᏔ
Ulasgvhi unohetlai
Hastings, what he told

ᎢᎵᎦᎢᎻᎡᎡ ᏣᏂᏃᎮᏍᎠ ᎠᏛ ᎠᏗᏩᎣᎠᎯᎻᎡᏂ ᎤᏝᎬᎯᎣᏍ ᎡᎬᎰ. ᎾᎾ ᎭᏍᏝ
   ᎠᏂᏗᏛ ᎠᏂᏣᎳᎩ.
Ilvhiyutsigesv tsaninohesgo ama aditasdinigesvni udwadisde elohi.
   Una nigada aninele Anitsalagi.
A long time ago, they talk about, water, undrinkable, surrounded
   by, the earth. That's where, all, lived, the Cherokee.

ᎾᏛ ᎾᏛᏓᎮ ᎡᎬᎰ ᎤᎾᎬᏌᏛᎦ ᎠᏛ ᎤᎳᏛᎵᎦ ᎠᎭᏩ ᏏᎵᎠᏓ.
Uhnadv ulenvhe elohi unawasdv ale uwodvlv atsila ganegotsv.
There, it began, the earth, to shake, and, the mountains, fire came
   out.

ᏣᏩᎩᏛ ᏣᏁᎳᎣᏍᎠ ᏣᏂᏃᎮᏟ ᎠᏎᏍᎩᏃᏌ ᎯᎵᏍ ᎮᎳᏦᎡ ᏃᏣ. ᎣᎩᏫᏃᏣᎣᎠ
   ᎤᏍᏗᎠᏉᏛ ᎠᎩᏃᎮᏗ.
Tsalagidv tsanadisgo yuninohetli asesgino yonega nigvnelv nowa.
   Sgihenoyusdi nustidolv aginohedi.
It was Cherokee, they used, when they told it, because of this,
   English, it was changed to, now. That is why, the things that
   happened, I must tell it.

ᎠᏤᏩ Ꮎ'ᏝᎠᏓ ᏧᏬᏛᎵᎦ.
Atsila unegotsv tsuwodvlv.
Fire, came out, the mountains.

ᎾᏝ ᎡᎬ ᎠᎬᏌᎬ ᎾᏛᏓᎮ.
Uhna elo agvsgv ulenvhe.
There, the earth, began, to drown.

ᎠᏂᎠᏛᏃᏬᎠᏃᏗᎵᏣ ᎠᎬᏱ ᎤᏂᏟᎣᏎ. ᎠᏂᎦᎣᎳᎣ ᎠᏃᏎᎰ ᎠᎫᎦᏍ.
Aniadanowodinatli agvyi wunilose. Aniwahaya anoseho kohiga.
The war fighters, the first, they went. The Wolf Clan, they call them,
   today.

DhᏠᏪᎣᏫᏯ DhᎠᎾ ᏔᏢᎾᎯᏗ ᎤhᎬᎦ4.

Anidanasgi, aniawi, talinehi wunilose.

The runners, the Deer Clan, the second, they went.

ᏩᏢᎥᎥᎦ ᎢᎠ ᎤᏍᏠᏟᏚ ᎤᏍᎾᎾᎩᎡᎡ.

Galigwoga igo unadatlaga unanagisv.

Seven, the total of, groups, left.

DhᎠᏢᏞᎾ Ꭴh ᎤhᎬᎦ4. ᎡᎬᎯ ᎤᏬᏫᎾ4ᎤᎯ ᎶᏞᎡ ᎤᎯᏯᏃ DhᎠᏢᏞᎾ.

Anigodagewi oni wuniloe. Elohi uhakasesdi tsigesv sgino
    anigodagewi.

The Wild Potato Clan, the last, they went. Earth, they took care of,
    used to be, those, the Wild Potato Clan.

ᎡᎬ ᎡᎢ ᎤhᎷᎯᎥᎤᎯ ᎶᏞᎡ.

Elo egwa wuniluhisdi tsigesv.

Earth, big, they had to arrive at, used to be.

ᏉᎬᎣᎠ ᏚᎥᎯᏞ ᎤᏍᎾᎤᏴᎣᎤᎯ ᎶᏞᎦ. ᏣᎾᎳᎣᎠ.

Doyudv ganvhida unanvgisdi tsigehv. Tsanadisgo.

Very, long, they had to walk, it was, they said.

ᎠᎯᏞ ᎤhᎬᎦ4, Ꭰ4ᎣᏯᎾ ᎤᎥᏯᎯᎢᏚ ᎶᏞᎡ Ꭴh ᎤᏍᏠᏟᏚ ᎤhᎣᏴᎷᎵ ᎤᎬᎤᎬᎣᎥ ᎡᎢ
    ᎤᎾᎠᎦᎢᏆ ᎡᎬ ᎡᎷ ᎤᎢᎥᎥᏉ.

Gohida wunilose, asesgina nvgineiga tsigesv oni unadatliga
    wunihalusa uwodvla egwa unagodvhe elo etsi uhegwotse.

A long time, they went, but, the fourth day, it was, the last, group,
    went to the top, mountain, big, they saw, earth, mother, sink into
    the water.

ᎤᏢᎣᎠ ᎤᏟᎤᎤᏆ ᎤᎡᏢ ᎫᏟ ᎠᎯᎬ.

Uhnadv udlenvhe wuyvtlv ditla anegv.

It was there, it began, toward the cold, that direction, they went.

ᎬᎾᎤᎣᏫᏟᎾ, ᎢᏚᏞ Ꮯ ᎬᎤᏢᎥᎣᏅ4 ᎬᎾᎾᏯᎡ, ᎢᏚᏞᏃ ᏛhᎬᎣᎠᏞ. ᎤᏘ ᎠᎤ ᎤᏟᏞ
    ᏚᏞ ᎤhᎠᎬᏔᎯ.

Yunalewisdana, igada tla yunaligwose yunanagisv, igadano
    wanilosge. Uyo ale uteda gada unigowatane.

When they stopped, some, no, join in, when they would go, some,
    they continued. Bad, and, good, land (dirt), they saw.

ᎤᏚᏞ ᎤᏟ ᎤᎾᎤᎣᏫᏔᎯ, ᎢᏚᏞᏃ ᎤᎡᏢ ᎫᏟ ᎤhᎬᎦ4.

Igada uhna unalewistane, igadano wuytlv ditla wunilose.

Some, there, they stopped. Some, toward the cold, that direction, they went.

ᎥᏍᎩᏛ ᏄᎳᏍᏛᏁ ᏩᎾᏂᏒ ᏭᏴᏢ ᏗᏝ.
Vsgidv nulasdvne wananisv wuyvtlv ditla.
That's the way, it happened, as they went, the cold, that direction.

ᎡᏆ ᎢᎾᎨ ᎠᏁᎯ ᏚᏂᎪᏩᏔᏁ ᏩᎾᎢᏒ. ᎢᎦᏓ ᏓᏂᎷᎨ ᏧᏂᎩᏍᏗ ᎠᎴ ᎤᏂᏝᏦᏛ ᎠᎴ ᏧᎾᏬᏍᏙᏘ ᎤᏰᏟᏗ.
Egwa inage anehi dunigowatane wanaisv. Igada daniluge tsunigisdi ale unitlatsodv ale tsunawosdoti uyetlidi.
Big, forest dwellers, they saw, as they went. Some, they killed, to eat, and, shelter, and, clothing, for that purpose.

ᎯᎠᏃ ᏙᏳ ᎡᏆ ᏂᎾᎨ ᎠᏁᎯ ᏥᎨᏒ, Ꮭ ᏱᏗᎪᏘᎰ ᎪᎯᎦ.
Hiano doyu egwa ninage anehi tsigesv, tla yidigotiho kohiga.
These, very, big, forest dwellers, they were, no, don't see them, today.

ᎪᎯᏓ ᏥᎨᏒ ᏭᏴᏢᏗᏝ ᎠᎾᎢᏒ, ᎤᏂᏬᏂᏍᏗ ᎤᏁᏟᏴᏎ.
Gohida tsigesv wuyvtlvditla anaisv, uniwonisdi unetliyvse.
A long time, it was, toward the cold, they walked, their language, it changed.

ᎠᎾᎢᏒ ᏭᏴᏢ ᏗᏝ ᎤᏁᎦ ᎤᎶᏛᎸ ᏭᏂᎷᏨ. ᎠᏎᏍᎩᏃ ᎠᏃᎯᎵᏁᏎ.
Anaisv wuyvtlv ditla unega ulodvlv wunilutsv. Asesgino anohilinese.
As they walked, toward the cold, in that direction, white, mountain, they arrived to, however, it moved.

ᏔᎵ ᎢᎦ ᏧᏒᎯ ᎤᏁᏙᎳ ᎤᎿ.
Tali iga tsusvhi unedola uhna.
Two, the total of, those nights, they ventured, there.

ᎠᏎᏍᎩᏃ ᎠᏂᎦᏴᎵ ᏗᏂᎪᎭᏘᏍᎩ, Ꮭ ᎣᏍᏗ ᏱᎦ ᎠᎭᏂ, ᎤᎾᏛᏁᎢ. ᎨᏍᏗ ᎣᏍᏓ ᏱᎩ.
Asesgino anigayvli dinigohatisgi, tla osdi yiga ahani, unadvnei. Gesdi osda yigi.
However, the old ones (elders), the seers, No, good, it is, here, they said, it isn't, good, it is.

ᎤᎾᎮᏃ ᏗᎧᎸᎬ ᏭᏂᎶᏎ.
Unaheno dikalvga wunilose.
There it was, where the sun comes up, they went.

ᏗᎧᎵᎦ ᏗᏝ ᏩᎾᎢᏍ ᎡᏆ ᎧᏃᎩᏂ ᏭᎾᏩᏔᎠᏍᎥᏢᏁ.

Dikalvga ditla wanaisv egwa kanogeni wunatosvtlvne.

Where the sun comes up, in that direction, they went, big, river,
    they crossed.

ᎤᎾᎭᏛ ᏚᏂᏩᏜᎮ ᎤᎶᏛᎸ ᏗᏃᏢᏍᎦ.

Unahadv duniwadvhe ulodvlv dinotlvsga.

That is where, they found, mound, makers (builders).

ᎦᎳᏃ ᎠᏁᏙᎮ ᏍᎩᎾ ᎤᎶᏛᎸ ᏗᏃᏢᏍᎩ.

Galano anedohe sgina ulodvlv dinotlvsgi.

Already, they were there, those, mound, makers (builders).

ᎪᎯᏓ ᎤᏁᏙᎸ ᎤᎾ ᎤᎶᏛᎸ ᏗᏃᏢᏍᎩ ᎠᏁᎲ, ᏌᏬ ᎤᎾᏍᏛᏁ, ᎠᏂᏣᎳᎩ ᎠᎴ
    ᎠᏂᏳᎶᏛᎸ ᏗᏃᏢᏍᎩ.

Gohida unedolv una ulodvlv dinotlvsgi anehv, sawu unasdvne,
    anitsalagi ale aniulodvlv dinotlvsgi.

A long time, they ventured there, at that place, mound, makers
    (builders), where they lived, one, they became, Cherokees, and,
    mound, makers (builders).

ᎨᏍᏛ ᎤᎶᏛᎸ ᏗᏃᏢᏍᎩ ᏱᎨᏎ ᎠᏎᏍᎩᏃ ᎤᎾᏂᏕ ᏙᏳ ᎤᎶᏛᎸ ᏗᏃᏢᏍᎩ ᎨᏒ.

Gesdv ulodvlv dinotlvsgi yigese asesgino unanide doyu ulodvlv
    dinotlvsgi gesv.

Weren't, mound, makers (builders), they weren't, however, they
    knew, very, mound, makers (builders), were.

ᎤᎾᎮᎾ ᎤᎾᏓᎴᏅᎮ ᎠᏂᎫᏔᏂ.

Unahena unadalenvhe anigutani.

That was where, they began, anikutani.

ᏃᎴᏛ ᎤᎾᎾᎩᏒ ᏗᎧᎸᏓ ᏗᏝ.

Noledv unanagisv dikalvda ditla.

Once again, they began going, where the sun comes up, in that
    direction.

ᎣᏂᏃ ᏩᎾᎢᏍᎥ ᏗᎧᎸᎬ ᏗᏝ ᎤᏂᏩᏛᏁ ᏍᏫᏓ ᎤᎶᏓᎸ ᎠᎬᏱ ᏧᏁᏅᏒ ᎤᏍᏗ.

Onino wanaisv dikalvgv ditla uniwadvne swida ulodalv agvyi
    tsunenvsv yusdi.

At last, as they walked, where the sun comes up, in that
    direction, they found, many, mountains, first, where they
    lived, like.

ᎤᎾᏛ ᎠᏂᏁᎴ ᎠᏂᏲᏁᎦ ᎠᎬᏳ ᏧᏂᎳᏨ.

Unadv aninele aniyonega agvyu tsunilutsv.

That is where, they lived, first, white people, they arrived.

ᏍᎩᏛ ᏄᏍᏔᏂᏙᎴ ᎠᏛᏱ ᏦᎩᎶᏒ ᏣᎾᏗᏐᎠ.

Sgidv nustanidole advyi tsogilosv tsanadiso.

That is, the things that happened, first, where we journeyed from,
    that's what they say.

The Cherokee Migration

On a late summer afternoon, Sequoyah and I were roaming around Tahle-quah and found ourselves at the Heritage Center outdoor amphitheatre. Apart from some kids who were playing a game of chase in the brambles and woods behind the stage, we had the place to ourselves. We sat on the concrete steps and talked.

"You know, last night at the stomp grounds I was talking to someone about the migration story. He was saying, a long time ago the story was told in, like, seven nights," I said.

"Yeah," Sequoyah nodded, looking down.

"There was a seven-night version and a four-night version," I said.

"Mmhm. Yeah," Sequoyah answered. "What Gramma told me, she told me in two nights. And then when me and Hastings got together and com-pared notes, that's when it came to about three nights. When the whole thing comes together, you know. So. And I guess he was the same way, you could tell the whole thing in about two nights. And the stuff that he gleaned from me, I think it probably gave him that much more to tell. And there's a few other people that I've heard tell the story and they have a little bit that they've had in theirs we didn't have in mine or Hastings's. But I usually don't include their stuff since, being a traditional storyteller, Gramma's the one that told me these things, and the people that I hear the other parts from, they're not family. But Gramma was family and she charged me with the story and since Hastings is what I call my immedi-ate elder, you know, it felt right to go ahead and include his stuff. But the others that I've heard, some parts, they're not family so I don't include their stuff. It might be, you know, it might be just for that family. Maybe they were only telling me 'cause they thought that I'd be interested in it. Have you heard me tell that story?" Sequoyah asked.

"I've heard you tell the short version," I answered. "Not the long one."

"Like I said, Gramma, it took her, like, two nights to tell me. And, she would get so far and stop; it was like a serial, you know?" Sequoyah said and laughed. "She'd get to a good part and say, '*Come sunali usani.*' Or, 'Now. Wait till tomorrow night.'"

"For the exciting conclusion of . . ."

"Yeah! So, let me give you the *Reader's Digest* version so you can listen to it some time. Or rather, this is the comic book version!"

"Okay! So this is the thirty-five minute one . . ."

"Ten-, fifteen-minute one. What I'm going to tell you is, like I said, a mixture of what Gramma told me and what's been handed down in Hastings's family. And, still yet, I've been able to, over the last few years, cut it down to what I tell. I've noticed that most of the stories, when most of the storytellers that tell the story, they all begin about the same way. And so I'll go ahead and start it that way."

Sequoyah sat quietly for twenty seconds or so, the only time I'd seen him do that before telling a story. And then he began.

THE CHEROKEE MIGRATION STORY
Told by Sequoyah Guess

Ilvhiyujigesv.
In the great forever that was.
　　Our people lived
　　on land
　　that was surrounded by water
　　you couldn't drink.
And the people
　　thrived
　　on this land.
The different families
of the people
which later became known as clans,
they all had different jobs
that they were to do.
Like, one family
did all of the planting and growing.
Another might have been in charge of
the games, like marbles, stickball.
Another family might have been in charge of medicine
for everybody.

And then there was a clan that was in charge of medicine
only for children.
And then there was the architects, or the builders.
There was a clan that kept the fire.
A clan that were, like, scribes.
There were the messengers.
Of course, the warriors.
And then there was the knowledgeable clan, I guess you'd say.
    Unanti.
Which later on got mixed and they started calling 'em Kutanis.
And then there was the . . . there was four more.
There were fourteen families altogether.

All of the things that the people done,
it was great.
I mean, there was none that
rivaled what the people knew,
and how to grow things,
and how to build things,
and everything, everything was
the best on this island.

The architects, they built cities.
They built great cities
with temples that reached to the sky,
and pavilions that went on for miles.

And the farmers, they grew so much that
hunger wasn't known with the people.
And it wasn't tolerated.
If anybody needed food they could just
go out into the fields and pick whatever they wanted,
and leave the rest for whoever else wanted some.

The medicine was so great that
hardly anybody ever got sick.
And if anybody did, the medicine
was so great that they all were healed.

The knowledgeable ones,
the Unanti,
they were the greatest seers of that time.

And, one day,
the seers, they,
they looked into the future and saw
something that was gonna happen
years from then.
And so they got together,
they got all the families together and
told 'em to do the best they could and
get everything ready for
in seven years there was going to be something that,
something big, cataclysmic was going to happen.

But the architects, they went
to the architects, the builders,
they told 'em,
we need you to build us
seven vessels, that will not sink in the water.
And so the architects, they started working on these vessels.
And, according to the legend,
it took 'em seven years to build seven vessels.
But when they were done,
the vessels that they had created
were more like works of art,
rather than just ships or boats.
The railings and everything else,
they were covered with copper and brass,
and shiny material.
And each vessel just
gleamed inside.
And each vessel also had
huge sails.
And on the sails were written
the fourteen families.

In seven years,
the Unanti got together again,
and they knew that the time was getting close,
where this great disaster was going to happen.
And so they started getting the best
out of each family.

They recruited the best out of each family.
And when they had done this,
when they had gotten the best builders,
the best farmers, the best medicine people,
the best game keepers, the best fire keepers,
all these things,
when they had gotten the best ones out of
each family,
they put 'em on these boats
and sent 'em in different ways.
Different directions.

And, when they were gone it wasn't
too long after the boats left
that the ground started shaking.

And, the legend says that
the mountains that were on that land,
they exploded and started spewing forth fire.

The water that surrounded the land,
it started flooding in.
And the earth
     cracked.
Earth spewed out of the cracks.
And the legend says that
in one day over half the people
that was on the land, on the Mother Land,
died because of these different things that was going on.
Those that were left were running to the Unanti
and telling 'em, "*Save* us."
And the Unanti said,
"There is a way that we know
to get off of this land and go
to a bridge between the great waters."
And about that time,
the water just kind of flowed back
and it showed this rock bridge
going across from the land that the people were on
to another, greater land.

And so, one by one,
the families got together and started crossing the rock bridge.
Of course, the warriors went first,
to make sure everything was clear.
Not dangerous.
And then, after them, were the scribes.
And then after them were the messengers.
And so forth, until the last one were the builders.
And, it's said that the builders
stopped when they got across to the big land,
they stopped on a big mountain,
and they looked back at the Mother Land
and watched it go under water.
And . . . everybody cried.
There was a great cry that went out
because we had lost the Mother Land.
And, from there on,
the Unanti said we must go toward the
blue direction, which is the cold direction.
North.
And so, the people started walking towards
the blue.
And, every once in a while they would
stop
and rest.
And when they would stop and rest,
the builders, of course,
being builders,
would start building again.
And they would build temples and everything else.
And then the Unanti would say,
"It's time to go now,"
and the majority of the people would leave,
but there were still some that would stay
in the cities that the builders had built.
And this happened several times,
until they came to a river.
They crossed the river,
but on the other side of this river,

was land that was scarce of water.
And on this side of the river,
they saw animals that had humps on their backs.
And these they killed for food and clothing.
And the people kept on going,
and they crossed the land that was scarce of water.
And they crossed another river.
And, on the other side of this river
was land that kind of reminded them of the Mother Land
that had gone under.
And some of the people wanted to stay,
but the Unanti said we had to keep on going,
so they kept on going.
They kept walking towards the blue, or the north direction.
And one day it started raining
and then the rain turned white.
But they kept on walking, and walking, and walking, until
they came on a white mountain.
    A white mountain that moved.
Here again, the Unanti said,
"We got to turn toward where the sun comes up.
    Toward the yellow direction."
And so that's the way they started going.
And they came upon land again
that reminded them a lot like the Mother Land that they had lost.
And all the people wanted to stay there
because it felt like home.
And some people started to
settle down,
but the Unanti said,
"No, we can't stay here. This is a land of sorrow.
    The land cries up to us."
They said, "We got to keep on going."
And so, even though a lot of the people didn't want to,
they packed up and kept on going
toward where the sun comes up.

They kept on walking until they came upon another river.
    And, this river they called the "Long Man"

because it was so wide and so long.
They were barely able to cross this river,
and when they got on the other side of this river,
they came upon people
who were mound builders.
And they built great mounds
and they were really good at it.
But they, uh, shared secrets
or shared knowledge with our architects,
to where they built even greater mounds after that.

And then one day, something happened.
A prominent person,
    of our people
was found dead.
And . . .
they noticed she had no
    blood.
And the people started wondering what happened.
And then they realized that these mound builders
    were cannibals.
And they sacrificed humans.
And with this prominent person being found dead,
and everything pointed to these mound builders
being the ones that killed her,
our people had a great war with them.
And they, well, you might say they wiped 'em out,
but there were still some that were left
and they had married into our people.
But most of the others were killed.
After this happened,
the people,
the Unanti said, "We must keep on going,"
so they kept on going towards
where the sun came up.
And, during this time,
as they walked toward where the sun came up,
the Unanti started becoming really, really . . .
    great in their own eyes.

They thought nothing could harm them.
They thought they held power over the people,
which they did because everybody was scared of 'em
because they were, back then, the most powerful
medicine clan there was.

As this time went along,
from the time the Mother Land went under water
to this time,
the original language was lost.
And the writing that we had back then was lost, too.
And the only ones that remembered anything about it was the
       Unanti.
And that was one of the reasons why they thought
they held such great power over the people.

One day, there was a man named Nicotani
who kidnapped the War Chief's son's wife.
The War Chief's daughter-in-law.
Nicotani wanted her for his own.
And, uh, the War Chief's son retaliated.
And a lot of the rest of the people,
they joined in, and they
massacred the Kutani clan, or the Unanti.
And from then on there hasn't been
another clan that was totally devoted to religion,
or the leaders of our medicine.
But during this time, also, a lot of the
other clans joined together.
The smaller clans joined the bigger clans.
Like, the panther and the bear, they became
the wildcat clan.
They all became one clan.
The raven and the pigeon clans became one.
There were a lot of other clans that came together
and made one bigger clan.
So by the time we reached
a land that reminded us so much of the
Mother Land that had been left so many years before,

the people decided this is where we are going to stay.
And the legend says that this is where we were
when the Europeans came over.

And also it ends by saying that
at that time
when we reached the new land that we were supposed to be at,
there were so many of our people
that we covered most of the eastern seaboard.
But over the years, of course that number dwindled,
and dwindled, and dwindled.
But, that is the migration story.

Clans

The ancient division of Cherokee society into families remains in the matrilineal clan structure. It is through one's clan that a Cherokee person traces his or her kinship. A Keetoowah person gains his or her clan identity from his or her mother, who in turn gained her clan from her mother, and down the line. A Cherokee man and woman are forbidden from marrying someone from their own clan. At one time not too long ago, the Cherokee family consisted of those who were related through one's mother's clan. This is still the case in some Cherokee communities. Even though a person's father was a member of one's immediate family, the father belonged to his own clan. A family's children, their home, and their domestic possessions all belonged to the woman of the family. It was through her that a Keetoowah person found belonging in the community. There was no concept of an illegitimate child because every child with a mother had a clan, and thus a place in the community. To be adopted as a Cherokee meant that one was adopted into a clan. But the clan system was also important to Cherokee concepts of law and social organization.

One evening at Hastings's home in Lost City, Hastings, Sequoyah, and I talked about the meaning of the clan system and its origins. Hastings's heart was acting up and he wasn't feeling well, so we'd decided to meet at his house instead of the chapel. When we'd arrived he'd been going over a list of bird names in Cherokee he'd been compiling. He set that work aside and we began to talk.

"The elders say, at one time the Cherokees had more than seven clans," he said. "Some say we had as many as twenty-six, others say fourteen and others say these were not clans as we know them today, but groups. The names of these groups or clans consisted of trees, plants, animals, birds, and the elements, like the wind, twister, hair hanging down and some of the ancient ones like the saber-tooth cat clan and the dragon clan. All this was B.C. ('Before Columbus') but today and through what we call modern history or A.C. ('After Contact') we have seven clans."

Hastings disappeared for a moment and returned from his workshop with a list he'd compiled. "All these, all these clans in here . . . ," I said, pointing to the thirty-three clan names he had written down. "How did clans come together? And how did they . . . go away?"

"They . . . like all these right here," Hastings said, pointing to the Raven, Hawk, Wren, Red Bird, Kingfisher, Pigeon, and Dove clans, "these right here, they all become Bird Clan. They all were absorbed in that one clan."

"All absorbed in it?" I asked.

"Even now and then you'll hear somebody say, 'Well I'm a *tawod*.' Hawk Clan, Anitawodi. But, in reality they're Birds. Anitsisqua. There was a Dragon Clan at one time, Aniugatena. Another name for this clan is Ani-kutena. Over the course of time this clan has gotten scarce. Every now and then you will hear one of the elders say he or she is from the Dragon Clan. They never talk about the clan; all they say is they never feared anyone. Even now the Turtle Clan is gone. See, all we have are these seven up here," Hastings said, pointing to the Bird Clan, Wolf Clan, Deer Clan, Wild Potato Clan, Blue Clan, Paint Clan, and Long Hair Clan. "But at one time we had these right here," he said, pointing at the other twenty-six clans.

"And this is within, like, historical memory?" I asked. "Nineteenth century and that kind of thing . . ."

"Yeah. Before. During. Right today, though, this is the modern one right here," he said, pointing at the seven clans.

"Were the people of these clans affiliated with these animals?" I asked.

"Yeah. Yeah."

"It's kind of what they did, too? Their vocations?" I continued.

"They became . . . ," Hastings said and paused a moment, "they could become what these were." He pointed to the names of all the clans. "The people of that clan had that ability. And people, see, people don't realize that."

"They could transform into those?" I asked. Hastings nodded.

"Even though they're still in this clan right here," he said, pointing to one of the seven clans we use today, "they still transform into that." He pointed to the other twenty-six clans. "See, they haven't lost that ability. Well, a lot of 'em don't practice it because of . . . religion. You know, modern religion has taken some of our activities, if you want to call it that, or things that we used to do. We're kind of away from it 'cause they say, 'No, that's not the way to do it. You can't do that anymore.'"

"And some probably lost the belief, too, right?"

"Yeah, well, some of 'em have," Hastings answered. "Some of 'em have actually thrown it away for the new, modern belief. You know. So . . ."

"Science tells you you can't do it," I said, echoing something I'd heard Hastings say before.

"Yeah. Science says we can't do it but we know we can, and I mean, then, there's that doubt. There's always . . . modern people always puts that doubt into it. 'Oh, you can't do that.' Science says you can't change into something that you're not. 'You can't do that.' Why not? My question is always, 'Why not?' What keeps you from it? Your own, your own *doubt* keeps you from it."

"Mmhm. We are just energy."

"Yeah," Hastings said. "That's all we are. And people, you know, they say, 'Well do it.' You can't do it in front of people. There are some things that we can talk about and then there's a point we can only go to here," he said, and made a stopping motion with his hand.

"I remember the last time I was at your place and you were talking about how a person will learn some aspect of tradition or medicine if they need to know it," I said. "You'll be taught it if you need it."

"Yeah."

"But if you don't need it you shouldn't be learning it," I said and laughed.

"Yeah. That's true," Hastings said. "Yeah, if you don't need it, why learn it? Like they say, curiosity killed a cat, you know? And there's so many things out there that'll hurt ya. Even the good things, you know. The medicine that we take. It'll *kill* ya. I mean, it's good for you, taken in the amount prescribed, but if you go beyond that, see, that stuff will kill ya. You know? It'll take away from you."

"How Much Are You?"

Along with our discussions about clan identity, the Liars' Club and I often discussed Cherokee forms of self-definition. Cherokee tradition attaches great meaning to blood, and it is common to hear folks speak with pride of being "full-blood." The meaning of that term isn't simple, and in the years since I first returned to Tahlequah I've seen its definition shift around. Sometimes "full-blood" means "traditional," or a person who lives a tra- ditional Cherokee life. To be "traditional" does not mean one has to speak

Cherokee or stomp dance—it means one has an approach to life and a way of being considered "traditional" by one's Cherokee peers. Other times "full-blood" means 100 percent Cherokee by descent. But once again, if one knows Cherokee history, one knows it is fairly unlikely that somewhere in the past there was not a Creek, Choctaw, or Euchee in the family tree—or another Native or non-Native ancestor. Definitions of "full-blood" shift back and forth between a way of being and a genetic heritage.

According to traditional Cherokee belief, to mix things that do not usually mix is a powerful and somewhat dangerous act. Hastings and I were talking about how traditional Cherokee values are changing, and he attributed some of these changes to the mixing of Cherokee and non-Cherokee people.

"But our blood is mixing. Once you start mixing things, it don't work," Hastings said. "That's what we always say. They used to say, 'You marry Indian.' For my grandma that was the main thing. She used to say, 'Boys, you marry an Indian girl. Girls marry who they want to. You boys, you marry an Indian.' And I always thought she didn't like whites. But what she was saying is that if I married a non-Indian then my children would not have a clan. But she didn't actually come out and say it. But she said the girls can marry who they want to. Women have a clan, that's why."

Living in this Middle World, we are surrounded by forces opposing one another, mixing and transforming all of us caught in their grips. The language. The fire. The clans. As I listened to Hastings and the rest of the Liars' Club, I began to understand how these three aspects of Cherokee culture, along with our homelands, were a constant of Cherokee peoplehood. Even so, the language, the fire, the clans, and our homelands changed and renewed through time. They provide a source for perpetuating our language, culture, and history.

Some stories tell of monsters created by the mixing of the Middle World; other stories tell of heroes such as Solegeh. Each has its place. Like more and more Cherokees, I am of mixed heritage. My physical characteristics don't necessarily mark me as Native. I got the recessive genes in my family: light eyes and light skin. The way I appear has granted me social advantages and shielded me from forms of discrimination and racism other Cherokees face on a daily basis because of the way they look. If I walk around a store in Tahlequah, I won't get followed like Sequoyah has been, the clerk thinking he's going to steal something.

Sometimes when I tell strangers I'm Cherokee they ask, "How much are you?" They're not asking if I know myself as a Cherokee and if I am considered by other Cherokees to be Cherokee. That would be a valid, though invasive, question. Instead, they're asking, "What percentage of 'Indian blood' do you have?" This question implies that the degree to which one is Cherokee is defined by racial purity. By this logic, the higher percentage of "Indian blood" you have, the more Cherokee you would be. It's a racist question because it implies that Cherokees are defined by race, not by culture. People tend to forget that "race" is a concept created by cultures. The concept of race continues to have power only because we continue to believe in it. Funny thing is, in all my life I've never been asked by another Cherokee, "How much are you?" Instead, the questions are: "Where do you come from?" "Who are your people?" "Who's your mother?" They are questions of beginnings and continuities, kin and relationships.

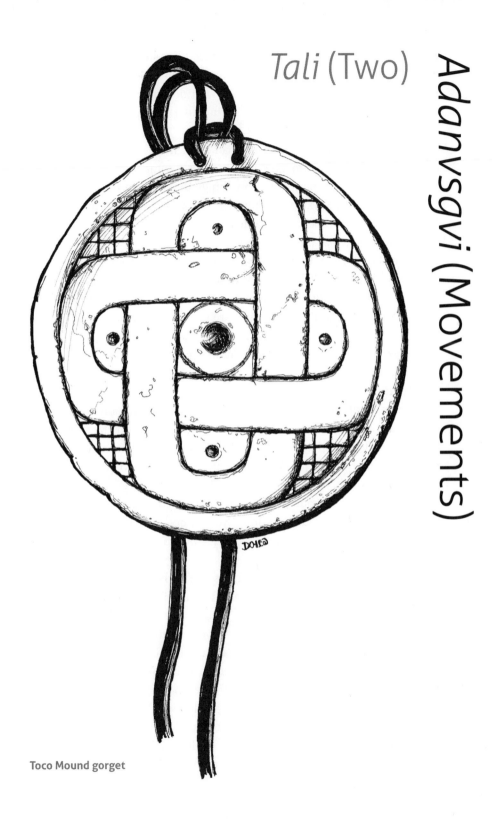

Tali (Two)

Adanvsgvi (Movements)

Toco Mound gorget

Hastings pointed his finger and traced the shape of a symbol on a piece of paper he'd brought to our meeting. "So this is another traditional southeastern design? What does it mean?" I asked. The image looked like two interlocking rectangular loops, each with separate put parallel lines carved in them.

"Well, you and I can walk this road right here," he said, pointing to one of the lines of the image, "and it's gonna come out the same place. But there will be so many different things that we can do. Individually. Even though we're walking down the same road and it comes out the same place. We'll never walk . . . the same road."

Hastings looked at me and I nodded.

"Even though, like I said, it comes out the same place. We can never walk the same road. See, that's what that means. Just like this trail here, this big circle," he said, tracing a line of the symbol, "we can walk in a circle. We'll never walk that same circle. Because of our different upbringings. People see things that I never see, and I'll see things that you won't see. I'll do things that you wouldn't do and you'll do things that I wouldn't do."

"Mmhm."

"But we'll still be on that same road. So we're not actually walking the same road. We got our own path, even though we're on the same trail. And people don't understand that. 'Why? How is that?' It's one road, two men. Two different people. You can't say nationalities. When it comes to humans, there's no difference. What makes you a different person or different nationality is your belief. What makes you human is you're the same—your organs, your breathing, your blood, everything's the same. There's a few that has mismatched organs, but there's a reason for it."

"Mmhm."

"But we're the same as far as humans. We're the same. But our beliefs, traditions, makes us . . . puts us in a different tribe, if you want to call it that. Or nationality, you know."

"Mmhm. And our perspectives. Everyone's is unique," I said.

"Yeah. Yeah. 'Course if we had the same idea this wouldn't be a good place to live," Hastings said and laughed. "You have to have that *diversity*. You wouldn't want to run around with me up and down the creek and freeze your tail end off all night long, you know?" We laughed together. "Which I like to do, you know. Or used to like it; I can't do it no more," he said, referring to his health. "Somebody could say, 'Yeah, I might enjoy it.' You might enjoy it once or twice, but if you do it all the time . . . And to me that's part of what we used to do. You know? That's part of our upbringing. There's certain things you do when you're out there."

"Mmhm."

"And I still have to do it, even though it may take me a while to do what I used to do. When it's time, I'll have to go out. Because I was told that's what you have to do, you know? I have to do it as long as I can. Until I can't do it. And then it's time for me to move on."

The stories in this chapter are about movements: the processes of maturing, growing, learning, leaving home, and returning home. We all tell these types of stories. We separate from our homelands, our communities, our kin and friends, and, of course, from our best selves. And we return home, reunite with each other, and reestablish connections with our communities and homeland. We learn something about the world, about diversity, and about each other in the process. These stories are important to us. We know neither our departures nor our returns are assured.

My grandmother and her family moved away from Cherokee country for work. Many of my relatives stayed in the Cherokee Nation and in Oklahoma; many others came back later. I was raised away from a Cherokee community. I did not grow up speaking the language. I was raised to know I am Cherokee, but I did not understand what that might mean till I came home to Cherokee country. And when I came home physically, I was searching for deeper paths of return.

Community

"Community. You have your family and community," Hastings said. We were speaking of his and Sequoyah's understanding of the roles of the individual and community in Cherokee society. "And most of the time, when a family gets a problem or something, the community's there. It's still like that around home. We don't let our neighbors . . . *want*."

"Yeah," Sequoyah said, "we take care of each other, which is opposite of the mainstream society."

"I hate to use this term," Hastings said, speaking of mainstream society, "but it's 'The hell with you.' That's a different society. That's their way of thinking. 'You got in that fix, now you get yourself out.'"

"Mmhm," I said.

"You know, a lot of our Mexican people that's working here, when a new one comes in, they take care of 'em. And that's how they prosper," Hastings said.

"And that's the way we used to be," Sequoyah said.

"Well, they've got their indigenous roots, right?" I said.

"Yeah. Yeah," Hastings said. "Like we was talking about, at one time our grandparents would go, when somebody was sick, they would go there and leave *their* things to be done later. Till that person either got well or, whatever. Then they would come back and take care of theirs."

"The way the system is now," I said, "everyone's fighting so hard just to keep what little they have that you're just stuck. You can't do anything for anyone. Because you've got to make your car payment, or . . ."

"Yeah. Yeah," Hastings said. "And you know, then, I don't agree with everything Chief Smith says, but he did make a point. You have to be able to take care of yourself first before you can take care of somebody else. And I agree with him there. You have to be at a point where you can at least take care of yourself before you can take care of somebody else. But, a lot of times, you know, we went anyway. Our problems became secondary. Their problems became the priority and our problems became secondary. And then we came back. And a lot of times a lot of people showed up. Communities, you know. *Gadugi*, they called it. That's where everybody's helping."

"Has that term been around a long time?" I asked.

"That term's been here since I can remember. But it's not how they use it down there," Hastings gestured toward the Cherokee Nation tribal complex. "It's *sgadug*. *Sgadug* is a county, state, or community. That's what that means. *Sgadug* is when they—*sgadudv dvdatlesuh*—that's when the whole, as a community come together. There's a difference, you know? There's points that can be argued, either way. But the way I've heard it is *sgadug*.

"But a lot of our elders, when they found out somebody was having problems, they'd go around and tell people. 'What can we do?' or 'How can we help 'em?' So. And that's how we were raised, both of us," Hastings said, referring to his wife Loretta and himself.

The Root Stays Alive

Hastings and I sat together at the chapel and talked about how changes in the Cherokee family affected traditional Cherokee culture. In 1906 the U.S. Congress passed the Act to Provide for the Final Disposition of the Affairs of the Five Civilized Tribes, which authorized the Department of Interior to subsume the Cherokee Nation's government; its nationhood lay dormant and was only awakened periodically for the so-called Chiefs-for-a-day to sign government documents. Much has been written about the

Cherokee up until Oklahoma statehood in 1907, but Cherokee life in the decades thereafter has received less consideration.

Hastings reflected on the Cherokee "Dark Ages," the time between 1907 and when the Cherokee Nation and the United Keetoowah Band of Cherokees began to reassert themselves as sovereign nations in the 1970s. We began to talk about what life was like for Cherokee people during that time when they no longer had a political presence as a nation of people. Hastings had told me that in the small Cherokee communities that dotted the northeastern Oklahoma countryside, Cherokee life and traditions continued.

"So in that time period from 1907 till, like, the 40s, was a sense of Cherokee identity within these communities still strong?" I asked.

"Well, all the traditionals was there. At that point. We started losing our tradition during World War I, 'cause one person left and one person stayed, you know? World War II, one left and the other one went to work. So that took both of 'em out. And at that point in time the father learned to speak English and the mother did, too. So, come back and they spoke English. Cherokee was kind of put to the side. So, that war, it was pretty much a killing time for our culture."

"Was the Great Depression?" I asked. "Did people leave during the Depression?"

"No, there was nowhere to go! I mean, I don't care where you went, it was the same. So everybody stayed and survived. Some of 'em left. Ninety percent of the people around here probably didn't leave."

"Mmhm."

"They might go off and work a little, but then come back. Because they had a family. Their home was here and not there. And then in the 40s they had that Relocation. That's where they took the young people and said, 'Okay, we're gonna send you over here and teach you a trade.' So they left in the 40s. The 70s, thirty years later, about time of retirement age, they come back. 'Where's my language?' You know? 'Where's the traditions?' So, the 70s marks a time when they begin to put language back in schools. That's about the time Loretta got into schools, teaching, what they call 'em? 'Teacher's aides?'"

"Bilingual teacher's aides," Loretta said.

"Bilingual teacher's aides. So, from I'd say, '17 to '45, we really lost a lot of the way we done things. Probably 50 percent of our language went within that period of time. And by then our elders, who were the ones we relied on to teach the culture and language, they were gone. And a lot of our culture, a lot of the traditional culture, went, you know? Because a lot of the ones at that age that they want to learn, they lost their grandparents and didn't have anybody that they could really go to. 'Cause that became a time of, more or less, a separation of people. Even though the war caused it. But it carried on into peacetime, also.

"Then you got your Korean War. By then, some of the youth went into boarding schools and a lot of 'em didn't get to come home. They went straight on into the services. That's what happened to my older brother. A lot of our kinfolks was in boarding schools. Chilocco. So that deprived us of what little was left. By the time they got back, their parents might have gone. Most of our grandparents that were born in the 1880s were gone in the 1960s. 50s and 60s. Back then, our life expectancy wasn't that high. Probably fifty, fifty-five years old. So, we lost a lot of our . . . *knowledge* . . . at that time.

"When the guys came in from Korea, wasn't nobody left. No language. The culture was kind of thrown back to the side. We were trying to get into the mainstream. We were trying to live in modern homes. Indoor plumbing. Indoor water. And it changed from that period of time. Vietnam wasn't quite as profound, because by then we were more into English. We were learning to speak English or learning to *think* English. To try to do what a different culture wanted us to do. We were trying to 'fit in,' I guess.

"Instead of bringing them to us, we were trying to go to them. 'Cause that's how it was presented to us: 'If you don't do like we're doing then you're going to be left behind.' That's what happened to a lot of our students. A lot of our students didn't finish school 'cause they got into that period of time where they got left behind. Because they couldn't fit. Either clothes. Mode of traveling. Not enough money. See, those three things . . . As kids, you know, we were getting to the point of peer pressure. But before then, we didn't care if you wore holey pants, you know? But then, if you didn't dress like this guy, you were ridiculed, you know? And kids, they don't like it. So we were trying to fit in. And it kind of pushed us away. Because we didn't have the, I guess, funds or whatever it takes to fit. I can't say it was all money. Style of living, I guess. House. See, I grew up in a log house up till after I got out of the service in '62."

"Were you in the Army?" I asked.

"Army, yeah. Went in '58 and got out '62. Actually got my discharge in '66. I got four years. Every day I'd go out to the mailbox and see if Uncle

Sam had called me back," Hastings laughed. "It wasn't I didn't want to go, but I was married then. Probably what kept me out."

"Vietnam," I said.

"Yeah. I was there pretty much at the beginning. Got out just before it got real bad. '62. 'Cause '64, '66, it was going then. But I never got called back. So. Went out there one day and my discharge was in there," he said and laughed again. He sat back and thought for a moment.

"We 'traditionalists,' if you want to call 'em that, we had to stay with it. That's how we survived. But a lot of the ones that was on the edge, that was leaning more, had already integrated into the different way of thinking, they kind of went that a way," Hastings said and gestured with his hand to the side, toward the mainstream. "But most of us stayed with the tradition, you know? We still know how to gather. We still know how to prepare things. And, that's what I was telling my boys. If you don't learn this one of these days you won't be able to feed yourself. So that part of it has never left us. And I don't know how many other people can say that. I mean, we actually still do the old way. Or, whenever we step outside we kind of put it off to the side till we come back. Then we pick it back up. It's not done openly, it's just within families a lot of times."

"Mmhm."

"Within. A lot of it done within the immediate family. And then, it's still being passed on. And I'll pass it on as long as I'm here. And, just like her, as long as she's here," he said, gesturing toward Loretta. "And, hopefully, my boys will pass it on as long as they're here. But it's going to diminish. I don't care how much they know, it's still going to diminish, you know? Over the years. Even what little I know has diminished from what my grandparents knew and what my parents knew. It has diminished a lot. 'Cause I've forgotten some of the plants. I know the name of 'em and I know basically where they at, but can I find 'em? They used to be here, but a lot of times a plant will move. Just like us, we kind of migrate; they kind of migrate. 'Course a lot of times I've had to look hard for a certain plant. I knew where it was at, but I'd find it way over here sometimes."

"Weather change, sun change," I said.

"Yeah, weather change. If you'll notice, land shifts. Land's always moving."

"We went to that creek today. Spring Creek. It changed. I looked, 'Wait a minute!' It looked different than when I was here last year,'" I said.

"It changes. I mean, our land is always . . . Mother Nature is alive, you know? She shifts around. And, just like plants. If something happens, it don't like it, it'll move. Wind blowing will move it. Water flood will move it. I mean, just little things, you know? Just like us, if we build in a flood-plain, we gonna get moved!" Hastings laughed, then continued.

"But, basically, the things that used to be a certain place, it's no longer there. You have to look for it. 'Cause I knew a plant behind my uncle's up there, and I seen it many times. Many times, I gone up there. Four or five years ago I walked it, but I never did find it. And I knew generally where it was. But where it moved to I don't know. Now I can't walk around like I used to. Back then I could still go up and down them hills pretty good. But now, I start going I'd run out of air and I'd be laying on the side of the hill there. See, again, we're losing . . . I've lost that ability to go out and look. So, I basically know where it's at. I could probably tell somebody, 'It's right here.' But would it be there? And would I give a good enough description for them to find it?"

"Mmhm."

"That's how come I tell my boys: 'You recognize this? You look at it, smell it.' 'Cause a lot of times you have to recognize it first. Just like right now, most of it's dormant. If you don't know what the stem looks like, you don't know what you're looking for. 'Cause the roots is still there, 'cause, basically, 90 percent of our medicine is root. And the root stays alive. But, identifying it . . . ," he said and laughed. "It looks different when it's green than it does when it's brown. The leaves are all crumbled up. Everything looks the same now. Leaves are all wrinkled up. One plant may . . . 'Oh, there it is!' When you get over there close it's not it. And it's something that needs to be taught."

"So, during that Cherokee Dark Age between statehood in 1907 and the rise of the Cherokee Nation in the 1970s, Cherokee culture continued to live on in the families and in communities. What about today?" I asked.

"Mostly families nowadays. At one time it was actually part of a com-munity. But anymore, we've gotten away from our community because we've had different cultures move into our communities. And, some-times, we have a community . . . everybody's invited, you know. We don't exclude nobody. But when there's different cultures, it changes the topic, I guess.

"We don't talk openly about certain things, like we would if everybody was Cherokee. There's certain things you can say to Cherokees that you cannot include with a different 'nationality' or 'ethnic group' . . . whatever you want to call it. 'A different way of thinking,' okay!" Hastings said and laughed. "That's probably the best way to put it."

"Today, what percentage of Cherokees do you consider traditional?" I asked. "Rough guess."

"Rough guess, uh, Keetoowah's probably got the most. I would say out of the 14,000 Keetoowahs, I'd say 65 percent of them are traditional."

"Traditional. But that's from language . . . ?" I asked.

"Language, culture, values. I mean, anything that has to do with why we're Cherokee. In the Cherokee Nation . . . the number is way down. Probably less than 10 percent. But, now we're looking at 14,000 compared to a population of 300,000."

"That's still a big number. 30,000."

"Yeah. Yeah. But, I'd say between 65 and 85 percent of Keetoowah's are traditionalists. And if you want a traditional Cherokee, I'd say Keetoowah. I'm a member of Cherokee Nation. That puts me in that 10 percent. And that's not very many. What is that, 30,000? Still, that's just a drop in the bucket. 'Cause you got 270,000 that's not."

"Do you think people can learn tradition? Or is it something you have to be brought up with," I asked.

"It's something that you would *want to learn*. You can learn it, but you have to *want to*."

"Want to learn," I said.

"Yeah. You can learn a language, but you have to want to. 'Cause you can learn any language that you want. You have to *want to learn it*. 'Cause if you don't, if you say, 'I'm gonna try.' That's all you're going to do is try."

"Is the language the lynchpin of tradition? Kind of the thing that ties it all together?" I asked.

"Yeah,. well, the language *is*. Everything we do traditionally, it starts with the language. Our stomp grounds. Our fire. It only understands the Cherokee language. Once the Cherokee language is gone we're going to lose our fire. 'Cause you know, that's what the Creator put here and it told us, 'Speak to it in Cherokee.' Once that Cherokee is gone, the fire's gone. That's how close we are to losing our true identity."

THE SPIRIT OF AN ANCESTOR
By Hastings Shade

As a young boy growing up along the banks of the Illinois River, I fished and swam in its waters during the summer, and I hunted and trapped along its banks in the winter. In time, as I grew older and began to venture farther up and down the banks of the river I decided I would go up the river and float back down, fish and camp along its banks at night.

I had travelled up and down the river banks many times and thought I knew every one that lives or had lived along its banks.

I picked out a place about seven miles from where we lived and figured it would take me about three days to get back to our place. I asked Dad if he would take me and the flat-bottom johnboat that he and I had built, and about how long it would take to get back, and he agreed.

The place I had picked out was right below one of the bridges that crossed the river. As we put the boat into the river and had loaded all the things I thought I would need, he said, "I'll look for you in a couple days." As he drove off, he said, "If you see a stranger and if he's hungry, feed him."

I watched him as he drove off down the road. This wouldn't be the first time I had spent the night on the river alone. I had camped on its banks many times. I pushed the boat into the river and got in. I was glad Mom had packed me something for the supper the first night. Tomorrow I would have to find food on my own.

There are many strange sounds at night when you are alone. Some I could identify, others I had heard but didn't know what they were: a bird, insect, or an animal. Maybe even a frog. There was one sound that night similar to something I had heard before. It was in a language much like the Cherokee language spoken by the people that came to fish and swim in the river.

I understood and spoke the language. The language I heard that night was Cherokee, but it was spoken in a dialect that I couldn't understand. Only the Creator could understand what was being said. I remember my grandpa saying, "If you hear something that you don't understand, the Creator knows what is being said."

Soon, they began to sing. As I listened to the songs, I knew they were being sung by someone a lot older than anyone I knew. They were more like chants. I listened to the songs, never understanding what they were saying but knowing that very few people had heard what I was hearing. I finally went to sleep and was awakened by the birds as they began to look for something to eat, reminding me I, too, was hungry.

I got my cane pole and put my line and hook on it without a sinker. Dad used to say, "The only thing a sinker is good for is to get you hung up." So I never use a sinker. Dad called it "drift fishing." I caught me a medium-sized crawdad, hooked him through the tail and threw it out where the water was swift. In about two minutes I had me my breakfast: a fat smallmouth bass.

I built me a fire, cleaned the fish, and sliced me up a potato that I had brought along just for this purpose. If you have never eaten fresh caught fish and fried potatoes along a creek or a river, you are missing out on some of the best eating that you can have. Along with a good cup of coffee, you just can't beat it. So I made some coffee.

After I had eaten my breakfast and cleaned up my mess it was about seven thirty. I thought, "If I'm going to make it home by tomorrow evening I better get started."

So off I went, letting the current take me down the river. Every now and then I would use one of the oars to straighten the boat and head it in the right direction. I would fish the headwaters where it was swift and ran into a deep pool. Sometimes I would catch a good-sized "lineside," as we called the largemouth bass, and even a channel cat every now and then. Once I hooked something that broke my line after it had pulled me and the boat around for awhile in one of the deep places along the river. Probably a big flat-head catfish, I thought. As I replaced the line on my pole I noticed that it was getting late. It was time to look for a place to camp.

I found a place and pulled the boat onto the gravel bar. It was time to catch me some supper. I found a good spot and didn't take long before I had a couple of bass and a nice-sized channel cat. I cleaned what I had caught and got ready to build me a fire to cook them on. I heard this voice that startled me; I wasn't expecting anyone along this stretch of the river. "You wouldn't mind sharing your supper, would you?" he asked. At first, I couldn't see him real good with him standing in the late-evening shadows. As he stepped from the shadows, I looked at him and a calm feeling came over me. I knew he could be trusted. I said, "Sure, come on," and began to build a fire. "Wait," he said, "I got a better idea. Let's go to my house and cook them. I just live across the field, not very far. Just tie your boat right there; no one will bother it."

When we got to his house it was real neat. A wood stove sat in the corner and a small table and a couple chairs in the middle of the room. "You don't need much when you live alone," he said.

By the time I got the fish battered and the potatoes peeled and sliced he had a fire going. We had two skillets with grease in them on the stove, one for the fish and one for the potatoes.

"Got any coffee?" he asked.

"Sure," I said, "let me get it." I poured water into this gallon can I carried to make coffee in and soon it was boiling away.

We sat at the table after we had eaten and drank our coffee. I don't know how long we talked into the night. He told me many things about the past and what might happen in the future. As I sat and listened to him talk I could almost picture what he was telling me.

When I told him what I had heard the first night I was on the river, he kind of smiled and said, "Oh that was just the Little People. They still know the Ancient Language; that is what you heard. Sometimes I go up there and dance with them. Their grounds is right below where you camped. It's been there for a long time." He said, "I remember when they first came there." It never dawned on me to ask him how long ago that was. I just listened.

He fixed me a pallet on the floor and I lay down and listened as he told me things that no mortal human being should know. I never asked him how he learned all of this. He even told me the name of the girl that I was going to marry. She and her family hadn't even moved into the area yet.

I never asked him how he knew these things, I just listened. Sometime in the night I fell asleep. When I woke up the next morning, I was the only one there. The old man was already gone. I looked for him but never saw him again. We never told each other our names, but he knew mine.

I didn't eat breakfast that morning. I wasn't even hungry, still full from the night before.

As I drifted down the river I kept wondering about the things he had told me. Everything seemed so peaceful as I went down the river.

It was late afternoon when I got to the place where I would leave my boat and go across the field to the house. As I approached the house, Mom came to the back door. Her first words were, "My, you look like you grew up these last two nights. Did you have a good time? Nothing didn't scare you?"

"No," I said, "nothing." I never mentioned the old man to her.

When Dad came home that evening, he said, "Let's go get your boat. It's going to rain tonight. If it floods you'll lose your boat and we'll have to build another one."

As we rode across the field he said, "Well, did you feed anyone?"

"Funny you should ask," I said. "I ate supper with an old man. You know where the big elm trees are? He lives across the field from there. I shared my fish, potatoes, and coffee with him."

"Did he talk like he hadn't had anyone to talk to for a long while?" he asked.

"Yes, he did," I said, "He also told me a lot of things. Do you know him?"

"I only met him once when I was young and floated the river like you did," Dad said.

"Did you spend the night with him?" I asked.

"Yes I did. He told me many things."

"Like what?" I asked.

"Like that I was going to have a son and what his name was going to be."

"What is the old man's name, Dad?"

He said, "I don't know. He died when your Grandpa was young." He then told me, "Don't look for the house where you stayed the night, because it isn't there. Someone burned it down right after the old man died."

I fished and floated the river many times after that, but I never looked for the house. Sometimes when I come by there I look across the field. I know there is nothing there, but I still think, "Maybe . . ." But I know better.

I did look for the Little People's stomp ground. All I found was a place where the grass was beat down in a round circle that looked like someone or something had stomped it down. Again, *maybe*. Maybe I was at the right place.

As the elders say, "The spirit never dies." The old ones, the ones that have gone on before, will always be with us. Sometimes they come and try to tell us something, but we have forgotten how to listen. Then again, maybe someday they will talk to me again.

Life Continuing

"So, one of the old beliefs regarding life and death is that there is no death?" I asked Hastings.

"It just goes on," he answered. "I mean, you know, we don't see them here, but they don't leave. The spirit never leaves. That's one thing we was always taught. The spirit is always going to be here. Although we don't see them."

"But it's not quite like reincarnation," I said.

"No, it's like the wind. Our elders tell us if you don't listen to the wind all you are going to hear is noise. A lot of times the wind is trying to tell you something. Or the rain, you know. If you listen to the rain. They may come back as the wind, the rain, anything. A bird.

"A lot of times if you listen to the birds they're saying something. I like to sit out here and just listen and see what's going on. The wind tells you a lot of things. It tells you what's going to happen. Fire. If you look at the fire you can see things. A lot of times you don't want to see what's in it. But there's things in there you need to look at."

"Mmhm."

"A lot of times when that fire starts jumping around there's things in there that's a part of your life, that went into your life. Some good, some bad. The water is a good place to sit down and listen. Where it ripples. That's the most soothing, most relaxing place you can sit. I go fishing down there and just throw a line out there. If it's got bait, alright; if it don't, alright. Just sit and listen to the water.

"There's so many other things that are happening and our kids are involved with it. Alcohol. Drugs. They go down there they don't hear nothing. All they hear is what they get from that, and it's not good. Marijuana is a medicine if it's used correctly. Alcohol is a medicine if it's used correctly. Drugs are medicine if they are used correctly. It's the abuse that makes them bad. Money is good. But you've got to use it like you are supposed to. And when you start throwing it away you want more and you want more. But if you use it correctly you always have enough to do with what we need."

"Right."

"Not what we *want*, but what we *need*. Want and need is two different things. That was the source of the beliefs that was given to us. Always look to Mother Nature for your answers. The younger generation, they need to hear these things. They don't hear them. A lot of our kids in school never hear this stuff. All my boys, grandkids, and my nephews and nieces they'll come over here and we'll come out here and put on a pot of dumplings and chili and sit our here and tell stories until way into the night. I got me an old woodstove right there. Turn the light on right here. Sit here and fight the mosquitoes. A lot of times we make baskets out here. But they want to hear these old things."

Kananesi Ugiladv (Webs)

"I read something in the paper that astronomers are starting to map dark matter, that stuff we can't see that makes up half the universe. The only way they can describe it is by saying it spreads across the universe like a spider web," I said.

"Yeah," Hastings said.

"So, even despite their disbelief in things, they're starting to see the same patterns."

"Well, my grandmother had a third-grade education and she said, 'One of these days this earth is going to be covered by a giant spider web.' If you could stand out in space and see all these satellites you could just see all these radio waves covering us, and to me that was her concept. The wires that's all over the place. Fences." Hastings sat quiet for a moment.

"And nowadays, you could look at it like the Internet," Sequoyah added.

"It's the web that weaves us all together," Woody said.

"You know, my computer's down but I could go in there and with a few clicks could be talking to somebody in Germany. And she said the world is going to get smaller. She wasn't talking about it shrinking in size, she was talking about our travel. A long time ago we'd go to Tahlequah and it would take us all day. I can leave here and I can be in Tahlequah in twenty minutes. If I'm in a hurry I can be there in ten minutes," Hastings laughed. "If there ain't the Highway Patrol sitting in the way somewhere. That's the difference. The world is getting smaller if you look at distance wise. But the world is the same size—it's the travel method that's made it smaller. You can leave here today and be overseas tomorrow some time."

"If they have enough gas," Sequoyah said wryly.

"But our teleportation they talk about," Hastings said. "Indians have known it for years. I mean, any Native American tribe knows how to get around. They move with nature."

"How is that?" I asked.

"It's something that's been taught. You have to have them look at you and see if you're worthy of it first. You don't learn something just because you want to, you learn something because it's been given to you. If you're not worthy of it, you won't learn it. You have to be worthy. There's no one that actually says, 'Yeah, I want to learn that.' If you're worthy of it then you'll learn it, if not then you never will. The worth, I guess you can look at it that way. What are you *worth*? Are you actually worth them teaching you, or what? See, a lot of these things need to be put into a book somewhere," Hastings said.

"But then somebody unworthy may try to learn it," I said.

"But they'd never believe it. Just like our medicine. They don't believe it because they can't prove it. Just like somebody said, 'You kill a deer there, they'll get you for killing a deer.' And I said, 'When I kill a deer it's for four or five different purposes: medicine, food, clothing.' Most of it is medicine. A deer has got a lot of medicine parts in it. Somebody said, 'Well, they'll still put you in jail.' And I said, 'Well, they'll have to prove that it wasn't what I killed it for.' The burden of proof is in their hands, not mine. I know what it can do for me. If I get a deer I'm going to eat it and use it for what I think needs to be done. There's a lot of cancer medicine in deer. And they can't prove that it isn't, you know? And I know it is because I've seen it work. But the burden of proof is in their hands."

Blood

We'd been speaking about tribal politics. This was only natural. Hastings was, after all, the former deputy chief of the Cherokee Nation. All the members of the Liars' Club had worked for either the Cherokee Nation or the United Keetoowah Band. And they expressed strong opinions about what the Cherokee Nation and United Keetoowah Band were doing right and wrong in terms of governance.

Today, the topic turned to the March 3, 2007, vote in which the Cherokee people voted to limit tribal citizenship to descendants of tribal members who were listed as having Indian "blood" in the 1907 Dawes rolls, the official roll of Cherokee tribal membership administered by the U.S. government. A crucial effect of the 2007 vote was to remove 2,800 descendants of the Cherokee Freedmen, those African Americans enslaved by Cherokees before the Civil War, from the Cherokee Nation tribal rolls. Since a separate Dawes Commission roll listed the Freedmen as not Indian by blood, their descendants no longer fit the criteria for enrollment. The club members discussed the results of the vote and its larger implications.

"So, a lot of our people, you know, I've heard preachers say, 'I don't want no . . .' I hate to use the word he used, him being a preacher, but he said 'I don't want no nigger in my tribe.' And I told him, 'What's going to happen if the Creator's black when you get up there? You gonna turn around and come back?' He just turned around and walked off," Hastings said.

"It's just blood," Woody said. "We're all human on this earth that walks."

"And this was a preacher, you know?" Hastings continued. "A preacher to me is . . . Whenever you preach and tell somebody what is in the Bible, do you skip the part about . . ."

"Yeah, it's about acceptance of everyone coming from one," Woody said.

"That was his exact words, though: 'I don't want no nigger in my tribe.' And I told him, 'If the Creator's black when you get there, are you gonna turn around and come back?'"

"Exactly," Woody said emphatically.

"And he just turned around and walked off. Didn't answer me," said Hastings. "To me, we don't know because if you go by the modern Bible it says, 'Let us create men in our image.' How do we know what he looks like? It don't say nothing about color, it just say, 'Let us make men in our image.' Out of the billions of people in the world, nobody looks alike."

"What language?" Woody offered.

"What language did he speak?" echoed Hastings. "All it says is, 'Let us make men in our image.' It didn't say, 'Let us make men look like me.' It said, 'Let us make men in our image.'"

"To me the key word is 'our,'" said Woody.

"Yeah. 'Our' image," agreed Hastings.

"It didn't say 'my' image. It said 'our,'" Woody repeated.

"How many were they?" Hastings said.

"Yeah. Man and woman?" Woody asked.

"Man and woman. So, who are we? What do we really look like?" Hastings laughed. "But if you tell a modern preacher that they'll kind of get after you, you know. They'll say 'Well, he looks like this: he's got a beard . . .' We don't know."

"And usually that's something they learned from the seminary. You don't hardly hear about preachers that are called to preach and talk by the spirit anymore," Sequoyah said. "They go to a seminary."

"Yeah," Hastings agreed. "They're *taught* how to preach."

"They're taught how . . . ," Sequoyah nodded.

"They're not called anymore. They've got a calling but they go to the seminary and learn it. To me, it's just like our treaties. I read them as I understand them. You take a lawyer and he'll tear them apart. The lawyer is the one that interprets it. Just like all of us could read one verse in the Bible and get five different interpretations out of it. To interpret what *we* want. To fit *my* lifestyle," said Hastings.

When the conversation hit a lull, Hastings leaned forward and spoke.

THE FOUR WARS WITH THE BLACKS

Told by Hastings Shade

The oldest legend I know is the Four Wars with the Blacks. It was while we was still on this island. Before we ever left the island. And we still had the Uk'tan at that time. This was way, way back.

And it was said the blacks came one day and they had a fight on the island and they were defeated. So they went back in their boats and left. They said they came in boats. *Jiyu*. To us, that's a boat.

So they come back again. They knew they'd come back. So, the next battle they had lasted a little bit longer. The third battle they had they almost defeated the Indians. The Cherokees. But they finally got run off.

So, they had Uk'tan, the mythical dragon. We call it "mythical" now but back then, at one time it was the real thing.

So, the captive ones, the ones they had captured, not the Cherokee by blood but the captives, the elders told them how to kill the Uk'tan and they killed it and they got this blood and put it where the blacks were on the land. I always said that was the first chemical warfare. Chemical warfare is nothing new. They were killed by absorption of the blood. The poison absorbed through their feet. That's how the blacks were defeated the fourth time.

And they took prisoners. We've had black blood in our tribe for, shoot, no telling how long. It's nothing new, the Freedman deal the Cherokee Nation is fighting. It's nothing new. There's been black blood in our tribe for years. I can't say I don't have any black blood in me. But, it's just like the priest clan. The blood comes out every now and then. And it shows, you know? It *has* to surface. The blood has to surface every now and then, I don't care how far you put it back, it has to come out.

Hawks

Woody and Sammy and their families had met Sequoyah and me at Spring Creek near Woody's home for a meal and storytelling. Just west of Highway 10 on Kenwood Road, a few miles north of Kansas, Oklahoma, Spring Creek is a beautiful stream the Hansens often swim in and upon whose banks they picnic. Several years before, my nephew, Matt, and I had gigged for crawdads down there with Woody, Sequoyah, Sammy, and their families. I remember standing in the stream and letting the pace of Denver wash away from me as Woody and I talked about Cherokee traditional beliefs and his Christian faith. This was before we had decided to write the book, and I had just talked to Woody about the idea. He had told me, "Well, we'll see. No need to rush it." At the time, I could see myself in Spring Creek. I could see a certain anxiousness and impatience that was a part of my normal life. Woody and I laughed as Matt threw bigger and bigger rocks into the creek, finally ending with boulders he could barely lift. "See, he doesn't know what to do with himself," Woody said to me. "He's bored. But give him a minute and he'll find something to do." Soon, Matt took to gigging again and wandered contentedly down the creek.

Today, Sequoyah and I arrived just at dusk when a storm was beginning to roll in from the southwest. We all gathered in lawn chairs around the fire on the rocky creek side and as the evening fell began to tell stories. Sammy told a ghost story about his uncle's house. Soon, the wind kicked up and the rain chased us to our cars. The next day, Sequoyah, Woody, and I met at Hastings's house, and we had this conversation:

"Oh! I forgot to mention when Lani first got to the creek there was a hawk feather laying there," Woody said.

"Oh yeah?" Sequoyah asked.

"We were just getting ready to set up the tables. I thought, 'Alright! Thank you. What a blessing.' You know? Hawk feathers . . . for me it's a personal sign . . . ," said Woody.

"Yeah?" Hastings said.

"Another one of my dreams, you know. I was probably a second or third grader when I had it. In my dream there was a real vicious dog chasing after me. And it was at the old homestead, in my dream. It's about a hundred yards from where we live now. That dog was just about getting me. And that yard where we lived, it had some walnut trees. And in my dream, they were there, the walnut trees. And as that dog was trying, just about to nip me, that walnut tree turned into a hawk. A red-tailed hawk. It enveloped me. And that dog couldn't touch me. And so I perceive that as a sign that a hawk would be my protector. So in subsequent years when I would have bad dreams a hawk would appear and take me out of danger, either by picking me up or it would swoop down and I would jump and I would start soaring behind it till I was out of danger. So when I found the hawk feather yesterday I thought, 'Alright. Good.' Throughout time, that hawk has always been there for me. Or to reassure me when something's up. So, I thought that was reassuring yesterday. And it turned out well. I told Lani, 'Whoever shows shows. If no one does, we're here. We have food. We have the creek. We'll enjoy it anyway.'"

"Mmhm," I said.

"When the clouds built up then I asked, 'Please have pity and hold off.' You know, I love the rain. I'm not saying, 'Rain, go away!' Just hold off. Because that was then my sister-in-law's last time with us before she leaves back for Illinois. I wanted her to have a good time."

"Did she make it? I mean, was she there last night?" Hastings asked.

"Yeah. She made it."

The Sequoyah Script

"We both speak, read, and write the language," Hastings said of he and Loretta. "I learned early and then I kind of let mine go. Almost had to relearn it. I learned way back. My uncle sat down with me one day and we was goin' to learn to read. My grandma got on to him about it. I was about twelve, I guess. Then I went into the service, done this working, raising a family. Kind of ignored it. It took me a couple days to get it back in my head. See, I used to write the old Sequoyah, the old version of it."

"Yeah, I heard that there was an old, old version of it," I said. I'd heard that Sequoyah never claimed that he invented the syllabary, but that he had developed it from an early Cherokee writing system that had been used by the Unanti priest clan. They had abused the people in part through their control of knowledge with writing. When they were destroyed, the story told, the writing went into hiding, passed in secret from generation to generation for safekeeping.

"Well there's a story. Again, a story. You know what the stories are . . . ," said Hastings. "But it was, back in the time Sequoyah was born. 1760s or 70s. There were seven elders that come from the Rocky Mountains that had some type of written form of language. And after Sequoyah got old enough to want to do the syllabary, they kind of presented it to him and kind of gave him an idea what to do."

"That's interesting," I said. "Scholars claim there weren't any indigenous phonetic writing systems north of Mexico until Sequoyah invented the syllabary."

"That's the only story I ever heard of the origins of the syllabary. *Galigwogi anigayvlige unilustv*. And that's what that means: seven elders came. And they wrote not on paper but on cedar or mulberry. That was their type of paper," Hastings said.

"And they came from the Rocky Mountains?" I asked.

"That's what they say. And what they were doing over there . . . You know, there's stories that have been told, you know, people had been to the Rockies, been to the West Coast. I mean, they traveled. I was telling my student, I said, 'You see a rainbow? That was a ladder. That was a pathway at one time for the indigenous people.' You know, to get from here to there. And somebody says, 'Well you can't even touch a rainbow!' I said, 'You can't touch it in *this* form.' But in our stories, it says we don't always stay in this form," said Hastings.

"Mm."

"You know? So, whenever they shape-shifted . . . they had that knowledge. See, they had that knowledge to do that. When the Winged One came, the time that they were trying to get the priest clan to quit sacrificing the Indians, it was when he gave them that ability to get around. To fly. So."

Warriors

One summer afternoon at Hastings's house in Lost City, the topic of discussion turned to the law. "I kind of notice a trend in lawyers and judges' interpretation nowadays," Woody said, "especially with Indian affairs. It's not what's written down. They're saying, 'This is what is *meant*.'"

"Yeah," Hastings agreed. "But if you'll listen to them, if they want you to do something, they'll say, 'This is what's been written. This is the way it's going to be.' When they look at treaties, they look at the way it's written. And that's the way it should be, but it's not. See, we read it as the laymen. We read it as we should read it. It's a difference between English and Cherokee.

"The way I understand things in Cherokee is they are *true*. Because there's no way you can get around the truth. That's how come a Cherokee trial don't last but five minutes, because you can't skirt the issue, you have to get right down to it. You actually get into the facts. There's no way to get out of it. The *word* is true. English can be taken and talked in a roundabout way all day long, but in Cherokee you can't do that. You have to get to the facts. That's how come our trials didn't last long a long time ago. The truth was there and it was dealt with."

"If someone lied in Cherokee . . . ," I said.

"You can't . . . ," Sequoyah said. "Like in English, you can use innuendo. You can't do that in Cherokee."

"So, if someone said, 'Were you there?' A person couldn't say, 'I wasn't not there,'" I said, and everyone laughed.

"No, you can't manipulate the Cherokee language that way," Sequoyah said. "And, if you say, 'I heard it.' I mean, again, hearsay is not admissible in a trial. Or if you say, 'I wasn't there.' I mean, there's no way to say, 'Well, I was close.'" Everyone laughed again. "In English you can say, 'Well, I was close. I wasn't quite there but I was close.' In Cherokee you say, *Tla yugedohe*. 'I wasn't there.'"

"So, if in English you can say something like, 'Did you hear something?' One could say, 'Well, I may have heard something.' In Cherokee it's either you heard it or you didn't?" I asked.

"Yeah. I mean, you can't do that in Cherokee. You were either there or you weren't there. You either heard it or you didn't hear it," said Sequoyah.

"But, see, there's no way of getting around it," Hastings said. "It's a precise language."

"And really that's the only way a Cherokee person could get a trial by their peers, you know?" Sequoyah said. "If they are Cherokee-speaking people then they should find Cherokee jurors."

"Jurors and Cherokee lawyers and a Cherokee judge that speaks Cherokee. And there's no such thing," Hastings said. "Now you can get some jurors that are Cherokees, but you can't get a judge. You can't get no lawyer that speaks Cherokee.

"It's interesting. We are fighting to keep our language, and it's just a fight. Because a lot of ours are going to Spanish or English. Right now in the state of Oklahoma they are doing the 'English Only.' But the law says, 'English Only,' but it doesn't apply to the Native languages. But, you know, that fine line could be changed to say, 'Well, this is what they meant.'"

"Yeah. Well, there you go . . . It's their out," Woody said.

"This is the concept," Hastings agreed.

"Give them about twenty years, they'll say, 'This is what they meant,'" Sequoyah offered.

"Yeah, 'This is what they meant.' But, the public needs to hear this stuff, you know. And you're going to get a public that's been indoctrinated with the culture they grew up in; it's going to be hard for them to understand what we're saying. We can put it out there and say, 'Here. This is our way of life. This is good. Take it for what it's worth.' We know what it is worth. But the non-Indians don't. They look at it like, 'Well . . . they do that and we can't control them.' They can't control us anyway. The laws, you know, the things we have to do . . . You can't go down the road no more than sixty-five. They post the speed limit but if you drive the speed limit people run you over.

"I was selling gigs at the Cherokee National Holiday a couple years ago. A game warden man came over and said, 'Hey, you're the one making gigs? You make them?' And I said, 'Yeah.' 'What kind of gigs you got?' 'Bass gigs.' He said, 'You're not supposed to get bass with gigs.' And I said, 'Well, you're not supposed to drive down the road at seventy miles per hour but a lot of people do. When I sell a gig I don't know what they're going to get, you know?'" Everyone laughed. "'I sell a product, it's up to you how you use it.' That man looked at me kind of funny. He told me I was a smart ass. I said, 'No. Not really. I'm a little bit smarter than you because I know my laws and you don't.' He said, 'What do you mean?' I said, 'I got treaties at the house that say I can hunt and fish and gather.'"

"Subsistence," Woody said.

"He said, 'Yeah, that's been ratified.' I said, 'There ain't no treaty that's been ratified. Congress had to do that.' I said, 'You better sit down and start reading some of your laws.' He don't like me very much. I don't care." Everyone cracked up again.

"There was a young man that was caught for fishing," Sequoyah said. "They took him to court and somehow or another he waited to get on the docket until he could get a final say so on whether we could fish or not, and they wouldn't do it." Everyone laughed again.

"See, they're afraid once they make a ruling they set a precedent," Hastings explained. "And they ain't about to do that. Just like I told that warden, I said, 'If you ever catch me you can take me to city, state, or county court.' He said, 'I can take you wherever I want.' And I said, 'Good. But we're going to end up in federal court.' I said, 'The city and county can't deal with these issues.'"

"It's a federal thing," Sequoyah said.

"It's a federal thing," Hastings agreed. "He said, 'You think you smart?' I know what I read, you know?"

"Next time you tell him, 'No, I'm not smart—you're just dumb,'" Sequoyah said quietly and everyone laughed again. "And that's the way the dominant society thinks, that we're not smart because we hold on to these things and live the way we do and think the way we do. But, it's just the opposite. Just like the way we talk. I think I told you that I got a phone call one time when I was working for the Cherokee Nation and a man was wanting to know how to say 'white wolf' in Cherokee. Because he was wanting to name his dog that, only in Cherokee. But he didn't say that. So, I asked him, 'Well, is it describing the wolf? Or is it going to be a name?' If it was just describing a white wolf is would be '*uneg waya*'—

'white wolf.' But if it was going to be a name it would be *'waya yuneg.'* So, you're actually saying 'Wolf White.' And that guy said, 'Hmm. I wonder why it's backwards?' And I said, 'I don't know why white people talk backwards.'" Everyone laughed. "But that's the way it is, you know? Even in our language. Even in the way we live. The dominant society thinks we live backwards, we think backwards. We think the way we're supposed to think. We live the way we're supposed to live."

"White society says if you ain't got a Cadillac behind your house you're poor," Hastings said. "But I'm satisfied with my old truck right there. It gets me where I want to go. It may not get me there as fast, but I'll be there right after they get there."

"And nowadays we get there cheaper than they would. They're driving in their Hummers and everything else, gas-guzzling things . . . ," Sequoyah said.

"And they say, 'Y'all eat that?' We say, 'Yeah we eat that.' 'I don't see how you can.' Well, you grew up with it, that's what you want. I like a hamburger every now and then, but I like my traditional food, too," Hastings said. After a moment he continued. "This was a bad place a long time ago to be Indian. Tahlequah still is. It's not a good place. A lot of prejudice."

"Yeah," Sequoyah agreed. "Even though it's the capital, there's still a lot of prejudice. But, like I've said before, I consider Hastings, Sammy, and Woody as warriors fighting to keep our culture and traditions alive, you know?"

"Warriors with a briefcase," Hastings said and laughed. "No longer bows and arrows."

"When we go somewhere to do presentations," Sequoyah explained, "it's fun and we like doing it. But, the underlying reality of it is we're teaching these people, we're still fighting to keep our cultural head above water, you know?"

"Nowadays, a lot of us Indian people are Wal-Mart warriors," Woody offered. "You know, you go get your meat at Wal-Mart and instead of growing gardens you go buy it. You don't hunt anymore, you just go to Wal-Mart."

"Seems the only place you see people is at Wal-Mart," Hastings mused.

"I've heard ladies don't know how to bake bread anymore, they just go to Wal-Mart or any store," Woody said. "I've been trying to get some ladies and some guys to learn how to can, pressure can like we used to."

"Mmhm," Hastings said.

"Too much work; they don't want to do it. It's cheaper to go to Wal-Mart," Woody said and laughed.

"Yeah," Hastings agreed.

"The knowledge of it. We may have to do it again," said Woody.

"We're *gonna* have to do it again," Hastings agreed. "Just like gigs, people say, 'How come you keep making them?' One of these days people are going to depend on them."

"That's what I told my wife," said Woody. "She said, 'How come you want two more?' I said, 'Well, Hastings is not going to be around forever.' I said, 'I don't know anyone else that's making them. We're going to need them one of these days.'

"Yeah. You know, it's like bows. You know, one of these days they may outlaw guns," Hastings said.

Seven Levels of Heaven

Hastings, Sequoyah, and I often talked about the Cherokee concept of the seven levels of heaven. "Heaven" is a translation of the word Galunlati, the Cherokee "Sky World." Traditional Cherokee thought holds that people progress through different levels of existence, represented by our interactions with the natural world. Moving on a journey from the water world to the world of the sky and beyond, we learned things along the way and brought that knowledge with us. We also make this journey as individuals.

"We were talking about the seven levels of heaven . . . ," I said.

"Yeah, that's the last step," Hastings said. "That's the one that everybody works for. That's that last place where the Creator is. There's no end there. That's continued. I mean, the living continues. But you're living in a different form . . . it's not this body. It's a body that doesn't hurt, a body that doesn't require food or anything like that. It's everlasting. There's no want for anything. There's no need for anything. It's just a continuation."

"Mm."

"See people—a lot of people don't understand that. They say, 'Well, death, that's it. They're gone.' No, they're *not* gone. They're not gone until we reach that seventh level."

"And can they come back?" I asked.

"Well, you know, now at that point in time they can. They travel. They have that ability to travel back and forth. Just like the wind right now. Now there may be . . . Who knows what's out there? A lot of times they travel in the wind. You can hear voices in the wind."

"Oh yeah. Yeah."

"You know, people say, 'I didn't hear it.' *Listen*. But you gotta listen with a different set of ears, not the regular daily noises, you know. You have to listen a little bit different. It has to be a little bit different, you know. Just like fire. You look at fire. You're looking at the fire, but you're also looking at what's in it."

"Mmhm."

"You know? Water. You look at water. But what's *in* it? Although it's clear, you see it as a liquid, but there's something in it. Earth, you know. There's always something in earth. You can see sometimes in earth that you look one way, you look back and there will be something there that wasn't there just a moment before. But people have forgotten how to do that. We don't take the time to go out with nature. Whenever we go out we always got something on our minds. 'Well, I'm going to go do *this*.' Instead of going out and saying, 'Well, I'm going to go see what I need to see.' Or, 'What do I need to hear today?'"

"Mmhm."

"I used to take my paper, pencil. Got a big old rock down there. I used to go down there and sit down. And just listen. And you hear things. But people are afraid of the unknown; if they can't describe what it is they're afraid of it."

"Yeah. Yeah," I said. I paused a moment and thought about the past few months I'd spent with my family in New Mexico writing this book while on fellowship at the School for Advanced Research in Santa Fe. "Well, being in New Mexico—in Santa Fe—this year, I go out on my deck at night and it's just crystal clear out . . . ," I said.

"Yeah. Yeah."

"You have a sense that you're in a different people's land. You can see it and you can feel it in the wind."

"Yeah," Hastings said and laughed.

"But those Pueblo peoples have been there for a long time. It's their land. It's their place. And the spirits of that place you can feel," I said.

"That don't leave," said Hastings. "I mean, you know, what we've done here on earth will never leave. I don't care if you was good, you was bad, or whatever. Whatever you've done is gonna be here."

Saluting the Flag

The members of the Liars' Club are friends, and I watched as they sometimes would disagree with one another, as friends, on important topics.

One afternoon, Hastings, Sequoyah, Woody, and I discussed the implications of saluting the American flag.

"Just like some tribes back west," Hastings said, "when the national anthem is played, they keep sitting. They asked me one day, 'Why do you stand?' And I said, 'Hey, I've had buddies killed, sacrificed their lives for that flag. That's my honor to 'em is for me to stand and salute the flag.'"

"It took me a long time to get over that," Woody said. "Because, growing up I read a lot of books. I read a lot of history. I read a lot of injustices. And it took me a long time to stand up and go like that." Woody saluted. "Because I don't feel like this was a just government, knowing what I know about the history of our relationship. But, as I got older, my brother died, who was a Nam vet. My uncle and father-in-law were Korean vets. And just like Brother Hastings said, it's a remembrance, an honor. They chose to do what they did."

"Mmhm," Hastings said.

"And I honor them for it," Woody continued. "Remembering. Not only just that military service, but their whole life. They came back . . . and my other brother who was also in Nam, they came back from Nam shattered and broken."

"Yeah."

"They said, 'Don't go to the military. Don't.' But it was their love for me, not so much antipatriotism. But the love for me 'cause they didn't want me to see and go through what they did. My brother's still shattered, but he's at a point where he's okay," said Woody.

"I've had old men come out here. Veterans. And talk about what they went through, just like it happened yesterday," Hastings said.

"Yeah."

"Vietnam. Korea. I had an eighty-three-year-old man come out here. And to him, it was like the war just happened. He has never came back. He's still fighting there, wherever that is. And our government kind of kicks 'em off to the side."

"Yeah."

"'Okay. We got your use,'" Hastings said.

"Kind of the nature of the beast," Woody said. "Just go on to another one."

Sequoyah, who had been listening, said, "See, I'm just a little bit different than you. To this day I *refuse* to pledge allegiance to the flag. I won't even put my hand over my heart. But I *will* stand up. But not for the flag, not for the United States, but for, like you said, the veterans. The soldiers that are still out there. That's who I'm standing up for. But, the things that I do, my standing, my removal of my cap, it's not for the flag. It's not for the United States. It's for our people, the ones that are in the army now, and the ones that have gone on before. That's who I'm doing it for. I will *not* do it for the United States."

"Me, it's different," Hastings said. "When I went in, they said this is what you have to do. And I took that oath. If they'd have called me I would have went. I was lucky; I didn't get called. I was in that Vietnam era. I was in that worst part, but I didn't get to go. And I had a buddy killed over there. Had two or three of 'em. But he'd come in, in December. He said, 'I'm not coming back.' I said, 'Yeah you will.' He came back." Hastings paused for a moment. "They *brought* him back. So, I still . . . I'll stand and honor them. Because I was part of it."

"I got a son-in-law who will be leaving out for the Baghdad area here in the next couple weeks," Woody said. "And he's my first grandson's father. He just turned two and I'm thinking . . . just remembering what my brothers both said about war. I just pray that he'll come back. I know he won't be the same person, mentally."

"Yeah," Hastings said.

"And emotionally. But there'll be a point where he will not be messed up so much. So, it is a concern."

"They say you walk over death," Hastings said.

"Mmhm."

"You step through death. You walk over it. Because it's there. It's there."

"He'll be with a combat unit, so I know he'll do things he has to do," Woody continued. "Like you said, he took an oath. So. I just pray that he goes in strong, with strength, and comes back with strength, too."

"Just like, three years ago, an old boy come and bought a gig from me. Pole and a gig. Eighty dollars. I still got it," Hastings said and laughed. "I asked a judge of the Creek Nation, 'How long am I supposed to keep that?' He said, 'What did you give him?' I said, 'My word.' He said, 'You're only as good as your word.'"

"Yeah," Woody nodded.

"So," Hastings laughed, "I still got it. One of these days he may come out there and he may not. But I'm gonna keep it. Because I gave my word. When he comes after it it'll be there."

"Mmhm."

"And I still got the pole and a gig. It's actually gonna be three years next month, in January."

"And, you know, that's the history and the nature that God has given us and Indian people, is our *word*. Look at the treaties; we kept our word. Who didn't? Who didn't?" Woody laughed. "The colonials; the Europeans."

"But who's gonna pay for it?" Hastings asked.

"Yeah."

"Not me," Hastings said.

"Yeah."

THE RETURN OF THE BEAR
Told by Sammy Still

"This is one that Grandma used to tell me when I was growing up. And I guess a lot of times, too, a lot of these stories did have teachings to 'em. And I guess this was sort of like a teaching she told me. And I tell this story sometimes to people. I don't tell this story when we tell stories to, like, groups of people. It's like individuals, like now when we're getting together, just talking to individuals.

"My grandmother used to, we used to sit outside in the backyard in the late evenings when it was warm. Springtime or summertime. And she told me this. Of course, a lot of times when you're young, you don't remember things or you don't keep up with things 'cause you're too young or you don't really listen to them till later on in life. And then you get to thinking, 'Hey, now I know what she meant, what she was talking about.' 'I know what my grandfather was trying to tell me, or my parents were trying to tell me.' You know, when you get older, you know, you finally realize that because you're going through that stage that they were."

Well, this story here,
I say it's a story, but I guess it's really about a bear.
She said, "You know,
    there used to be a bear,
used to live right around where we used to live.
And they were all scared of this bear.
They were all afraid of it 'cause they were all afraid it was going
    to come and do harm to them."

She said that people said,
"Oh, we got to get rid of this bear. We got to get rid of it."
    Somebody said, "We'll go out and try to find it and kill it."
She said, "No, no, don't kill it 'cause it lives here.

We just need to get it away from our families."
So, what they did was they trapped
that animal.
They trapped that bear,
and took it miles and miles away.

She said, when they took it miles away
    they let it go,
    and they all came back.
They were all happy, everybody was happy:
    "Well, the bear's gone now,
    We don't have nothing to worry about."

But pretty soon,
I guess that bear got homesick for its home.
It wanted to come back to where it was born and raised and all of
        that.
So, about a week or two weeks later,
that bear was back. Someone noticed it.
They come back and say, "Hey, that bear's back! The bear's back!"
    But it wasn't harming anybody.
So they all looked at it and said,
"Well, it really is not hurting anyone, and I guess if he stays over
        where he's at and no one bothers it he'll be alright."
So they let that bear stay.

But what she told me was,
"You know what, you're going to be just like that bear."
She said,
    "When you grow up."
And I kind of looked at her and I kind of thought,
    "Well, what does she mean?"
And what she was saying was that
when I grow up and get older, I'm going to be taken away from
my environment.
I'm going to be taken away from my home.
I'm going to be taught
    a different language.
And a different religion.
They're going to take me away from my home

and try to
make me something that I'm not.

So, as I got older I did.
I went to school.
They taught me English.
I lost my Native tongue.
Start speaking English and
I went away
and started going to schools and I got to learning
    their religion
    and how they learn.
And as I got older,
I lost my heritage and my culture.
I wasn't thinking about that anymore.
I thought about what's happening *now*,
    I thought about the *future*,
    what's going *on*,
    what's happening *present day*.

But one day,
it came back to me and I thought to myself, I said, "You know . . ."
And we did move, my family did move away from here.
We went to a different state and lived.
But, you know, after a while I got to thinking,
we came back home and it didn't dawn on me till later in life
what my grandmother was saying.
"That was right, they did take me away from where I used to live.
They did take me away from my culture and my language and all."

But, in the story she said,
    "You're going to be just like that bear.
    They're going to take you away.
    They're going to teach you things that they want you to know.
    But later in life you're going to return.
    You're going to come back,
    and you're going to teach your kids what you learned,
    and your culture and your history."

And so, I guess, like, today,
it's gone around full circle

because it did,
I finally came back home and I learned my history and my culture
again.
My language again.
And being with my own people.
And now I'm teaching this to my children and my grandchildren.

So in a way I guess I came full circle,
which is just like that story she told,
that one day we'll be taken away,
but that we'll always be coming back
to our old stomping grounds again, I guess you would say,
and I guess that's what really happened to me.

Now I understand what she was talking about.
I understand the stories that she tells
and what she explained to me when I was growing up
because, like I said, when you're younger
you really don't pay that much attention to 'em, you know,
but now you get to thinking, now I'm doing what she was doing.
I'm sitting there, talking to my kids,
talking to my grandchildren
about this story of the bear.
That they're going to be taken away,
but one day they'll return
to teach their grandchildren
our history and our culture.

So, you know, like I say,
it may not be much of a story
but it had meaning to it, you know?
It had a teaching to it.
What they would teach you.
And I guess that's why I hang around with these guys a lot because
things that they talk about,
even the stories that they tell,
it does have teachings with them.

"And that's what I learn," said Sammy. "And Sequoyah really made me
understand that 'cause, see, I wasn't a storyteller . . . I say I wasn't a story-

teller but, like I say, he brought me out to get in front of people and tell 'em stories. Stories that we were raised with. 'Cause I didn't know any stories. I mean, I said I don't, but I really did, but it took someone like Sequoyah and Hastings to bring me out to tell these stories. Because these are stories that we was raised up with and told. And so, that's what we share today. And I really appreciate that, because it's something that we cherish with our hearts, you know. That's our heritage; that's our culture; that's our language. That's who we are."

"Don't blame me for making you a liar," Hastings said wryly, and everyone cracked up.

Friendship

I remember Sequoyah telling me once when we had only known each other for a little while that there really is no Cherokee word for friend. He explained to me that there are no formalities or niceties in the Cherokee language. There's no word for "excuse me" or "pardon me." And that's because, Sequoyah said, politeness and respect for one another is an assumption within Cherokee culture. "As for friends," Sequoyah said, "if you're talking to someone then you're on friendly terms. You wouldn't be talking to someone if you weren't friendly with them."

At the Heritage Center chapel, Hastings, Sequoyah, and I were discussing Cherokee values, and the idea of friendship came up again.

"There's a lot of things that we as Cherokees do and expect that isn't recognized by other societies," Sequoyah said. "I think, typically, if you make real friends with a Cherokee, you got a friend for life. I mean, they will stick by you. If you are true. And, it don't matter if you're in the right or wrong, they will stick by you. And that's only if you make a friendship for what it is. To be friends. Not because of what you can get out of 'em, not because of what you can exploit from being friends with a Cherokee. But if you're just a true friend, and that's all you're in it for, your Cherokee friend will stick with you till the end. And that's something that mainstream society doesn't see anymore."

"Mm," I said.

"It's always, 'What can I get out of this? I want to be his friend because I can get another step up on the ladder.'"

"Mmhm," I said.

"But that's not how it is with Cherokees. Cherokees, they value true friendship for what it really is. Not what you can get out of it. Like you, just like Woody said last night. You're our friend. If you were to call from

El Reno and said, 'Hey, my car broke down!' We'd be on our way out there to go get you, you know? And you won't find that in mainstream society."

I nodded my head.

"If you call somebody else, they'll say, 'Well, hope you get out of there,'" Sequoyah said and laughed.

"Call triple A," Hastings chimed in.

"So, that's one value that Cherokees really . . . well, I guess, slowly we're losing that, too. 'Cause Cherokee people, they're starting to think the same way as the mainstream society."

Later, Sequoyah talked about how he's often approached by people when he travels and tells stories.

"A lot of the people that I meet from other places, they'll come and they'll say, 'Yeah, I'm Cherokee and I want to learn how to be more Cherokee.' And one lady, I asked her, 'Okay, you say you're Cherokee. You want to learn the language, which is good,' I said. She said, 'I feel I'm Cherokee in my heart. My heart's Cherokee.' And I said, 'Well, one thing you'll have to do is learn Cherokee values. They're totally different than how you're living your life right now.' Because this lady, even though her heart was going toward the right place, she didn't seem like she was willing to give up her hold on mainstream society in order to give herself over to really being a real Cherokee like she was saying she was wanting to be. And in order to be a Cherokee, I mean it's more than your language, it's more than just going to the stomp dance, you know, every once in a while. It's just like we've been saying before, it's a total different way of thought. Our values are so much different from mainstream values. And our stories reflect these values. Just like the friends I was talking about a while ago. If you're my friend, then we're friends until the bitter end. But if you're just my friend just to see what you can get out of me, I'm not going to . . ."

"Mm," I said.

"Just like Hastings was saying, if you need something and I got what you need, you're more than welcome to have it," Sequoyah continued. "And, a lot of people will say, 'Well that person will give the shirt off their back for you.' A real Cherokee friend will do that if they know you need it. And you won't even have to ask. They will do it. If my friends are in trouble and I can do something to help 'em, I'm going to drop everything I'm doing right now to go help 'em. And that's the difference. If you were driving back home and your car broke down in El Reno or maybe even Amarillo, we'd be in the car right away to go help you."

"Right," Hastings said curtly. "I expect you at the house Monday morning then." Everyone burst out laughing

"Except for Monday morning," Sequoyah said.

"Make an appointment!" I said.

"Except for Monday; I'll be busy Monday," Sequoyah continued, laughing. "But, that's how you can tell the difference between a person that just wants to play Cherokee and somebody that really, really truly does have the heart of a Keetoowah. It's just like we said a while ago. The needs of the many doesn't always outweigh the needs of the few. In the old days, if one village was under attack, all the other villages came. If one person was in trouble, all the village came. If one family member was in trouble or needed help the whole family gathered together. So."

"I always tell 'em, 'If you knew how Cherokees lived, you wouldn't even want to be a Cherokee,'" Hastings said, and everyone laughed and nodded.

As the conversation shifted, I thought back to a time when on the way home from Hastings's house Woody's car started to act up. He lost a fan belt in Tahlequah and didn't know if he could make it home. Sequoyah and I had just pulled in to Little Kansas from the half-hour drive from Lost City when we got Woody's call. As Sequoyah got off the phone he looked over and said, "We got to head back to Tahlequah. Woody's got car trouble." There was no hesitation on Sequoyah's part. No griping about inconvenience. We spent the early evening driving to Tahlequah and following Woody back to Jay. We cross distances to help each other get home.

THE COPPERHEADS AT THE FOUR CORNERS OF KENWOOD

Told by Woody Hansen

Woody looked at Hastings and asked, "Did I tell you that story about when I got hit? Well, there's actually like two or three stories in that one incident. On the surface is, yeah, like you said earlier,"

"Yeah?" Hastings said.

"I got hit by a car chasing a snake, and that's what everybody says, you know? And that's basically the story," Woody said and began to laugh as Hastings chuckled. "In a nutshell, as they say. But the second story is . . ."

> up in rattlesnake country.
> This happened on a Monday night,
> April 23rd last year of '07.
> And

I had hunted rattlesnakes . . .
Well, I left I think
Thursday evening and went to southern Oklahoma and . . .
    When you're rattlesnake hunting
    you do a lot of walking. A lot of walking.
So we did that Thursday morning
    and come back in for lunch,
then we go back and go out in the evening.
So, actually you hunt
twice a day.
And so we did that Friday
and we did that Saturday
and we did that Sunday.
The weather was wet
    and we covered many,
    what seemed like many miles,
    but actually, you know, it's not.
It's, you know, terrain and rocks and hills.
So we did that for three days in a row
and I managed to catch one rattlesnake.
And it was disappointing
because I had a snake presentation, you know,
the following Friday.

"Uh-huh," Hastings said.

But I did have a rattlesnake,
but I didn't have a copperhead
and a couple other species I didn't have.
But anyway,
we come back Sunday night.
I got in about eleven o'clock Sunday night.
Just threw my gear aside and went in the house,
showered, and went to bed.
Went to work Monday morning, you know,
my full eight hours,
I think I might have drove to Tulsa, you know, for my job.
And that evening, Lani had choir practice in Tahlequah.
Joyce said, "You going?"

And I almost said, "Naw, I'm gonna rest."
But since I was gone three or four days I thought,
well, we'll have family time on the way down, on the way back.
And so,
    she finished up
    probably about eight thirty or so
    and went to Wal-Mart.
    And it was about nine.
    You know, in April, the sun's about going down about eight
        forty-five,

"Yeah. Yeah," Hastings agreed.

    you know, and it's still dusk.
    So it was around nine o'clock
        we went on to Moody,
            come out at Lowry and Rocky Ford.

"Yeah," Hastings said.

    Get on Leech Road and go to Kenwood and go east.

    Well, Joyce was driving.
    And when we got to that Leech/Kenwood road
    we go east to my house ten miles.
    I told her, "I'm going to rest a little bit."
    And so I, uh, I just closed my eyes.
    It was right there at that section,
    she turned,
    and I just
        really relaxing,
    but I could hear her talking.
    I could hear the radio on and everybody else talking and stuff.
    And we drive about two miles. Straight stretch of road near Falling
        Buzzard's house . . .

"Yeah," said Hastings.
"Chumalukey's," Woody said.
"Chumalukey's, yeah," Hastings nodded.

Straight going east.
She goes, "There's a copperhead in the road.
    Want to stop and look at it?"
And I said, "Yeah." And I kept my eyes closed the whole time.
I was just really tired and relaxed by then.
And she turned in, and I could tell she pulled off.
I said, "Turn your flashers on."
    And so she did,
    and I get out.
And I go out and this big, long copperhead.
He was just laying there.
Which was . . .
    first that should have been a red flag right there!
    Usually they're gone.
Just laying there.
Just look like he shed.
And I thought, "Wow."
A real vibrant red and cream color.

Woody looked at Hastings and said, "Dang, kind of wanted to go and
get you 'cause I didn't have . . . I just had tennis shoes on, I didn't have
no snake-hunting equipment cause it was at home. And they're, they're
pretty tricky to try to catch."

So, I walk back to the car
and there's a floor mat.
I say, "I'm going to get that floor mat and just squish him and try
        to . . ."
    That was my intent.
And I was talking to it, you know?
    "Oh, you're pretty."
    You know.
    "I'm thankful you're here because I got a presentation,
    I don't have a copperhead and you're a nice one . . ."
Just as I was gonna put that mat on it,
    Boom!

And that was the end of *that*.

Well, fast forward,
I'm in the hospital four or five days later
by myself,
    the only time I was by myself.
I was watching TV just kind of painful and stuff,
and leg swollen, hurt.
Anyway, I was watching that history channel or something
and it showed a rainforest.
An Indian man going through a rainforest.
It had sun rays through it
and it was yellow as he was walking through it.
And I said, "I seen that!"
I seen that light the night I saw that copperhead.
    And it started coming back to me.
    And here's the third part of this story.

It was, when I opened the door
my eyes were still closed.
But my mind . . .
when I got out it was almost like I was hypnotized.
And when I did open my eyes there was that yellow light,
just like I saw that guy in the rainforest in.
It just followed me
    to that snake.
And that's why I think maybe that yellow light just brought out
        those little bright colors.
And I was talking to that snake, you know,
    "I respect you.
    I don't want to bite you.
    I got a snake presentation." You know?

"Yeah," Hastings said, listening intently now.

And, then I thought,
"I'll get that mat."
And I go back and that light follows me.
You know, just kind of a light glow.
You know, a little bit more than this.

Yellow.
Then I go back and,
same thing,
just as I go to put that mat down, that car hits me.
And soon as I get hit, that light's gone.
And I know I'm back in reality
    and I feel myself hitting her hood,
    and hitting her windshield.
    Then, Boom!
And my granddaughter, my first granddaughter,
four months old at the time,
she was right there,
she just smiled at me and just kind of giggled and then she
        disappeared.
    And it just kind of calmed me.
About that time then,
Joyce and the girl that hit me come running up, you know,
and everything just went wild then.

    But that amber light . . .

Fast forward,
I'm out of the hospital, I'm laying in bed at home.
And I was just feeling bad
so I opened the Bible. Random.
And it opens to Ezekiel.
    Chapter one.
And it talks about Ezekiel seeing a vision
    in the distance, you know.
    Clouds coming.
Then, he recognized this to be angels of the Lord
and as they were getting closer he says they were cast in an amber
        light
as representatives of God.
And, just the amber light was the light that I saw that night
    of the accident.
So I felt like, "Well, God was there because I'm still alive."
Even though I got hurt really bad.
And, just seeing that amber light that night,
    feeling no pain,

even though it was all busted up and they was wanting to
        amputate it.
    Feeling no pain.
    And seeing my granddaughter appear to me was like an angel.
Then again, like I said, when Joyce and the girl that hit me come
        running up,
it was all reality then.
    Tears.
    Sorrow.
    Grief.

"Hurting?" Hastings asked.
"Hurt on their part, I wasn't . . . ," Woody said.
"You wasn't?"
"At the time I lay just barely hanging on," Woody continued. "There was
no bones, it was all inside."

    They were crying.
    Each of us crying.
    It was a terrible, sad scene.
    But, uh, an ambulance rolls up.
    Well, first responders come.
    Then the ambulance rolls up and
    I was glad it was Cherokee Nation, you know?
    It kind of comforted me knowing because I trained with them.
    And one of the guys rolled up and I recognized him and he
        recognized me and the girl, too. "Woody, what were you
        doing?!"
    "Trying to catch a copperhead."
    I was laying on that backboard and said,
    "It's laying right over there somewhere."
    And they said, "Copperhead! Oh my god!"

Woody and Hastings laughed.

    "Let's get this man out of here!"
    Boy they loaded me,
    and I say they just kind of threw me in the ambulance because they
        did.

And it was just kind of a light moment,
to see them do that, because, professionals, you know . . .

"Yeah," Hastings said.

And, of course there was a lot of people, there, too!
I thought, "My gosh! Where did all these people come from?"
But in the meantime that copperhead,
with all that commotion,
dove under a big old log by the ditch.
And he got in there and, boy, he was all flustered, and scared.

"Yeah?" Hastings said.

And three or four other copperheads were under that log, boy, and
he said,
"Guys! Guys! Guess what!"
And they said, "What's the matter with you?"
He said, "Guys, I almost got run over by a car tonight . . .
but a *human* jumped in front of me and saved my hide!"

Hastings, Woody, Sequoyah, and I erupted in laughter as Woody continued,

That was me.
So *any*way . . .
That's the end of *that* story.

That story came to me
about three months later as I was laying there,
and I was like, "There has to be . . ."
I was just laying there.
And then the copperhead came,
and it was like, this is what happened to *me*
while that was going on with *you*.
And so, anyway . . .
The copperheads at the four corners of Kenwood owe me one.

"People ask me, 'Well, I guess you're not going to be chasing snakes
anymore.' I said, 'Number one, I wasn't chasing it. It was just lying there,'"

Woody said and laughed. "'But if I was a bull rider, bull riders get hurt, they get back on the bull.' I said, 'The athlete on the football field, they break a leg or an arm,' I said. 'They go back to play. I'm no different. I'm going to do it, you know?' I said I just won't take anything for granted, even on a straight stretch of highway, you know? During that time the light was on I didn't hear anything. I didn't hear them hollering at me 'Car coming!' They saw it coming closer straight toward me. They were screaming and I didn't even hear the car. You know, you can hear a car go by. Totally, totally relaxed and focused. That probably saved my life. Along with the Great Spirit, the Creator. Didn't hear nothing. And then the light was gone."

"I told him one time that copperhead was a hit copperhead, with a contract on him," Sequoyah said.

"Yeah?" Hastings said.

"And people would bring me dead or alive snakes instead of flowers or candy or anything, they'd bring me snakes to cheer me up," said Woody. "Had a lot of phone calls from different organizations that heard about my accident. Wished me a speedy recovery. Next question would be, 'When can you come out? When can you bring the boys out?'

"So, through the years, I've had people say, 'I don't run over snakes anymore because of your presentation and how you view them as part of nature and part of the world and creation.' I've heard some say, 'I used to hate all snakes and now I know the difference between poisonous and nonpoisonous because of your presentation.' So, I feel like it's been worthwhile."

I wondered whether Woody was talking about his work with snakes, or getting hit like a snake on the road. Maybe both.

ᏧᏍᏗᏥᏍᏔᏟ
TSUSTATSISTATLI
COPPERHEAD
ᏗᎪᏪᎵᏍᎩ ᎤᏃᎮᏢᏂ
Digowelisgi unohetlani
Woody, what he told

ᏓᎵᏈᏩᏛ ᏬᎨᏙᎸ ᏥᎨᏒ ᏀᎯᏯ ᏙᏩᎴᎵ ᏣᎬᏫᏂᎸ.
Daligwadv wogedolv tsigesv nahiya dowaleli tsagwvnilv.
Was Tahlequah, we had gone to, it was, at that time, wagon
  (vehicle), hit me.

ᎠᏆᏍᏔᏴᎲᏍᎩ ᏎᎵ ᎠᎴ ᏔᎵ ᎠᏂᎨᏳᏣ ᎣᎩᎾᏤᎵ ᎠᏤᎢ ᎠᎴ ᎠᏂ ᏦᎦᎵᎪᏒ.

Agwastayvhvsgi seli ale tali anigehutsa oginatseli atsei ale ani tsogaligosv.

My cooker (wife), (no translation) Joyce, and, two, the girls, belong to us, New (Jade), and, Strawberry (Lani), we were all together.

ᎩᎾᏭᏓ ᏗᎧᎸᎬ ᏗᏝ ᏦᏣᎢᏗᏍᎬ.

Kinawuda dikalvgv ditla tsotsaidisgv.

Kenwood, where it rises (east), that direction, we were going.

ᏙᏳ ᏥᏗᎠᎩᎠᏪᎦ. ᎣᎾᏗᏝᎦ ᏣᏯᏉᏢ. ᎮᎴ ᏂᏥᎸᏍᎪ.

Doyu tsidiagiawega. Onaditlvga tsayagwotlv. Hele nitsilvsgo.

Very, I was very tired. In the back, I was sitting. Almost going to sleep.

Ꮒ! ᎢᎾᏓ! ᎤᏛᏁ ᏎᎵ. ᏧᏍᏔᏥᏍᏔᏟ ᏅᏫᏍᏓ! ᏣᏚᎵᏍ?

Ni! Inada! Udvne seli. Tsustatsistatli nvwisda! Ysadulis?

Look! Snake! s/he/it said, (no translation) Joyce. Copperhead, it appeared to be! Do you want it?

ᎾᎯᏳᏃ ᏥᎨᏒ Ꮭ ᏯᎩᎧᎮ ᏧᏍᏔᏥᏍᏔᏟ. ᎰᏩ, ᏥᏲᎮᎴ.

Nahiyuno tsigesv tla yagikahe tsustatsistatli. Howa, tsiyohele.

At that time, was, no, didn't own one, copperhead. Alright, I told her/him/it.

ᎤᎴᏫᏍᏔᎾᏃ ᎾᎠ ᏗᎦᎾᎥ ᎢᎾᏓ, ᎠᎩᏠᏒ ᏙᏩᎴᎵ.

Ulewistanano naa diganav inada, agidlosv dowaleli.

S/he/it stopped near, where it lay, snake. I climbed down, wagon (vehicle).

ᏙᏳ ᎤᏬᏚ ᏥᎨᏒ ᏧᏍᏔᏥᏍᏔᏟ. ᎭᎴ ᎠᏍᏔᎷᎩᏍᎨ ᎩᎦᎨ.

Doyu uwodu tsigesv tsustatsistatli. Hale astalugisge gigage.

Very, pretty, was, copperhead. Almost, shining, red.

ᎠᏎᏍᎩᎾ Ꮭ ᏱᏥᎾᏙᎮ ᎫᎱᏍᏗ ᏥᏒᏛᏙᏗ.

Asesgina tla yitsinadohe guhysdi tsisvdvdodi.

However, no, I didn't carry, something, to trap it with.

ᎾᏃ ᎠᎳᏍᏛᏙᏗ ᎠᎵᏭ ᏱᎬᏔ, ᏣᏇᎵᏒ.

Nano alasdvdodi aliwu yigvta, tsagwelisv.

What about, what you stop on (mat), possible, I can use, I thought.

ᎤᏟᏍᏗ ᏥᏩᎩᏁᏒ ᎠᎳᏍᏛᏙᏗ ᏥᎦᎳᎥ ᏓᏩᎴᎵ.
Utlisdi tsiaginesv alasdvdodi tsigalav dawaleli.
Quickly, retrieved, what you stop on (mat), it was in there, wagon (vehicle).

ᏙᏳ ᎤᏍᏆᏂᎦᏗ ᏄᏍᏔᏂᏙᎴ, Ꮟ ᎤᎦᎾᎥ ᎢᎾᏓ ᏥᏩᎩᎷᏨ.
Doyu usgwanigadi nustanidole, si vganav inada tsiwagilutsv.
Very, interesting, happened, still yet, it lay there, snake, when I returned.

ᎷᏓᎴᏛ ᏱᎨᎮ ᎢᎾᏓ ᏳᎳᏘᏎ. ᎠᏎᏍᎩᎾ ᎯᎾ ᏧᏍᏔᏥᏍᏔᏟ ᎥᎦᎾᎠ.
Ludaledv yigehe inada yulatise. asesgina hina tsustatsistatli vganaa.
Different, if it was, snake, would've run away, however, this, copperhead, still laying there.

ᎤᎾᏛ ᏥᎦᏜᏍᏛ ᎢᎾᏓ Ꮭ ᏯᏆᎾᏔ ᏄᏓᏍᏔᏂᏙᎸ ᎠᏎᏍᎩᎾ ᎩᎶᏰᎪᎯᏓ ᎦᏙ ᏫᏥᎾᎥ.
Unadv tsigatosdv inada tla yagwanata nudastanidolv asesgina kiloyegohida gado witsinav.
There, I was watching, snake, no, know, what happened, but, very quickly, ground, I was laying.

ᏝᏍᏇ ᏯᏫᏕᎶᏎ ᏙᏩᎴᎵ ᎠᏋᏮᏂᎸ.
Tlasgwa yawidelose dowaleli agwvnilv.
Didn't, notice, wagon (vehicle) hit me.

ᏝᏍᏇ ᏯᏇᏍᏔᏁᎮ ᏥᏰᎸ ᎤᏅ ᏥᎾᎥ ᎦᏙ.
Tlasgwa yagwestanehe tsiyev uhna tsinav gado.
Wasn't, in no pain, my body, there, laying, ground.

ᎠᏎᏍᎩᎾ ᎠᏇᏥ ᎠᏧᏣ ᎧᏃᎭᎵᏙ ᎤᏤᎵ ᎤᏍᏗ ᎠᎨᎱᏣ ᎡᎵᏏ ᏧᏙᏫᏓ ᏥᎪᏛᎲ.
Asesgina agwetsi atsutsa kanohalido utseli usdi agehutsa elisi tsudowida tsigotvhv.
But, my egg (offspring), boy, Hunter (Jake), s/he/it own, little (baby), girl Alise (granddaughter), s/he/it name is, I saw her/ him/it.

ᏝᏍᏇ ᏯᏆᎾᏔ ᎮᎳᎢᎪᎯᏛ ᏥᎾᎥ ᎤᏅ ᎦᏙ ᎠᏎᏍᎩᎾ ᏥᏭᏂᎷᏨ ᎠᏂᎦᏅᎦᏗ ᎠᎾᏓᏍᏖᎵᏍᎩ.
Tlasgwu yagwanata helaigohidv tsinav uhna gado asesgina tsiwunilutsv aniganvgadi anadastelisgi.

No way, don't know, how long, I lay, there, ground, but, they
 arrived, doctors helpers.

DӨSᏫᎢᏞᏍZ ᏅᏏᏎᎦᏀ ᏅᎾᏍᎫᎢ VGᏕᏞ ᏣᏍᎳᎻᏛᎤᎳᏔᏟᏟᏫC EӨ DᏂ
ӨᎥᏛᎦᏛᏀ4Ꮰ.
Anagastelihvno unigalvgi unatsodii dowaleli tsustatsistatli gvna ani
 navtsidetsiyoselv.
As they were helping, those who are sick, where they ride, wagon
 (vehicle), copperhead, lying, here, near, I told them.

ᏛᎤᏎᏛ ӨᏎᏕᏒ ᏅᏟᏍᏛᎤᏛ ᏆӨᏍᏝᎯ ᏣᏛ ᏓᏎᎤᏎᏛᎢᏒ VGᏕᏞ ᏣᏢ.
Sgidv nagiwesv utlidusdv nunadvnelv hale wenagedaisv dowaleli
 ditla.
That, when I said, quickly, they acted, almost, they threw me,
 wagon (vehicle) in that direction.

ᏣᏂᏎᎦᎦ ᏅӨᏝᏣ ᏣᏛᏫᎤᎢ ᏛᏛᏝ ᏣᏟᏉᎯ.
Junigilvgi unadlvdi tsutsiyai sgwida tsunedolv.
The sickly, where they lay, when I was in there, many, came walking
 around.

TᏚVZ ᏗᎠ ᏆᏂᏛ94.
Igadono hia nuniwese.
Some, here, what they said.

ZGᏛ4 ᏛᎨWAᏛ TӨᏝ ᏚᏗᏂᏍᏛE.
Nowadvse tesulagotsi inada dehinisgv.
Now I suppose, you are going to quit, snake, you catching them.

Ꮈ, SᏛᏛᏀ4Ꮑ. ᏝᏛᏛ TӨᏝ ᏛᏛ4 CᎬᏂW. VGᏕW ᏛᏛR.
Tla, degetsiyosehv. Gesdv inada yigese tsagwvnila. Dowalela
 tsigesv.
No, I was telling them. Wasn't, snake, it wasn't s/he/it hit me,
 wagon (vehicle), it was.

D4ᏫᏎӨ, Ꮈ ᏂᏚᏝ ᏒᎩ ᏛᏛᏁᏛE.
Asesgina, tla nigada yigi tsiohesgv.
However, no, everything, it is, what I'm telling.

ӨᏁZ ᏣᏫᏝᏛᎤᎳᏔᏟᏟᏫC ᏛᏛᏛᎯVᏁ ZᏗG ᏅRᏗ ᏗᎠ ᏆGᏛᏝᏛ.
Naheno tsustatsistatli tsitsikenidohv nohiyu usvhi hia nuyudvnele.
That, copperhead, I was chasing, that, night, here, what s/he/it did.

ᏧᎵᏍ ᎤᏴᏴᏴᏴᏃ ᏛᎥᎥᎣᎿᎵᏗ 9ᏈᏯ ᎤᎴ ᎠᏂᎱᎢᎢ ᏧᏍᏔᏫᏂᎣᏛᏪᏟ ᎠᏂᎥᏂᎧᎡ.

Ditlaga uweyvsv hawinaditla wulose uhna ansoi tsustatsistatli aninatlae.

Tree, fallen down, underneath, it went that way, there, others, copperhead, they lay.

Ꭿ! Ꭿ! ᏉᏓᎸ ᎤᎣᏗᏘᎥᏗ ᎣᎳᎣᏪᏞ, ᎤᎾᎲᎢᎡ Ꮎ ᎠᎬᎤᎣ ᏧᏍᏔᏫᎳᎣᏛᏪᏟ.

Ni! Ni! Doyu usgwaikadi nagwastasi, udvhe na agvyi tsustatsistatli.

Look! Look! Very, interesting, it happened to me, s/he/it said, that, first copperhead.

ᏉᎤᎣᎥᎠᎢ? ᎤᎵᎤᎲᎢᎿᎣ ᎠᏂᎱᎢᎡ ᏧᏍᏔᏫᏂᎣᏛᏪᏟ.

Dousdi? Unadvne aniso tsustatsistatli.

What is it? They said, the others, copperhead.

ᏉᎠᏌᏞ ᎤᎥᎦ ᎣᎬᎲᏍ Ꭰ4ᎥᎣᏯᎣ ᎠᎣᎠᏍᎦᎣ ᎠᎣᎬᎯᎥᎠᏟ ᎣᎤᎥᏰ!

Dowaleli hale nagwvniga asesgina asgaya ayagvhaditla nadvgi!

Wagon (vehicle), almost, ran over me, however, man, in front, s/he/it did!

ᏉᎠᎤᎤ4 ᏏᎣᏛᏆᎰᏞ ᏧᏍᏔᏫᏂᎣᏛᏪᏟ. ᎣᎥ ᎣᎥ!!

Doyudvse tsistelvhe tsustatsistatli. Ha ha!!

Very possible, I helped s/he/it, copperhead. Ha ha!!

ᎥᎣᎤᏯᏴᎤᎣ Ꭰ4.

Vsgiwudv ase.

That's it, possible.

"My Pact Is with Rattlesnakes"

As we sat and whittled down staves under the roof of Hastings's shed, Woody, Hastings, Sequoyah, and I discussed Woody's accident and its implications for his work with snakes. Like other folks, I wondered if the snakes had taken vengeance against Woody for capturing them. Woody seemed to anticipate my question.

"Sequoyah was telling me that one of the reasons I got hit, even though it was a straight stretch, even though I had reflective clothing on, even though we had flashers on, is that it was a copperhead. My pact is with rattlesnakes."

"Yeah," Hastings nodded.

"You know, my educational role. The rattlesnake in my vision years ago, that big one sitting on that rock asked me, 'Why are you catching my kin-folk?' I told him, 'For *education*. To help people understand they don't really have to kill you.' He said, 'That's good.' And that's when I woke up.

"And that little bitty snake that led me into the dream, I think I've seen him maybe twice in the past twelve years. And that first was in the dream. This was about a year or two after I started hunting snakes in '92. So it was about '94, '95. Little bitty old yellowish-looking snake, a rattler. And boy I can't catch him and it's kind of laughing at me. I can't catch him, you know? And he goes into a rock wall and he sticks his head out, laughing again. So I get my catcher and I was shaking it around him and the hole falls in and there he is. Just kind of taunting me.

"So I chased him in and he goes around a little curve like that and when I went around, there was rattlers all around. Going 'ch-ch-ch-ch-ch.'"

"Yeah?" Hastings said.

"And I went like, '*Ohh.*' I didn't get scared. And there he was, just around that bend. And in my dream I just walked real slow and come around an-other little curve in a big room, in a cave. And he was sitting on a rock about this big," Woody said and held his hand waist high. "*Big* old rattler. And he asked me in English, 'Why are you catching my kinfolk?' And just like me to you, I said, 'To educate. Not to kill. Not to sell. Nothing. Just to educate people. To learn more about you.' He nodded his head and said, 'That's good.' And I woke up."

Woody began to laugh and we all laughed with him for such a powerful and good dream.

"Yeah, it was strange," he said. "You know, he didn't have a human face, he had a rattlesnake face but we spoke English. And since then, like I said, I've seen that little yellow snake a couple times. And ever since then I felt more comfortable about hunting them, talking about 'em. Just like it was . . . my gift, you know? They can still bite, though!" Woody said and laughed.

By Word of Mouth

Sammy, Sequoyah, and I were talking about all the places they've visited as storytellers as well as all of the Cherokee communities they knew out-side of Oklahoma. We talked about North Carolina, of course, but also of communities in California, Texas, and New Mexico. Sammy explained how they get invited to tell stories: "It's just by word of mouth," he said. "People say, 'Hey I know a storyteller that knows his history . . .'"

"And that's one of the reasons why I put my voice in there," I said of the book. "Because there's a lot of Cherokees that are not in Oklahoma."

"Oh yeah. Yeah."

"And not in traditional Cherokee territory," I continued. "And, those are people interested in the traditions because they don't have access to traditional culture in that way."

"Yeah, exactly," Sequoyah said.

"So maybe I can be a voice to introduce them back. To say, these are the teachings you can . . . think about, you know?"

"Yeah," Sequoyah said.

"Stories you can learn."

"And I like that because, you know, somewhere along the line in the book, if you haven't already mentioned it, we're all full bloods," Sequoyah said.

"Mmhm."

"Yeah," Sammy said.

"And here you are . . . ," Sequoyah said.

"Mixed-blood guy . . . ," I said, finishing his thought.

"Yeah, mixed-blood guy," Sequoyah said. "And somewhere in there we need to take a group picture with you. And people can say, 'Hey, he looks kinda like me! He's got the same kind of skin!'"

"Yeah," I said.

"Maybe even put it in the back of the book."

RUNNING BEAR AND FALLING ROCK
Told by Sammy Still

As a long evening of storytelling at the Heritage Center began to wind down, Sammy got quiet a moment and then spoke. "There's this other one I always tell," he said. "And, uh, of course this is a *serious* one."

"Serious?" Hastings asked.

"Serious," Sammy continued.

> And it's about these two young boys playing out in the Indian
>   village.
> This is way back in the 1600s.
> They're out there playing around and this elder,
> this elder standing out there says,

"You two boys. Come here."
So he calls them over.
　　He says, "Come with me."

He goes up in the center of their village and he gathers all the
　　　　villagers,
all the elders and the young adults and the children.
He gathers them all in a circle.
　　And he says, "It's time for these young men to become young
　　　　warriors.
　　But they have to pass this test to prove they can be warriors."

So he tells 'em.
He says what they'll have to do is travel through rough terrain,
　　inclement weather,
　　face wild, dangerous animals,
　　and be gone for several days to seek this precious stone.
　　And when they find this precious stone and bring it back to me
　　　in this village,
　　they'll be worthy to become young warriors.

He said, "Do you understand that Running Bear?"
He said, "Yes, I do."
He said, "Do you understand that, Falling Rock?"
He says, "Yes, I do."
He said, "Alright. Then be on your journey."
So they both leave.
Running Bear takes off one way, and Falling Rock runs the other
　　way.

Well, pretty soon, several days pass,
　　here comes Running Bear.
Running Bear comes back into the village.
His clothing all ripped up, and he's all scraped up and bruised up.
And finally he comes back and says to the elder,
　　"Is this the precious stone you seek?"
　　And the elder says, "Yes it is."

So he gathers all the villagers back around again
and he tells the villagers that this young man brought this precious
　　stone.

"Now he's a young warrior."
And they all celebrate, they all get up and dance and they have a
    meal for him.
They have a party for him.

But, they had no sign of Falling Rock yet.
He hadn't returned.
So they kind of worried about him.
Some of the women, they kind of looked for him
and some of the men, they look around outside the village to see if
    they see him coming.
But still no sign of Falling Rock.

So several days pass.
Pretty soon the elderly women, they get real concerned,
so they start praying and dancing and whooping for his safe return.
    Whooping and hollering and trying to pray to the Creator for his
        safe return.
But again, several days go by and still no Falling Rock.
So, finally they say, "We wonder what has happened to Falling
    Rock?
    He hasn't returned.
    I hope nothing has happened to him."

And even today, they're still looking for Falling Rock.
And you know how you know they're still looking for him?
You drive down the road and there's a yellow sign says:
"Watch For Falling Rock."

After a pause, I began to chuckle and Sequoyah clapped his hands
together. Sammy leaned over and slapped Sequoyah and Hastings on their
knees. Hastings leaned back with mock derision on his face and Sammy
cracked up, delighted he had fooled the other liars.

Toad swallowing Moon

"**M**ost of the traditional stories are teaching tools," Hastings said. "They're not stories, per se, that kids would really, really prefer to listen to when they find out what they are," he said and laughed. "But they're actually teaching tools. They teach a value, some kind of value. I guess that's how we were taught our values, without actually come out and say, 'Hey, this is what you gonna do.'"

"Mmhm," I said.

"'You goin' do it like this,' or, you know, they would tell you in a story. And that way, it wasn't saying, 'You . . . do . . . this.' It kind of brought it real . . ."

"Subtle," Sequoyah said.

"Yeah. Subtle. 'Cause a lot of times you tell somebody, 'You goin' do this,' it just puts a wall." We all laughed at the truth of that. "And we were no different than ordinary kids, you know. I mean, when we were told, 'Don't do this,' a lot of times we done it anyway," Hastings said, and we laughed again.

"But these right here are something that you can live with every day," Hastings continued. "Like the walk. How you present yourself, you know? My grandpa used to say, 'When somebody's coming towards you, don't ever look where he's been. Look at that person. Let him prove who he is. 'Cause if you look past him, you may not like him. And he may be the best man around.' He said, 'Don't look at his past 'cause if people looked at our pasts they wouldn't want us around neither.' So, that's another good teaching. Always look at the man, or the person. And let them prove to you who they are."

"Mmhm," I said.

"I think what I'd like to see in this book is, like Hastings was saying, you know we've lost that, we've lost that where we sit and speak with kids, with our young ones, and tell our teachings," Sammy said. "We lost it to TV, to video games, to other things that's out there. And maybe if this is done in a book, maybe if someone can pick it up and read this and read the teachings, they'll get interested and say, 'Hey,' and pass this along to others and show 'em. Maybe this will be another tool that we can use to teach our kids again the teachings they should know. And like I said earlier about the story about the bear making full circle. Well, maybe this will be what happens to them. Maybe they know who they are, they realize where they come from. Maybe as they grow older and read this book with the teachings in it, they'll come back to it and say, 'Hey, maybe it's time I come back and start teaching my kids.'"

"It's gonna happen to 'em. I mean, it's not 'if,'" Hastings said. "And they may not move as far. They may move within a mile away from where they grew up. And they may move a thousand miles."

"Or in their own head . . . ," I said.

"Yeah. Yeah," Hastings and Sammy both said.

"So I think that would be good to do that," Sammy said.

"That time we talked about the ice storm," Hastings said, after a moment. "Our electricity . . . We were lucky. I think we lost about eight hours. But the community around there, just houses right around us. For two or three weeks we had kids, we had neighbors over at the house. I enjoyed it, 'cause they'd come around and say, 'Tell stories. Tell some more stories.' We'd sit around there and put a cot up, put a pot of beans on and coffee, and we'd sit there until, shoot, two or three o'clock in the morning. Telling stories. They was wanting to hear stories. That was something that they really wanted to hear.

"And it lasted for two or three weeks, even after the electricity come on and they got back into their routine. Their video games and stuff like that, when they knew the electricity was going to stay on," he said and laughed.

"The thing about it is . . . ," Hastings paused for a moment and looked away. "Our kids . . . I think if we could do it somewhere once or twice a week. If we could just sit down together and talk. We don't raise them anymore. We don't talk to them.

"I think it's the influence of different cultures. And the modern technology that we have has influenced a lot of the things that we do, even how we teach our kids anymore. We used to sit around like this a long time ago and this was our classroom. Listen to the elders speak and tell us these things. Anymore, they can go inside and click the computer on and all the knowledge is right there, or the knowledge they *think* is true. But I always said, the computer is only as smart as the man that designed it."

"That's true," I said.

Hearing versus Seeing

"Hey, I was put here to like everybody," Hastings told me once. "You can be the worst person in the world. I still like you as a person, I just don't like what you *do*. And that's the thing about it. I always say, 'I'm not the most honest man in the world, but I won't cheat you or lie to you.' But, a lot of people will look right at you and say this, with all intention of not doing it. That's how come Indians will not look at you in the eye, because he wants to take you at your *word*, not what he *sees*. Somebody say, 'He didn't look at me.' Well, he didn't want to see you. 'Cause a lot of times, you know, especially the elders. We've learned anymore to look at people. Our elders, they look down when they talk to you. And it's not, it's not disrespectful to who you are. It's they want to *hear* what you are going to say. They didn't want to see the truth, 'cause they could look at your eye and see the truth. But they wanted to hear it from you. They want to hear it from your mouth. And what you were going to do. Until this day, a lot of our elders, they'll talk to you like they're not paying attention to you. And, modern society says, 'If you're not looking at me, you're not listening.'

"Like that little boy says, 'Teacher says, "Look at me when I'm talking to you!"' He says, 'Teacher I hear with my ears, not my eyes.' And that's basically what we do. And a lot of kids . . . I know this when I'm teaching. Kids are playing around, but a lot of them, no. Because they're listening. A lot of times, you know, they'll say, 'What'd you say?'" Hastings laughed and then paused.

"Even in school, especially with little ones, you know? I'll be talking about something. Kid'll be there and a teacher will get on 'em and I'll say, 'Leave him alone.' 'Cause they're listening. And I'll get through and he'll say, 'What'd you say about this word?' And that tells me then they're *listening*. At least I was reaching 'em, you know? And if I'd have got on to 'em or the teacher'd got on to 'em, they would have cut 'em off. And teacher said, 'I don't see how you could talk with all that noise.' I said, 'What noise?' Kids is not noise," Hastings said and laughed again. "To me. They're kids. I *enjoy* kids. I mean, I just like to be around 'em."

HOW THE TERRAPIN LOST HIS WHISTLE!
By Hastings Shade

One day while Quail was walking around in a field, he heard a whistle. He wondered, "Who can be whistling?"

He thought he knew all the ones that whistled. So he started to look for the whistling. As he got closer, the whistling got louder. Soon he came to a small clearing in the field. This is where he found the source of the whistle. And it surprised him to see who it was! It was Terrapin.

"I didn't know who was whistling. I just wanted to know who it was," said Quail. "You really have a beautiful whistle."

"You really think so?" said Terrapin.

"Yes, you do. I just wished I had one," said Quail.

As Terrapin went back to whistling Quail had an idea! "Maybe I can borrow Terrapin's whistle! If I borrowed his whistle I could hear more of that beautiful whistle. I can get around faster than Terrapin," thought Quail.

Quail said, "Terrapin, can I borrow your whistle?"

Terrapin said, "No."

"I won't use it long and I will give it right back to you," said Quail.

"No! No! I can't let you," said Terrapin. "You may not give it back! Where is your whistle?" asked Terrapin.

"My whistle is not as beautiful sounding as yours. See?" said Quail. "Let me borrow yours just for a little while; I'll give it right back," he pleaded.

Terrapin thought for awhile. "Would you really give it right back?" asked Terrapin.

"Yes," said Quail. "I'll give it right back. If you don't believe me, I'll try it out right here."

"Right here where we are?" asked Terrapin.

"Sure," said Quail.

"Okay," said Terrapin, "just this one time."

So Quail got Terrapin's whistle and tried it. It sounded beautiful. Terrapin listened and it did sound beautiful.

"When I first heard it, I didn't see you," said Quail. "It really sounded beautiful. Let me back up a little bit so you can hear it better."

So Quail backed up and whistled.

"It does sound better," said Terrapin.

"Let me back up a little farther and you listen again," said Quail.

"You are getting too far away," said Terrapin.

"But it does sound better when you are farther away," said Quail.

Before Terrapin knew what happened, Quail was gone. Now Terrapin couldn't see Quail.

"Where did you go?" asked Terrapin, but all he could hear was his whistle.

This is how Terrapin lost his whistle. Terrapin still looks for his whistle and Quail still uses it. Quail knows he took something that wasn't his, so he still hides. That is why to this day we can hear him but we can't see him when he is whistling. We can see Terrapin crossing the road or in the field. He's still trying to catch Quail and get his whistle back.

WHY THE TOAD SWALLOWED THE MOON
Told by Hastings Shade

I got one that's never been written down. It's about the toad.

You know, a long time ago when there was an eclipse of the moon the Indian would say a giant toad is swallering the moon. And when all the animals and birds and everything was casting a spell on the Indians for sickness, the toad spoke up.

He said, "I want this to happen. I want this to be one of their ailments." And somebody said, "You know, the Indians always looked at you whenever the eclipse comes. You was the one swallering the moon." And they would beat on drums and everything to chase it off, you know?

"I don't know how many has heard this," Hastings said to us, "but this is what they said a long time ago."

During the eclipse, the toad was opening his mouth to swallow the moon, and they would take drums and noisemakers and make noise to run it off.

So, they told him, "Why would you want to do something like that?" And he said, "Well, look at me!" He said, "I have all these sores and warts on me. A long time ago my skin was smooth."

Everybody said, "What happened to your skin?!" "*Gado nigv-hasda janegila*?!"

He said, "I was complimented on my skin because it's smooth, you know?" Then when the Indians came out and got on top of the land (because they used to say we came out of a hole to where we at today) and as they marched along (and you'll notice, the toad, when he goes underground he won't go real deep, just get under a little dirt or something) and as these Indians was coming he tried to hide and he done that, he went under a little ground, you know? And as they walked they were stepping on him. And it worked that dirt into his skin.

He said, "They didn't even look down to see where they were stepping! They just walked all over me. So I want an illness, I want this to happen to them. 'Cause if it wasn't for them my skin would still be real smooth and real pretty." But, to this day, if you look at a toad, the dirt got under his skin and got infected. And he never has had smooth skin since then. They look like warts, but if you look at 'em real close they look like scabs. And that's what happened. He got sores and they got infected. Scabs are what's left.

And that's how come he wanted to be one of the people that cast evil, sickness upon the Indians. And that's when the plants come in, you know? But that's another story. The plants come in and everything that the animals—birds, reptiles, whatever—cast on Indians, the plants say, "Well, we got something to counteract it."

So, today, that's how come we use most of the plants. We still use animals for medicine, too, but most of it's plants. But that's a story I ain't never seen written down anywhere. It's an old story.

"Mmhm," I said.

"But that's why the toad looks like that today. So, make something out of that!" Hastings said.

"Oh, yeah. All of them!" We both laughed.

HOW THE DOG CAME TO BE WITH THE INDIAN
By Hastings Shade

Many, many years ago the Indians had no dogs. They were all wild. And as evil began to come into the world and danger was everywhere, the dog saw that the Indian needed something that could warn the Indian of these things that were present.

A dog can sense and see things the human cannot.

So the dog came to the Indian and told him he would stay with him and if anything bad or dangerous was coming toward him, the Indian was to throw the dog between him and the danger.

Just for a kind word, food, a pat on the head, the dog would sacrifice his life for his masters.

Again, the dog chose the Indian; the Indian did not choose the dog.

So the animal must be treated with respect.

"If You Want to Learn You're Going to Learn"

"The mainstream society, you know," Hastings said. "The mainstream society says, 'Hey, I know this. And you don't know it and I'm going to *keep* it.'"

"Mmhm," I said.

"But, to me, I do a lot of different crafts and stuff. And I'm willing to teach. Because, why should I not teach it? One of these days I'm going to take it with me. If I don't teach anybody, that's going to be lost. I mean, it's just going to be like taking this chair and throwing it in that river. Nobody can use it. If we don't use it, there's no use having it.

"Somebody asked me, 'What do you charge to do that?' And I say, 'Well I *could* charge a whole lot. If you can afford it, pay it. I will charge you. But I'll teach you.' The only charge I have is you *learn*. That's *my* charge. And, now, some of them pay me. I'm not going to say I do it for free all the time, you know? And it's out of the goodness of their heart. It's not because I say, 'Hey I'll charge you a hundred dollars an hour or fifty dollars an hour.' Whatever, you know.

"I'm willing to teach 'em. If they're willing to learn then I'm willing to teach 'em. Because, like I said, why should I take it with me? When I can leave it. 'Cause I've heard a lot of 'em say, 'Well I ain't going to teach 'em. They should have learned way back when they were younger.' But maybe they didn't have a teacher back then. Who was there to teach 'em?"

"Mmhm," I said, thinking of my own learning.

"Just like, you know, somebody come to the house say, 'I need to make a bow. I want to learn how to make a bow.' Well, there's a piece of wood right there. Let's get started. But you're going to have to split it. I'm gonna *show* you," Hastings said and laughed. "If you want to learn, then you're going to learn like I did. You're going to learn it the *right* way. I'm not gonna *do* it for you. I'm gonna *show* you. That way you'll *know*. When you learn that way you'll *have* it.' My grandpa said, 'I'm gonna show you how to make a gig, that way you'll know how. Then you won't have to depend on me.' And I see his point now. And he said then, 'If I make gigs for you that's all I'll be doing.' And sure enough!" Hastings laughed at the memory. "But, when you learn something like that, take it from a piece of metal or a piece of wood and fashion it with your hands, that way the knowledge is implanted. And when you pick up something, you'll say, 'This is what I see in it. I see a gig.' Or 'I see a bow.' 'I see a carving.' 'I see a piece of wood I can start a fire with,'" Hastings nodded at the stick Sequoyah was whittling, and we all cracked up. "But you always see something in it. And basically that's what I tell 'em. I say, 'Pick up something. What do you see in it?'

"My granddaughter. She's what, six? I said, 'Look at this? Now what do you see in it?' 'Oh,' she say, 'I see a bird' or 'I see this . . .'" Hastings laughed. "And a lot of times we'll carve it. If that's what she sees we'll carve it out. Sometimes I have a hard time seeing, but she'll show me, say 'Right here!'

"But, that's what you got to have. You have to *see* what you're looking at. The old saying, 'Can't see the forest for the trees.' That's a lot of people. They can look right here and not see nothing. I can look right here and see Mother Nature all day long."

"Mmhm," I said.

"But a lot of 'em look out there. 'Yeah, well, leaves. Dead trees and all that.'"

"No McDonald's, so . . . ," I said.

"No McDonald's. I don't see no golden arches," Hastings laughed. "But, the best way to learn is to *do* it. I teach gig making. And I taught my boys, taught my grandson. They can go out there and they can teach somebody else. And I said, 'Whatever you do don't let it . . . don't let it die.' And if I live long enough, I'm gonna have a granddaughter, the only girl gig maker around Oklahoma!" Hastings laughed. "*Learn. Learn* what to do. Learn *how* to do it. Then do it."

"Mmhm."

"That way you'll *have it*, you know? Look at it. What do you see in it? Do you see a bowl? Do you see a gig? Do you see a knife? What do you see in it? Whatever it is, then you have to bring it out. I said, 'The hard thing is seeing it.' See, I can't draw. I'm not an artist. But you give me a piece of wood and if there's something in it I'll bring it out," Hastings said and laughed.

"Mmhm."

"And I think that's how a lot of our elders viewed us. 'If you want to learn you're going to learn. If not, then I ain't going to mess with you.'

"And that's what they used to tell us, you know? '*Nijadolihvi jadetlos-gwasdi. Tla yidetlosgwasdi.*' 'If you want to learn you're goin' to learn. If you don't want to learn you won't learn.' And if you learn, it's going to be yours. And if you don't learn it, that knowledge belongs to somebody else."

"Right."

"Yeah. Maybe it wasn't yours to learn."

"And you're going to have to pay for it . . . ," I said.

"Yeah. Yeah. Well, they used to say . . . even some of our medicine, he'd say, 'This right here. I'm gonna tell you one time. If you learn, it's yours, and if you don't it probably belongs to somebody else.' And I don't know whether at that point I listened more or what. I don't know if he was using psychology on me or what," Hastings said and laughed. "But I paid attention to him. I wanted to learn it. And I can see his point. Maybe it wasn't mine? If I didn't learn it, maybe it belongs to somebody else. Because not everybody knows all the plants. I don't, she don't," Hastings motioned toward Loretta. "We don't know all the healing qualities in 'em. We know a few. So maybe that same plant and its other knowledge belongs to another person.

"Grandpa used to say, 'Let's go hunting.' That was his way of getting *me* to go *with him*, 'cause I liked to hunt. I used to like to hunt. Still like to hunt, can't go. But, he says, 'Let's go hunting." *Iniyohalvga.* I'd go with him. And while we walked along, he said, 'This right here is *this*.' He'd point at a plant. Sometimes I looked at it and sometimes I studied it. But nine times out of ten I was hunting," Hastings laughed. "I was wanting to look around. So I missed a lot. I learned a lot but I missed a lot also. Just by doing what *I* wanted to do, not what he was teaching me. Then, later on as I got older, then I began to say, 'Hey, when I go again I need to listen to what he's teaching me.' And he also said, 'When I'm teaching you . . . One of these days you may use it, and you may just throw it away. It's going to be your choice.' And sure enough, I was about thirty years old before I decided, 'Hey, what he's talking about I better hang on to.' So, it took me a while."

"Started to get some maturity . . . ," I said.

"Yeah. Yeah. Maturity. Basically, that's what you need. They want us to teach kids. We can teach the language to kids. We can teach foods. When you start getting into medicine, it's a *little* bit different. Might be too young.

"Best thing to do is just kind of introduce the basics to 'em. Stomach aches, the headaches, this and that. Let 'em learn. Then, let 'em grasp it, then begin to add more. But the foods, you can teach 'em. Because that's something daily. And medicine is not daily. But the food is daily. Got to have food every day, you know? But we can teach 'em. But, introduce it a little bit at a time. Don't just say, 'Here. Here, learn this.' But, a little bit. And that's what they done with me. When they first started I was young. Taught me just a little bit, said, 'This is this.' And maybe next time, he'd say, 'You remember this? What was it for?' That's how he would check me."

"Hmm."

"And that was his way of teaching. I mean, that was interesting. After I decided, 'Hey, I want to learn!'"

What Is an Elder?

"I was writing down a bunch of notes and thinking about what readers might be interested in knowing. So, since we're on the topic, what is an elder in the Cherokee sense?" I asked.

"I used to kid around a lot and used to say it's somebody that's older than I am," Sammy said and laughed. "But this is the way I look at it. This is my opinion. To me an 'elder' is someone who is wise. Who's learned the ways of life. It's not someone that's ninety or eighty years old, it's someone that's got wisdom and shares that wisdom with you. That, to me, is an elder. Just like Sequoyah and Hastings. I consider them my elders. But it's not because they're older than I am or they remind me of my grandparents. It's because they taught me a lot of things. Just like when I speak with the elders out in the communities, they're my *teachers*."

"Mmhm," I said.

"It's not about age," Sequoyah agreed. "It's about wisdom and the respect you have for that person. To me, that's what an elder is. And just like Sammy, you know, I consider him my elder, and mainly because he's older than me!" Sequoyah said, and we all cracked up.

"I'm not either!" Sammy said.

"Nah. He says I taught him something, but he's taught me, too. And Hastings, of course, has taught all of us. Even Woody, who's the youngest. I consider him an elder. Because he's taught me things, you know? One of the main things is he taught me to grab a rattlesnake behind the head!" Sequoyah said and laughed. He was referring to a time when, during a reptile-safety demonstration, Woody forgot that Sequoyah had never handled a rattler and handed one to him, which Sequoyah, strangely enough, took.

"Trial by fire, hunh?" I said.

"I held one rattlesnake in my life, and that was thanks to Woody. But, a lot of the knowledge and a lot of the reasons for stories that Gramma told me, is because of Hastings. He tells some of the same stories but he tells his in a way which makes me think, 'Ah, that's what that's about.'"

"Mm."

"And, then Woody, as I've told you often, he's the level-headed one of us all. He's like the logical one. He'd be the Mr. Spock," Sequoyah said, and we all laughed. "But, you know, we've got . . . of us four, I think we have, each person has their own niche that they offer to each person. And, when I'm just somewhere by myself telling stories, yeah, I have fun. I like telling the stories and everything. But I always feel like I'm lacking, mainly because Sammy's not there. Hastings ain't there. Woody's not there. Because we've been doing this nearly twenty years."

"Every time we do a presentation somewhere, somebody remembers something new," Sequoyah continued. "Something they hadn't mentioned before. I mean, it was stuck in there but it took to this certain time for it to come out. And it might be the first time we heard it. It might be first time I've heard it; Sammy might have known it."

"So telling stories together can kind of spur on your memory . . . ," I said.

"Yes," Sammy said.

"Yeah. You know that 'Wolf Wears Shoes' story?" Sequoyah asked. "That just popped into my head. Me and Hastings was heading out to Tulsa when he was campaigning for deputy chief. And we were talking, and there came a time when everything just got quiet and all of a sudden I started hearing Gramma, in my head. Talking. And she was telling me this story. And I would laugh, because, you know, I could hear Gramma doing these voices like she'd always done. And she was telling me this thing in Cherokee. And I'd laugh, and out of the corner of my eye I'd notice Hastings, he'd kind of look over there and wonder what I was laughing at, you know? And finally . . ."

"He thought you finally lost it!" Sammy said.

"Yeah. Finally, I told him the story that I remembered my gramma had told me. And he started laughing. He said he hadn't heard that story since he was a boy. That just came from me and Hastings driving up to Tulsa. Out of the middle of nowhere it came to me. I don't know what triggered it. But since then I've told that at different places. At an intertribal elder conference in Oklahoma City, when I got through telling the story 'Wolf Wears Shoes' these two little old Cherokee ladies come walking up to me and one of 'em kind of had a glassy eye like she'd been crying or about to cry. And the one told me she hadn't heard that story since she was a little girl. And she was glad that I remembered it and told it. And it took her back. And so, those are the times that really make me feel like I did honor to Gramma. Because I remembered the story. And it touched somebody else's life. So, through me, Gramma was able to touch this woman's life. So, in a very real sense of the way that they say, Gramma still *is* around."

SEQUOYAH'S GRAMMA: MAGGIE TURTLE
Told by Sequoyah Guess

Ilvhiyu jigesv,
nigada inage
anehi
jalegi
janiwonisgv . . .

That's how my gramma always started her stories.
    And she told me those stories over and over and over.
    All my life.
From the time that I can remember,
    when I was about five or six,
    I remember her telling me all these stories.
    Over and over and over.
There were some other things she tried to teach me, too,
but it seemed like the stories were the ones that always caught my
      ear.
I can still remember
sitting
on the floor
next to her rocking chair.
She'd be sitting there just rocking,
and I'd ask her to tell me stories, and,
uh, she would always tell me scary stories, too.
It seemed like at night
were the times when she would always
call me over and tell me all these scary stories.
We lived just across the yard from her.
Oh, it was probably around,
not even thirty yards from our house to her house.
And, uh, when she got through telling me these scary stories,
I'd have to walk back across the yard
and I would tell her, or I would ask her
to watch me as I crossed the yard.
I'd get about halfway and turn around and make sure she was
      standing at the door watching me.
And she'd be standing there,
    just smiling,
    because she knew she had scared the something out of me.

But that's what I remember about Gramma.
Her name was Maggie Turtle.
And she was really my great-aunt.
But we called her Gramma.
As I mentioned,
    she told me these stories all my life.

And, it never really occurred to me
to wonder why
    until after she was gone
and then Mom told me one day
    that she had picked me,
    from my brothers and sister,
    she had picked me to carry on these stories.

Even when I was in Mom's
    belly,
Mom told me that Gramma came up to her
and pointed at her stomach and told Mom
that this was the one
that was going to carry on the stories.
And that was me.

Gramma died when she was ninety-eight years old.
    Ninety-eight years old.
So, she saw a lot of things happen in her lifetime.
I figured it out once.
She was born back in 1883.
And so that was a long, long time ago.
She saw everything from horse-drawn wagons to
men being blasted off into space.
And she saw, what, microwave pizza and cable TV.
So, you know, she lived a long full life.

Storytellers Have Something to Say

One evening over dinner, Sequoyah and I spoke with Sammy about how
he came to see himself as a storyteller:

"It wasn't until I met Sequoyah. And one day he told me, 'You know, I'm
going to go do a storytelling. Why don't you come up with me? Maybe you
could even tell a story.' I never told a story before. I always heard stories
from my grandmother and everybody else. And I guess, in a way, I kind
of would tell stories like to my family and stuff like that. So I got to thinking, 'Maybe I *am* a storyteller.' I didn't realize it. But I never got in front of
people or would ever talk to people about storytelling. So Sequoyah said,
'Ah, it's easy. Get up there and tell a story. Just don't even think they're
there. Just get up and tell a story.' I'm sitting there shaking like crazy and
thinking, 'Golly, I don't know if I can!' But I told my first story, and I

can't even remember the first story I told. But, that's how I got to know Sequoyah.

"And through Sequoyah, then I got to know Hastings even more better. And when we worked at the Cherokee Nation cultural center we really got all together and we started going doing presentations. I used to follow them. I used to listen to 'em. And then, later on, then Woody came into the picture and we started working with him."

"Can I ask you a question about storytellers?" I said. "Did you grow up knowing of people who are designated storytellers? Or is it kind of just a role that exists within community; some people just tell stories?"

"If you want to consider or say that there were designated storytellers, it would have to be your grandparents. They're the ones that started it all. You would listen to them and there's many times that, like now, when it got dark, we'd be sitting out there in the back. My grandmother would be telling us stories, speaking in Cherokee. My mom would, too. I remember many times going to Stilwell on weekends and visiting our cousins. And we'd have what we'd call a meal, but it was a pretty good-sized feast! And afterwards, they would go outside and they would sit around the tree and they would sit and just tell stories. And a lot of the kids would be running around playing. But if the story caught their attention, you'd sit there and listen.

"So there really wasn't a 'designated' person to tell stories. But if there was, I would have to say, like Sequoyah said, grandmother. 'Cause she would always say, 'Come here. Let me tell you this story. Let me tell you this.' And just like she told me the one about the bear leaving and that I would one day be that bear and it did come around and you can see that. Like Sequoyah said that now, as you get older, you realize and you see that, see? But when you're young, 'Yeah, yeah.' Sometimes it was just to keep you quiet. Sometimes it was just to make you behave. But then, you get that memory back."

"Yeah," I said.

"And you start telling those stories. But yeah, I don't think there really was a designated storyteller. Because sometimes my grandfather would tell stories," Sammy said.

"Was there any gender divisions in storytelling, like men tell certain stories and women tell certain stories? Or, it sounds like you were saying it was mostly your grandmother, but sometimes your grandfather, too?" I asked.

"It was both. It was both. I know that we'd go to Swimmer Church and sit there before church and some of the ladies, the elder ladies, they'd be sitting there. They would be telling stories. And we'd listen to them. One of them told about the Little People. Around their house. So, it was both. It was women storytellers and man storytellers, too. It just depended who you listened to. Because, like I said, in the summertime when we'd go visit our cousins, there would be women and men sitting around talking."

"So there's not really any kind of strict divisions?"

"No. No, there wasn't really no, 'You tell stories.' Or 'You're the one that tells it.' There wasn't someone like that. It just all got together. Just like we're sitting and we start telling stories. You know? It just so happens . . . My daughter tells stories, and Woody's daughter, she's beginning to tell stories. See, there's women out there, too, that tell stories. It just so happens that it's just the four of us men in the Liars' Club. Just crazy enough to get together and tell things. But . . ."

"Well, do you all get together with other storytellers?" I asked.

"Oh yeah," Sammy said.

"Like from other communities?"

"Oh yeah. Well, we still do sometimes. My daughter works at the Job Corps center and they got a lot of other tribes, like Navajos, Hopis, Cheyennes. They say, 'Dad, they want to listen to stories. Can you have a storytelling night at the house?' Said, 'Sure. Come on over.' We'd feed 'em and they'd come over and they'd sit around and tell stories. And then we'd listen to their stories. Then somebody would say, 'In our culture, our tradition, this is a story that we tell.' And we'd listen to their stories, and they tell us stories, too. So, it was just an exchange of stories. No, we just don't gather around and have people listen to us. We listen to them, too. And there's one story that was told to me and I remember the story, but it was a long, long time ago. And I had forgotten about it.

"I went to a Sallisaw school and I was sitting there and this young boy said, 'Hey. I got a story.' He was nine. I said, 'Yeah? What's that story?' He told the one about Runs Like the Wind. And I said, 'I remember that story!' So see, even the young ones, you learn from them as much as they learn from you. So you listen to them. Now I still remember that story 'cause of that nine-year-old boy telling me that story. And I remember it, but I lost it way in the back of my mind. Until he brought it out."

"Hm."

"So see? There's really no designated storyteller. It's just someone who has something to say, you know? And I think that's real important that you listen to everyone. You probably have stories to tell, you know? You can tell us stories and we learn from that, too, you know?" Sammy said.

"Mmhm. And I'm learning these ones, too," I answered.

"Yeah. Then down the road somewhere, 'Do you know this story?' 'Yeah, I know this story,' and I'll be telling the story you told, you know?!" Sammy said and laughed.

"One thing I was thinking about, and this is something I brought up to Sequoyah, and I just want to address it 'cause it's probably going to come up. When we publish this book, I'm careful to say, the Liars' Club is just a group of people that come together and tell stories, and they're humble about it. Because the tendency is for people to think, 'Oh, well they're try-ing to say this is what Cherokee storytelling *really* is.'"

"Yeah," Sammy said.

"And I hope it comes across that that's not true, and that there's other Cherokee storytellers all around. And that there are so many different other stories . . . ," I said.

"Oh yeah," Sammy agreed.

"This is just a slice of it."

"Yeah. And we *share* stories. We share stories that we've heard from other people. Like that rattlesnake story. That's just not a traditional Cherokee story. It's been told by Navajos. It's been told by other tribes. And so, see, it's not just a Cherokee story. We tell stories that we've heard and that was told to us. The reason why we call ourselves Cherokee story-tellers is we're Cherokee."

"And I think, you know, my opinion is this kind of sharing has always occurred," I said. "We've always shared knowledge across tribal traditions."

"Oh yeah. Yeah. We cross that line between tribes, and we listen to them as well as they listen to us. So, even with this, I could read this book and say, 'Hey, there's a story I want to tell.' Because I read it and this lady told it, but we always give credit to the people who told it. We don't say, 'Oh, this is a story that I know, that I made up' or something. We don't do that. We just share stories. We have a good time sharing stories. We laugh at each other; we're always laughing at each other. We're always making fun of each other. And so, I guess that's what people don't understand . . . you know, Native Americans, we like to *laugh*. And we do. We do.

"Matter of fact, like I was saying, we go to Stilwell it seemed like every weekend. And we'd go visit our cousins. We'd eat, and then they *had* to watch *Gunsmoke*. You know that old TV show? I mean, here's grown people sitting there watching *Gunsmoke*. And they'd say, 'Oh, Chester's going to get it! Chester's going to get it!' 'Yeah, he got it last week and . . .' I mean they really get into it! It's like they're part of that show. Then after *Gunsmoke*, 'Okay, let's go out.' And then they go outside and sit down under the shade tree and all night long spit, chew, and smoke and talk. Tell jokes and stories. And that's where we learned it. See? That's how we come to it. This is part of it. I mean, we don't watch *Gunsmoke*," Sammy said, and we all cracked up. "We watch *Andy Griffith*!" he said, and we burst out again. "But no, you know."

Later on that same evening, Woody came by the room where I was staying and he, Sequoyah, and I talked about storytelling as well.

"We're all made of stories. And everything's a story. Science is a story. Our religions are stories. Everything's a story, it's how we tell it; we narrativize our world. But there's a flipside to that, right?" I said. "'Cause a story is something you make up. And I think that comes out in that term 'liar.'"

"Right," Woody said.

"Is it a lie or is it true?"

"It's up to you."

"It's a matter of perception. It really is. All the stories that we all hear, we have to think about them and see what we get out of them," I said.

"Yeah," Woody said.

"And so, that's what I'm going to play on with the name 'Liars' Club.' How do you deal with that truth? And that time we spent out at Hastings's house recording, and how he was talking about there's people who, if they have some kind of knowledge or grew out of a Cherokee belief system they'll believe these stories. And some won't. Some who don't come out of that tradition will just think these are lies."

"Yeah."

"Or curiosities."

"Yeah. Yeah."

"And that's fine for them. But I think there will be some that, maybe it will open their minds."

"Well, you know," Woody said, "we'd love to have someone pick it up and carry it on to the next generation. And we can't force no one to do it, you know?" Woody laughed. "Just by continually going to different places, like Sequoyah does, somebody, somewhere out there will pick up the torch and carry it."

"Yeah. Yeah. Or go find their own stories," I said.

"Yeah, I hope my daughters are. Because they've been exposed to

Sequoyah and me and Sammy for many years. But, as kids are, you know, they're doing their own thing. But yet, they still have . . ."

"Well, your daughter was there at Hastings's. She was sitting quietly, just listening the whole time."

"Yeah," Woody laughed. "And I'll probably never know until I'm gone and she gets to be a mature person that she may tell her kids and grand-kids, 'I got a story that . . . Woody or Sequoyah, I used to hear all the time when I was a little girl.' So. Unfortunately, we won't be around to hear that, but I bet and I'm hoping that will happen," he said and laughed again.

"Yeah. Yeah. Well then, that's what will be great about a book like this. Reading or something, someone could pick it up two generations down the line and go like, 'I remember that!'"

"Yeah. 'I remember them guys!'"

"Maybe they just heard a piece of it maybe, but now here's the whole story here."

"Lani might be saying, 'Well, at least that's what Sequoyah said!'" said Woody.

"Yeah," Sequoyah laughed and said, "instead of 'Gramma.'"

"But you know, these past couple days I had two young people, nine, ten, eleven years old, didn't know 'em, but yet, 'Hey Woody! How ya doing?' One of 'em says, 'You still got any snakes?!' And I said, 'No, it's too late in the year.' And the other one says, 'When are you all going to do some story-telling?' And I could not place him anywhere. I was like, 'Where did I see him?' And you know, I don't want to ask. Like, 'Hey, who are you?'" he said and laughed. "Even as an adult, like I don't want to be embarrassed in front of a kid!"

"That's something that happens to me all the time," Sequoyah said.

"It kind of reinforces a good feeling. Those type of boys like that will do something in their own little area, growing up. Their own community."

"Yeah," I nodded.

"One day."

Let It Ride

At the last meeting we had together with Hastings, I asked him a question about how to present the stories in the book. I was wondering about whether or not I should explain or interpret the stories for readers. I knew that some readers would know very little about Cherokee culture, while others would know a great deal. I didn't want to be disrespectful toward either audience. So the Liars' Club and I had a talk about it.

"You know, one last thing before we wrap it up," I said. "I have a question about how you interpret the stories. When you tell a story, do you ever explain it, or do you just let it ride?"

"We just let it ride," Hastings said.

"So that's what I want to do with the book, then," I said.

"Yeah, because each one is going to get something different out of it. Not everybody's going to get the same. Just like reading a story. Each one that reads it is going to get something different out of it; they're going to get a different meaning out of it."

"But you might want to put *that* down," Woody said.

"The only one that I ever kind of point out the lesson to is about how the rabbit got his long legs, and the lesson is so obvious," Sequoyah said. "You gotta be nice. But, the main time that I do point that out is when I tell it to little kids. 'Cause, you gotta kind of explain it to them."

"My stories and presentations are about respect. Respect nature, God, and respect his creatures," Woody said.

"Usually, it's kids at a certain point of age, then you want to kind of tell 'em what this story is about. Adults or teenagers, kind of hang it out there. 'Cause they're gonna grasp what they want to anyway," Hastings said.

"Plus, it gives them a chance to think about the story," Sequoyah agreed.

"It's not sticking it down their throat," Woody said.

"Yeah," said Sequoyah. "And if they think about the story, they're gonna remember the story. And that's my main focus is for them to remember the stories that I tell 'em. I always tell 'em, 'Try to remember these stories and share 'em.'"

"Yeah," Hastings said.

"Yeah. To me all the stories is just like a day," Woody said. "We still have the sunrise, we have the time, you know? But it's a different day. But yet we still have the same overall . . ."

"But the meaning is still the same," Hastings said.

"Yeah," Sequoyah said.

"The meaning's there. But how do you get there?" I said.

"The journey," Woody said.

"Just like we was talking about a while ago," Hastings said. "Two men can walk the same path, and they'll go to the same place, but they'll get there two different ways. Although one road, we'll have two ways of getting there."

"And they'll usually see different things," Sequoyah added.

"Yeah," Hastings said. "It's hard to understand. Somebody say, 'How can that be?' I say, 'We're two different people. We may take the same steps, the same length of steps. We may breathe the same air, but we're gonna do things different when we go down that road.'"

"Just like being in a car," Woody said. "One's a driver, one's a passenger. One sees something more, the driver sees something more focused."

"Like I told my wife once," I said, 'You know how to get there. You've been there a dozen times.' She says, 'Yeah, but you've been driving. I've been looking out the window.'" We all laughed.

"Same way with a story!" Woody concluded.

"Listening to You Telling Stories Was Better Than Watching TV"

"Here, couple of months ago," Sequoyah said, "they had an Indian Territory Days, where they bus in different kids here and they can go through the museum and through the ancient village at the Cherokee Heritage Center. And, they always have me tell stories in the council house, out there in the ancient village. This last time they did that I was in there telling stories and I got one of the greatest compliments of all my storytelling. An eleven- or twelve-year-old boy come up to me and he said, 'I really enjoyed that. Listening to you telling stories was better than watching TV.' That really got me; I mean, that's a compliment right there! He liked the stories better than watching TV. He asked me, 'When are you going to tell stories again?' And I told him, so, hopefully, he'll be there. But that's the best thing anybody's ever told me."

HOW THE RABBIT GOT HIS LONG EARS AND LONG LEGS
Told by Sequoyah Guess

This is a story that
Gramma used to tell me after I got through fighting with my
      brother.
I don't remember
her telling my brother this,
but she would sit me down
and she would always tell me this story.
I don't remember
her telling my brother this story.
And, later on I started thinking about it
and I think it's because I was the one that usually started the fights.
So, that's why she would sit me down tell me this story.

Rabbit's long legs

This one is called, "How the Rabbit Got His Long Ears and Long
    Legs."

A long time ago, back when the animals could talk,
    they all spoke Cherokee.
At least that's what Gramma said.
But back then,
you know a lot of the animals
they didn't look the way they do today.
    The bear wasn't big and strong.
    The eagle couldn't fly as high.
    Skunk didn't smell.
    And the rabbit,
    the rabbit didn't look the way he does today.
He didn't have the long ears and long legs, and,
uh, he didn't have that cute little cotton tail.

Well one day, there's this person that we call Unetlvnv.
That's his Cherokee name.
Unetlvnv.
Some people might call him "God" or "Creator" or "Supreme being,"
but in Cherokee we call him Unetlvnv.

One day he was looking down at the world
and he saw how this *one* day,
all of the inhabitants of the world,
all the people that lived on the world,
and animals and everybody,
they were being nice to each other.
And he liked that!

He said, "Hey, look at that!
Everybody's being nice to each other!
Nobody's eating each other, nobody's fighting.
Everybody's helping out with each other's chores.
I *like* that!
I think I'll just go down there and give everybody one wish."

And so that's what Unetlvnv done.
He come down from among the stars
and he came to earth and he told all the animals,

"You guys have been so nice to each other,
I'm gonna give everybody one wish.
No matter what you ask for, I'm gonna give it to you."
And so all the animals, they said, "Yeah!"
And so Unetlvnv said, "I want you people,
I want you animals to line up!"
And so those animals, they lined up.
And there were animals for as far as you could see.
That line of animals probably went around the world once or twice
there were *so* many animals.

And one by one,
they came in front
and stood in front of Unetlvnv.
And when they were there in front of him,
Unetlvnv would look down and say,
    "Well, what is your wish?"
And whatever animal was there would give him their wish.
Like the bear, you know,
the bear wasn't big and strong.
And so he said,
    "Well, everybody's always pickin' on me
    and they're always beating me up and everything,
    I was just wonderin' if you can help us?"
And so Unetlvnv said, "Sure!"
So he went,
    POOF!
Today, the bear is one of the biggest and strongest animals in the
        woods
so nobody picks on him no more.

Well here comes the eagle.
And Unetlvnv said,
    "Well, what is your wish?"
And the eagle said,
    "Well, you know we'd like to be able to
    fly better.
    Even turkeys fly better than us right now."
And so Unetlvnv says, "Sure. Okay."
So he went,

POOF!

Today, the eagle is probably the highest-flying bird in the world.
I mean, when that eagle got his wish he took off and he started
    circling
around and around and around.
He went up into the sky
higher than the clouds until he was nothing but a little dot up
    there.
And that's the way the eagle is today.

Well, here comes the Skunk.
Now the Skunk come waddling up.
Unetlvnv said,
    "What is your wish?"
And the Skunk said,
    "We want everybody to leave us alone!
    Everybody's always bothering us,
    borrowing money from us and everything else.
    And so we just want to be left alone!"
And so Unetlvnv said, "Okay."
So he went,
    POOF!
So you know what happened to the Skunk?
    He got stinky!
And Gramma said you better leave him alone, too, or you'll be
    stinky and everybody will be leaving *you* alone.
And she's right!

Well, finally, here comes Rabbit.
Now, Rabbit didn't come hopping up like he would today.
Instead he come waddling up because all his legs were short,
like his front ones.
And he didn't have the long ears.
He had these little, bitty short ears.
And he didn't have that cute little cotton tail.
Instead he had a long, bushy tail.
Well he come waddling up and stood in front of Unetlvnv.
Unetlvnv looked down at him and said,
    "Well, what is your wish?"
The Rabbit looked up and said,

"Well, sir.
We have two wishes if that's alright."
And Unetlvnv thought a second and he said,
    "Uhh. Well, yeah, o-okay.
    I feel good. I'll give you two wishes."
And so Rabbit said,
    "Well, we have these short ears
    so we can't hear anybody when they're sneaking up on us.
    And when we finally do hear 'em,
    we have these short legs and we can't run away fast enough.
    So everybody's always eating us for breakfast, lunch, and dinner.
    Can you help us?"

And so Unetlvnv said,
    "Yeah, I can help you.
    But I can't POOF you like I did everybody else.
    We're gonna have to do you
    a different way."

And so Unetlvnv said,
"I don't want anybody to see what I'm gonna do to the Rabbit."
So he made everybody turn around.
    All the animals that were still waiting on their wishes,
    they all turned around.
    All the animals that had already gotten their wishes,
    they all turned around.
When he was sure that nobody was watching,
he reached down there,
picked up old Rabbit.
And he grabbed those short ears . . .
    and he yanked!
And those ears they come stretching out
and old Rabbit went "Eh-he-he-heww!"
And when those ears come stretching out,
    that long bushy tail he had,
    it come up.
And that's where he got that cute little cotton tail.
Now, Gramma said if you pushed those ears back in,
that tail will come back out.

But it don't work.
All you do is get bit on your finger; I still have the scar to prove it.

Well, then he turned Rabbit around
and he grabbed those short little back legs.
    And he yanked!
And those back legs,
they come stretching out.
But you know what?
    While he was stretching out those back legs,
    he looked down the line of animals that were waiting on their
        wishes.
    And way down there,
    the Owl
    was watching.
You know how an owl can be looking one way and he can turn his
        head around and he can look behind him?
That's what he had done.
And when the Owl saw those back legs come stretching out,
his eyes got real big; he couldn't believe what he was seeing.

Now Unetlvnv, he dropped the Rabbit
because he saw the Owl watching and he said,
    "Oh, that's it.
    No more wishes.
    The Owl messed it up for everybody.
    I asked everybody not to watch,
    but the Owl saw what I was doing.
    And because he disobeyed,
    I'm gonna make his eyes
    stay that way!"
And so that's why the eyes of the Owl are always big, to this day.

Well, Unetlvnv said,
"No more wishes.
I'm gonna go back home."
And so he started going back to among the stars,
and while he was going up,
the Rabbit started jumping around saying,
"Wait a minute!

Wait a minute!
What about me!
You still gotta stretch out my front legs!"
Untelvnv said,
    "Someday,
    when all of the inhabitants,
    all the people,
    all the animals of the world
    are nice to each other again,
    I'll come back
    and I'll stretch out your front legs."
So that's what the Rabbit's waiting on.
For all of us to be nice to each other,
so he can have his front legs,
stretched out.

At least that's what Gramma said!

TERRAPIN AND WOLF RACE
Told by Hastings Shade

At one time, everything spoke Cherokee. All Cherokee stories were told in Cherokee. That is how we know these things. The animals told us these things. They still speak Cherokee, but we have forgotten how to listen.

Wolf used to go around bragging about how fast and how far he could run. Every time he got around the other animals he would say, "There is no other who can outrun me or run farther than I can."

In Cherokee lore, Rabbit is a trickster and he was getting tired of hearing Wolf brag all of the time. One day Rabbit came up with an idea on how he could get even with Wolf and get him to quit bragging. He got with Terrapin and told him what he was planning. Terrapin, remember, at one time had won a race with Rabbit. He set everything up and went to find Wolf. Rabbit found Wolf bragging to the animals, as usual. He came to Wolf and said, "I know someone who can outrun you, right now."

Wolf asked, "Who?"

"Terrapin," said Rabbit.

"Terrapin?" said Wolf. He laughed. "The last time I saw Terrapin it took him a while just to crawl from my back feet to my front feet."

Rabbit said, "I have to respect Terrapin. I remember who won when I raced him."

Wolf said, "But I'm not you."

"Are you scared to race him?" asked Rabbit.

"No!" declared Wolf. "Anytime, anywhere . . . You just name it!"

"See those six hills?" asked Rabbit.

Wolf said, "Yeah."

"That is where the race will be," Rabbit said. "The reason we chose that course to run on is that you two will be running so fast we won't be able to keep up with you. So as you two get to the top of the hills, whoever is leading will have to whoop, so we will know who is ahead."

Wolf thought that was a good idea, so the race was set for two days later right at daylight and Rabbit got busy with his plan. He went and found six cousins of Terrapin's because they all looked alike and were hard to tell apart. He took them to the top of each hill and told them his plan.

The morning of the race, Wolf was at the starting line when Terrapin arrived. He looked at Terrapin and came toward him. Terrapin pulled his head back into his shell just as he does today when you get close to him.

Wolf said, "Look at him . . . He won't even look at me."

"He's meditating . . . clearing his mind so he can outrun you," Rabbit said, and Wolf just laughed.

Rabbit got them on the starting line and he said, "Get ready!"

Wolf crouched down and Terrapin hadn't stuck his head out yet. "Set!" Rabbit shouted.

The muscles in Wolf's legs bunched up as he got ready to leap. Terrapin's head finally began to stick out.

Rabbit said, "Go!!"

Wolf leaped and landed ten feet away. When he landed he looked back and saw that Terrapin hadn't even moved yet, so he leaped again. Once more he looked back and saw one of Terrapin's legs move.

"This isn't even going to be a race," Wolf thought, so he began to lope. He looked back again and he couldn't even see Terrapin.

Wolf was getting close to the top of the first hill and he could see where the top was marked. Then, all of a sudden, he heard a whoop. He looked and there went Terrapin over the hill. All he saw was the back end of Terrapin going over the hilltop.

So, now, Wolf speeded up and was running even faster now and he thought, "How did Terrapin pass me?"

It was the same thing on the next hill. Just when Wolf thought he was ahead and nearing the top of the hill, he heard another whoop! And there went Terrapin over the hill. Now Wolf was really running and passing the slow-moving Terrapin as he went down the hill.

"I can't let Terrapin beat me," Wolf kept thinking.

Over the next three hills it was the same thing. Just as Wolf would get ready to whoop, he would hear Terrapin whooping and see him just as he was going over the hill. Now it was down to the last hill and Wolf was running all out. His tongue was hanging out, his sides were hurting and his muscles burned.

He kept thinking, "I can't let Terrapin win!"

But as he got to the last hill and the finish line, just like before, Wolf saw and heard Terrapin whooping as he crossed the finish line. All of the animals who were at the finish line began to laugh at Wolf and tell him he had gotten beat by Terrapin.

To this day, Wolf does not come around the animals and brag like he used to. You'll see him out in the fields hunting, usually by himself. Never brag about yourself; people don't like to hear it. Let your accomplishments speak for themselves.

RABBIT AND POSSUM LOOK FOR WIVES
Told by Sequoyah Guess

"You know among the Keetoowah Cherokees and probably most other tribes, the stories usually have some kind of moral or lesson to 'em. And then there's 'How and Why' stories. And I kind of figured this is probably a 'Why' or 'How.' I don't think there's any moral or lesson in this story, but it was fun to listen to Gramma. So this one is entitled . . . well I call it 'Rabbit and Possum Look for Wives.'"

Rabbit and Possum, they were like best friends.
They grew up together.
From the time that they were little bitty babies,

they grew up playing together.
They'd stay over at one another's house and everything else.
Sleep over.
And they'd play out in the woods all the time.
And Rabbit, he found out at a early age that he like to play tricks
        on people.
    On anybody.
    And old Possum, on the other hand,
he liked everybody.
He was always trying to be helpful.
Wanting to help.
And that's the way they grew up.

But just like you,
just like me,
just like everybody in this world,
Rabbit and Possum,
they kept getting older . . .
    and older . . .
        and older . . .
            and older . . .
                until they were really,
                    really,
                        old.

Well Rabbit and Possum, you know, like I said, they were friends.
They were best buds, you know.
And so, as they grew older,
while they were growing up,
Rabbit kept getting smarter because he'd always get into fixes and
        everything.
Among Cherokee stories, Rabbit is always a trickster;
he's always getting into trouble.
And so that's how he grew up.
So by the time he was really old,
he was really, really smart.
On the other hand, Possum,
while he was growing up, like I said,
he's always wanting to be helpful and everything else.
So he started learning medicine.

And when a Keetoowah or Cherokee man,
an Indian man, learns medicine they call him a
    "medicine man."
If a woman learns medicine, an Indian woman learns medicine,
        they call her a
    "medicine woman."
And since Possum learned medicine
the other animals,
they always called him
    Medicine Possum.

So anyway,
    they got really, really old.
Now, out by where they lived there was this big old shade tree.
And they'd sit under there every day.
And every once in a while they'd go to sleep
while they were watching others going in and out of the village.

Well this one day,
    while they were sitting under the tree,
    dozing in the summer sun,
    Rabbit jumped up,
    looked down at Possum and said,
    "Possum!
    You know, I was thinking . . .
    I was barely able to get out of bed this morning."
And old Possum looked at him and said,
    "Yeah. I know what you mean.
    I was barely able to cook my breakfast."
Well old Rabbit said,
"Possum! You know, I was thinking . . .
maybe it's time we got married."
And old Possum said, "Huhn?!"
And old Rabbit said,
"Not to each other!
We need to find us some wives."
And so Possum thought that was a really great idea.
And so they went into the village where they lived
and they started asking everybody they saw,

"Will you marry me?"
"Will you marry me?"
"Will you marry me?"
"Will you marry me?"
But everybody they asked said no.
Like one said,
"Don't be silly, you're a possum and I'm a squirrel. That's not gonna
    work!"
Another one said,
"You're stupid! You're a Rabbit and I'm a Bear! Just go away."
And so they couldn't find any wives there in their hometown.

And so they went back outside, you know,
and sat under the tree.
And old Possum, he was kind of a crybaby type.
He was sitting under there saying,
"Uhh. Nobody likes us.
We're never gonna find any wives."
And remember old Rabbit,
he's always thinking he's smart.
And so after a little bit, he jumped up and said,
"Possum! You know I was thinking . . .
maybe if we go to the next town,
maybe we'll find us some wives there!"
And so Possum thought that was a really great idea.
And so they got out on the road
and they started heading to the next town.
And there were cars going up and down that road
and they were dodging.
And old Rabbit, you know, he's quick.
So he wouldn't get hit.
But old Possum, he's kind of slow,
so a car was coming at him
and he couldn't move fast enough and he got hit and got
splattered out!
But . . . remember . . .
    he's a medicine Possum!
So he fixed himself up
    and they took off again.

Well they got halfway to the next town and old Rabbit
    took off!
    Took off running.
    Left old Possum just barely going.

Well Rabbit, he got to the next town in no time at all
and he got all of the animals together.
And he jumped up on this big old rock and he said,
"I have a message from the Chief.
The Chief said that he wants everybody in this town
to get married right now!"
And boy howdy, everybody started grabbing each other
and taking off and getting married.
It didn't matter what they were.
A squirrel grabbed a duck and took off and got married.
A coyote grabbed an eagle and took off and got married.
Even a dog grabbed a cat and took off and got married.
    That one didn't last long, though, 'cause they were always
        fighting.

But even old Rabbit, he found himself a cute little bunny and got
    married.

Well here comes Possum.
Finally made it to the village.
And he started asking everybody,
    "Will you marry me?"
    "Will you marry me?"
But everybody he asked said no.
Why?
Because they were already married!
Well, he couldn't find no wife there in that village
so he found himself a big old shade tree outside of town
and he was sitting under there,
"Uhhh. Nobody likes me!
Even Rabbit found himself a wife but nobody likes *mee*!"

Well old Rabbit heard
old Possum crying and he kind of felt sorry
that he had played this mean trick on him.

And so he went out there and sat next to old Possum
and after a little bit he jumped up and said,
    "Possum! You know I was thinking . . .
    maybe if we go to the next town,
    maybe we'll find you a wife there."
And Possum thought that was a really, really great idea.
So they got out on the road again,
and again they were dodging cars and everything else.
Possum still slow and he got hit and got splattered out again.
    But again, he fixed himself up
    and they took off.
Well they got halfway to the next town and Rabbit
took off running!
Left old Possum just barely going.
Now Rabbit, when he got to the next town
he got all the animals together again.
He jumped up on this big old stump and he said,
    "I have a message from the Chief!
    The Chief said that this is one of the laziest towns he's ever seen
    and he wants everybody to start fighting.
    Right now!"
And boy howdy everybody took to fighting, right then and there.
It didn't matter what was going on.
Two of 'em ganged up on one and three on one.
Just throwing sticks and stones and everything.
And even some of 'em knew that hii*yah*! stuff.
It was awful!

Everybody in town fighting.
And old Rabbit, he didn't want to get beat up
so he ran out of there real quick.

Now here comes Possum.
Finally made it the village.
Well, when he got there he saw these animals
rolling around in the dirt and he thought to himself,
    "Oh boy! I'll be able to find me a wife here.
    There's a party going on here."
And so he went up to the first animals and he said,

"Will you m . . ."

But before he could finish, somebody yelled out,

"Look! There's Possum! Get him!"

And everybody jumped on Possum and just started whupping
the tar out of him. Everybody taking turns kicking him and
hitting him and everything else.

Biting and scratching.

And old Possum didn't know what was going on.

He was just laying on the ground going,

"Ewh! Ach! Ihh! Ah!"

After a while he thought to himself,

"I gotta think of something or they're gonna kill me."

After a while he got real still.

And when somebody would hit him he'd just roll over.

When somebody else would kick him,

he'd just roll over.

Finally somebody noticed that he wasn't making any noise or
moving around anymore.

And they said,

"We KILLED him! Oh no! We killed the Medicine Possum!"

And everybody started crying and

right when they were crying the hardest,

old Possum jumped up and ran out of that village

and never went back again.

And there's a trick that we learn from Possum that day.

And that is,

playing Possum,

or playing dead.

But you know what?

Gramma said that Possum never did find himself a wife.

He's still looking to this very day.

You know how you can tell that he's still looking for a wife?

When you're going down the road somewhere,

you see him splattered out on the road.

He's headed for the next town to find himself a wife!

At least that's what Gramma said.

CROSSING SAFELY

By Sammy Still

One day my oldest daughter, wife, and I had traveled to a town about fifty miles away. My daughter had to attend an event so we went with her as chaperones. The event began around 7 p.m. in the evening. We were provided with a nice dinner, listened to speakers, and then my daughter was introduced and she did her presentation. She is a very fine musician; she played a flute when she was in grade school band and throughout her high school years, traveling with her school band and competing in individual music competitions. Along the way she had learned to play an Indian wooden flute and she was known in our area as a wonderful flutist. So she would be asked to come and entertain at conferences and special events.

Well this one particular evening as we were traveling back home, we took a short cut, driving on a rural paved road. We had just driven through a small community town and by this old lime-mining plant. It was a straightaway for about a mile, and with all the lime being mined there was dustings of white lime along the road. It looked like snow on the trees and roadway.

As we drove down the straightaway, I had my headlights on bright and could see over one hundred feet in front of us. I noticed a huge object by the side of the road. I thought it was a huge stone but as I stared at the object it began moving. My wife and daughter also noticed the object and my wife said, "Do you see that? What is it?" As we drove closer we noticed that the huge object was a large raccoon. But (now this is where the story becomes a little unbelievable, but true) as we drive up to the raccoon, the animal stops in the middle of the rural road. I slow down to a stop to avoid hitting the animal. My wife says to me, "What is this raccoon *doing*?" I tell her that I probably blinded the poor thing with our headlights and the raccoon cannot see.

To our amazement, the raccoon raises its front paw, telling us to stop. I think to myself, "What the heck! What is this raccoon doing?" Then all of a sudden three little baby raccoons come running behind her, crossing the road to the other side. My wife, daughter, and I looked at each other with amazement. After the three baby raccoons safely crossed the road, the mother raccoon lowered her paw and looked our way and it sure looked as though she gave us a wink and went her way with her babies. We all looked at each other and began laughing, telling each other that no one would believe this. We continued home and never told anyone for a long time. When I finally decided to tell our friends about this incident, they just laughed and told me that it was a great story. And to this day they still don't believe me. But honestly, it's a true story!

Ө ᎡᏢ ᏓᎲᏃᎮᏣ
NA KVLI DATSINOHETLI
THAT, RACCOON, I'M GOING TO TELL ABOUT
ᏏᏩᎢᎢ ᏫᏃᎮᏢᏢ
Siquotsi unohetlv
Sammy, what he told

ᎤᏫ ᎢᏍ DEᏛ ᎡᎦ DᏮᏂ DᎨᏠᏠ, DᎢᏞᏢ DᏯᏃ ᏯᏴᏬᎠᏯ ᎢᏍᏣᏠᎫ ᏝᏏᏂᏲᏬᏣ ᏝᏚᏍᏒᎡᏴ ᏫᏀᏞᏬᏣ ᏏᏜ.
Saquu iga agvyi ehi aquetsi ageyutsa, agwadali, ayano higisgohi iyutlilodi oganigisdi digadusvyv wogedasdi gesv.
One, day, first, living, my egg (my offspring), girl, my wife, and me, fifty, measured, to travel, where the town is, we had to go there, it was.

DᏮᏂ DᎨᏠᏠ ᎠᏟᏬᏣ ᏧᏬᎢᏒᎡᏝᏀ ᎩᏆᏞᏬᏣ ᏏᎡᎢ, ᏝᏬᏣᏞᏣᏠᏀᎡᎢ ᏝᏬᏟᏞᏍ4ᏬᏣᏗᏍᎩ.
Agwetsi ageyutsa gohusdi tsunisgwalvehv wuwedasdi gesvi, osdidawadvei osdagasesdidegi.
My egg (my offspring), girl, something, event happening, s/he/it had to go there, the way it was, we were followers, we were care givers.

ᏍᏞᏤᎩ DᏣᎢᏞᏒ ᏫᏞᏛᏅ ᏏᎡᎢ, ᏫᏛᏣ ᏝᏞᏪᏬDᏔᏅᎢ, DᏂᏪᏂᏬᏒᏃ ᏪᏣᏬᏝᏬDᏔᏅ ᏃᏬᏃ DᏮᏂ DᎨᏠᏠ ᏓᏂᏃᏣᏝᏅ DᏕ ᏂᏛᏫᏂᏞᏏᎢ.
Galigwogi atliilisv udalenvdi gesvi, utedi ogelastanvi, aniwonisgino dotsidvdastanv noquuno aquetsi ageyutsa datsinotsalanv ale nidvdvnelisvi.
Seven, it was going along, it was beginning, the way it was, excellent, they fed us, speakers, listened to, and also, my egg (my offspring) girl, announced, and, what s/he/it was about to do.

ᏍᎣᏛᏃ ᏗᏍᏴᎩᎣᎵᏍᏫ, ᏗᏴᎹᎭᏍᏗ ᏌᏁᏣᎣᏍᏫ ᎩᏒ ᏥᏌᏍᎬᎢᏍᏫᏒᎢ,
ᎨᏔᏗᏍᏬ ᏗᏁᏍᎬᏦᏍᏏ ᏓᏁᏬᎵᏍᏬᎢ ᎠᎾᏓᎤᎥᎣᏍᏫᏍᎨ ᎠᏂᏐ ᏦᏁᏍᎬᏦᏍᏗᎢ
ᎲᏂᏏᏴᎣᎵᏍᏫᏒᎢᎢ.

Osdano dikanogisdisgi, atseluhisdi dinelodisgi gesv
tsidadelogwasgvi, getadidohv dinadelogwassgi danedolidohvi
anadagonvdisgv aniso tsunadelogwasdii daninogisdisgvi.

It was good, able to make a melody, a flute, player, it was when
s/he/it went to school, taking them around, learners, in their
walking around contesting, the others, schools, in making
melodies.

ᎤᏍᎬᎢᎢ ᏓᏛ ᎠᏇᏬᎤ ᏗᏴᎹᎭᏍᏗ ᎤᏫᏗᎢ ᏓᏛ ᎢᎣᏛᏙ ᎤᎧᎮᎧᎥ ᏍᎣᏛᏛ ᏧᏂᎬᏩᎵ
ᎡᏒᎢ ᎠᎦᏍᏗ ᏣᎰᏕᎢᎨᎡᏪᏧ ᏓᏍᎧᎧᎲᎣᎥᏗ ᏧᎾᎴᎤᏗ ᏗᏴᎹᎭᏍᏗ.

Udelogwai ada gotlvtanv atseluhisdi utodii ale vsgi unanadv
osda tsunilododi gesvi gohusdi yunisgwalvela agadvdvhvsgo
tsunelvdodi atseluhisdi.

S/he/it learned wood, made from, flute, to blow, and, that, in their
knowledge, good present, the way it was, something, when they
have an event, they would ask s/he/it, to play flute.

ᏌᏫ ᎤᏒ ᎧᏊᎥᎠ ᏔᏗᏍ ᎤᏂᎮᎧᏝᎥ ᎠᏍᏆᎳᎯᎨᏍᏗ ᏔᏗᏍ ᎤᎩᎶᏏᎢ.

Saquu usv tsogenvsv ididla wotsigvdv asqwalahigesdi ididla
wogilosvi.

One, night, where we came from, direction, heading for, the
shortest direction, we went that way.

ᎤᏍᏗᏗ ᎾᎢ ᏄᎾᏓᎴᏫᏒ ᏍᏴᎩᎶᏒ ᏓᏍ ᎠᎣᏗ ᏔᎦᏍᏗ ᎤᏃᏢᏗ ᏍᏴᎩᎶᎤ ᎢᎤᏒ.

Usdi nav nunadalewisv ogilosv ale gosdi iyusdi unotlvdi ogilosonv
gesv.

Little, near, community, went by, and dust, like where they make it,
had passed, it was.

ᏘᎥᏛᏎ ᏴᎧᏗᏉ ᏺᏣᎦᏗ ᏘᏐᎤᎠᏛ ᏍᎯᏃᏛᏛ ᏍᎤᎤᎤᏤ, ᏂᎬ ᎠᎣᏗᎢ ᏔᎦᏍᏗ ᏍᏕᎷᎢᏴ
ᎤᎥᏃᎮᎷᏗ ᎢᎤᏗᎾ ᏂᎬᎤᎥᏛ ᏗᏝᎥᏕ ᏕᎷᎤᏇ ᏍᎤᏗᎢ ᏓᏛ ᏍᏍᎤᎤᎤᎢᎢ.

Tlvdvse ginudiyv sutlilodi iganvhida gatsinosda ganvnv, nikv kosdii
iyusdi galageyv nvnohulidi vnvtsiquu nigvwisdv atlahv deluyv
gadui ale deganvnvi.

Probably not, quarter, measured out, about the length of, straight,
road, everywhere dust, like, lay, blown around, it was snow,
appeared to be, it lay, the trees, on top, and, there on the road.

ᏥᎢᎵᏒᏃ ᏥᏳᎪᏗ ᎦᏅᏅᎢ, ᏓᏍᎪᏍᏛ ᏂᏓᏋᏁᎸ ᏓᎩᏨᏍᏛ ᎢᎸᏢᏛᏎ ᏍᎪᎯᏥᏡ ᎢᎳᏏᏗ ᏪᎦᎪᏩᏛᏗ ᎨᏒᎢ ᎢᎬᏯᏗᏟ, ᎪᎲᏍᏗ ᎤᏔᎾ ᎠᎲ ᏅᏃᏳᎸᏗ ᏣᎩᎪᎲᎢ ᎤᏔᎾ ᏅᏯ ᎨᎵᏍᎬ ᎠᏎᏃ ᏥᎦᏙᏍᏛ ᎤᏢᏅᎲ ᎠᏓᏅᏍᎬᎢ.

Tsiilisvno tsiyugodi ganvnvi, dasgosdv nidaqunelv dagitsvsdv ilvtlvdvse sgohitsitlu ilasidi wegagowadvdi gesvi igvyaditli, gohvsdi utana ahv nvnoyulvdi tsagigohvi, utano nvya gelisgv aseno tsigatosdv utlvnvhv adanvsgvi.

As I steered, straight, road, bright, I made them, the lights I had on, it was about, about 100, footsteps, possible to see, the way it was, in front, something, big, it sat, beside the road, I saw it, it was big, rock, I thought, however, as I watch, began moving.

ᎠᏆᏓᎵ, ᎣᎩᏁᏣ ᎠᎨᎤᏣᏃ ᎥᏍᏊ ᎤᏂᎪᎲᎢ, ᎠᏆᏓᎵᎢᏃ ᎯᎠ ᏄᏪᏒᎢ “ᎯᎪᏩᏘᏍ? ᎦᏙᎤᏍᏗ?” ᎾᏂᎨᏍᏗᏃ ᏭᎩᎷᏣ ᎬᎵᏊ ᎣᎨᏒᎢ.

Agwadali, oginetsa ageyutsano vsquu unigohvi, agwadaliino hia nuwesvi “Higowatis? Gadousdi?” nanigesdino wugilutsa kvliquu ogesvi.

My wife, our eldest, the girl, also, they saw it, now my wife, this, what she said, “Do you see?, What is it?” Nearer we got there, just a raccoon, it was after all.

ᎾᏍᎩ (ᏃᏊᏃ ᎯᎢᎾ ᏍᏓᏱ ᎰᏩ ᎡᎵᏍᏗᎢ ᎠᏎᏃ ᎰᏩᎢ) ᎾᎥᏃ ᏭᎩᎷᏣ ᏗᎦᏙᎬ ᎬᎵ ᎦᏅᏅ ᎠᏰᏟ ᎤᏢᏫᏍᏔᏅ, ᏚᎴᏅᏃ ᎠᎴ ᎣᎦᎴᏫᏍᏙᏗᏃ ᏃᎦᎵᏍᏓᏁᎸ ᎣᏳᏂᏍᏗ ᏂᎨᏒᎾ ᎬᎵ.

Nasgi (noquuno hiina sdayi howa elisdii aseno howai) navno wugilutsa digadogv gvli ganvnv ayetli utlvwistanv, dulenvno ale ogalewisdodino nogalisdanelv otsanisdi nigesvna kvli.

That (now, this, hard, real, to think of however, it's real) there, we arrived, where it stood, raccoon, road, middle of it stopped, it stood, and, we had to stop, it caused us, to kill it not to happen, raccoon.

ᎠᏆᏓᎵᎢᏃ ᎯᎠ ᎾᎩᏪᏎᎸᎢ “ᎦᏙᎵᎨ ᎠᏛᏁ ᎯᎢᎾ ᎬᎵ?”

Agwadaliino hia nagiweselvi “Gadoike advne hiina kvli?”

Now my wife, this, what she said to me, “Just what, doing, this raccoon?”

ᎯᎠ ᏂᏥᏪᏎᎸ ᏕᏥᎨᏩᏗᏍᏙᏗᏛᏎᏥᏕ ᏥᏴᏍᏓᏏ, ᎣᎩᏍᏆᏂᎪᎯᏍᏙᏓᏅᏃ ᏚᏎᎵᏔᏅ, ᎾᏍᎩᏊ ᏦᎦᎴᏫᏍᏙᏗᎨᎢ, ᎠᏋᏒᏊ ᎠᏆᎾᏛ, ᎪᏓᎢᎨ ᎠᏛᏁ ᎬᎵ ᎨᎵᏍᎬ?

Hia nitsiweselv detsigewadisdodidvsetside tsiyvsdasi,

ogisgwanigohisdodanvno duselitanv, nasgiquu tsogalewisdodihoi, agwvsvguu agwanadv, gadoige advne kvli gelisgv?

This, what I told her/him/it, blinded it, I caused it, it interested us very much, it raised them up, as though, it was stopping us, I ran out, my knowledge, just what, doing, raccoon, I was thinking?

ᎩᎳᏉᏴᏃ ᏦᎢᏯᏂ ᎬᎵ ᎠᏂᏗ ᎤᏂᏄᎪᏨᏢ ᎣᎾᏗᏜ ᎦᏙᎬ ᎤᏂᏥᎢ ᎠᎴ ᎦᏅᏅ ᏚᏂᏂᏗᏫᏒ.

Gilagwoyvno tsoiyani kvli anidi uninugotsatlv onadidla gadogv unitsii ale ganvnv duninidiwisv.

Suddenly three of them, raccoon, offspring, came out, behind, stood, their mother, and road, they crossed it.

ᎠᏆᏓᎵ, ᎣᎩᏁᏣ ᎠᎨᏳᏣ ᎠᏯᏃ ᏙᎦᏓᎧᎾᏅ ᎣᏥᏍᏆᎾᎪᏍᎩ, ᏂᎦᏗ ᎬᎵ ᎠᏂᏗ ᏚᏂᎾᏗᏫᏏ ᎦᏅᏅ ᎤᏓᏥ ᎬᎵ ᎡᎳᏗ ᏂᏚᏩᏁᎸ ᏚᏎᎵᏛᎢ ᏙᏓᏲᎦᎧᎾᏅᎢ ᎠᎴ ᏦᎦᏔᏍᏓᏁᎶᎢᏃ ᏂᎬᏫᏍᏛᎢ.

Agwadali, oginetsa ageyutsa ayano dogadakananv otsisgwanagosgi, nigada kvli anidi duninadiwisi ganvnv udatsi kvli eladi niduwanelv duselidvi dodayogakananvi ale tsogatasdaneloino nigvwisdvi.

My wife, our eldest, girl, now me looked at each other, we wondered, all of them, raccoon, offspring, they crossed road, the mother, raccoon, low, caused them to be, raised, looked at us, and winked, it appeared to be.

ᎢᎾᎨ ᏭᏃᎶᏒ ᏧᎾᏍᏗ ᏗᏘᏁᎢ.

Inage wunilosv tsunasdi ditinei.

Woods, they went, the little ones, it kept with it.

ᏂᎦᏓ ᏓᎦᏓᎧᎾᏅ ᎠᎴ ᎣᎩᏰᏨᎢ; ᏝᏛ ᎩᎶ ᎰᏩ ᏱᎦᏰᎵ ᎣᎦᏛᏅᎢ.

Nigada dogadakananv ale ogiyetsvi; tladv gilo howa yigayeli ogadvnvi.

Everyone, looked at one another, and, we laughed; no way, anyone, real, believe it, we all said.

ᎣᎦᎾᏂᎩᏒ ᏦᎨᏅᏒ ᎢᏗᏜ ᏬᎩᎶᏒᎢ ᎠᎴ ᎪᎯᏗ Ꮭ ᎩᎶ ᏲᏥᏃᏂᏎᎴᎢ.

Oganigisv tsogenvsv ididla wogilosvi ale gohidi tla gilo yotsinoniselei.

We left, where we came from, direction, we went, and, long, no, anyone, didn't tell it.

ᏓᎤᎪᏛᎾᏃ ᎧᏍᎵ ᏕᏒᏃᎵᎣᎠᏞᎯ ᎨᎶᎢᎠᏪᏂᎦ ᏫᏃᎵᏓᏁᎳᎹᏬ ᎠᏎᏃ ᎭᏗ
ᎲᎬᎩᏪᏎᎸᎢᎢ, ᎤᏙᎯᏳ ᎤᏍᏓᎶ ᎦᏣᎳ ᎧᏃᎮᏗ ᏳᎩ.

Dawugodvnino tsogali gatsinohisedi nulistanidolv unolidanelvquu
aseno hia nigvgiweselvi, udohiyu osda sgwala kanohedi yigi.

I decided, my friends, to tell them, what happened what came to
us, however, this, they told me, very, good, short story, it is.

DᏏ ᎠᎫᏃ ᏂᏴ Ꮣ ᎲᏜ ᏆᏗᎶᎣᎠᎢ. D4Z ᏂᎦᏚᏃ ᏂᏂᏃᏞᏆ!!

Asi gohiyv tsigi tla howa yanelisgoi. Aseno howaino tsitsinohe!!

Still, today, it is, no, real, don't believe. However, it is real what I'm
telling!!

Laughter as Medicine

Sammy, Sequoyah, and I sat in my room in the Best Western motel in
Tahlequah. Sequoyah and I had gotten takeout from Del Rancho and were
busy munching away when Sammy came over after work. Sequoyah is a
great lover of hamburgers—the bigger the better. For a man with a slight
build he's got a big appetite. I've got before and after pictures I took of
him in Denver when we went to a local burger joint that serves monstrous
burgers. Before: Sequoyah with a big smile on his face, a burger about the
size of a dinner plate in front of him. After: nothing but scraps on the plate
and another big smile on Sequoyah's face, with two fists in front of him
giving a thumbs-up.

"IS THIS VOICE SENSITIVE?" Sequoyah said as he chewed his burger,
his mouth close to the digital recorder. We all laughed.

"Yeah, they can hear you chomping now," Sammy said. Now he talked
into the recorder: "THAT'S SEQUOYAH EATING. TRADITIONAL FOOD."

"Traditional hamburger," I said.

"What is it?" Sequoyah said and thought for a moment. "'Cow meat between two fry bread?'" We all laughed.

"Roots," Sequoyah said and held up a french fry.

"Roots! Yeah," Sammy said.

"Traditional Incan food, right? Potatoes," I said.

"We get it from the original, traditional Sonic," Sammy said. "Oh, that's
Del Rancho, isn't it?"

"Del Rancho," Sequoyah corrected.

"Oh, sorry. Wrong tribe."

Throughout the process of working on the book, the members of the
Liars' Club would often talk about the importance of laughter, both to

themselves and to Cherokee community. Popular cultural stereotypes see American Indians as stoic, serious people. When Indians do laugh, non-Native folks often think they're laughing at their expense. Sammy had a story to tell about this:

"I think it's real important for people to realize and to know that Native Americans are people that likes to laugh. Like to *enjoy*. And, when I got married to my wife, Dama, who's white, my mother and me, we'd be speaking Cherokee. She'd be sitting there looking at us and we'd be laughing or something. And she'd be looking at us real mean. We get back home. 'You were talking about me, weren't you? You guys were talking about me.' I said, 'No, we weren't talking about you!' But see, that's how they get paranoid. What we do is, when we talk we more or less just talk about each other or funny situations that happened to us. We talk about that. Or we cut down each other. But, because that's just the way we are. We just enjoy laughing and having a good time. And, a lot of people don't understand that. But, we're just funny people. I don't mean funny looking, either," he said and we all laughed. Woody came into the room and sat down.

"Well, me, Sammy, and Hastings were at a school once talking about the culture," Sequoyah said. "And, they had us in the gym with other people in booths and tables and stuff. There were people walking around looking at crafts and everything. And there we were. We were all by ourselves; nobody was coming by us because we were like laughing and everything else. And finally, the principal came by and thought that we were laughing at everybody going by. And Hastings said, 'We're not laughing at you guys! We ain't even paying attention to you guys, we're laughing at each other!'" Sequoyah said and we all laughed. "We were making fun of each other. But those people thought that we were laughing at them. Making fun of them, you know? But, that's the way it always is when you get a bunch of traditional Cherokees around. They laugh and . . . at each other most of the time."

"Yeah. Just having a good time," Sammy said.

"I tell some folks, you know, they call it the 'Trail of Tears.' But I believe there was laughing. Because it's true you know, the Bible says it and everything, but laughter is a good medicine. And I believe that our people couldn't have made it this far from our homeland without some laughter. You know? Because I think the laughter gave 'em the courage and the strength to keep on going. And so, laughter is a very important part of our culture. When I see people laughing, it makes *me* feel good. I think, 'Alright. They're on the same level as I am.' Then we can get into the stories.

And I know people might say it's blasphemous to think that we laughed on the 'Trail of Tears.' But, I believe so."

"Oh yeah. I think so," Sammy agreed.

"I've always thought that," Woody agreed. "You know, because that's just the way we are. We're created that way! We understand the good of life and the bad of life. And it can happen all in the same time, I think."

"Mmhm," Sequoyah nodded.

"You know, there's really no delineation or separation of laughing and crying at the same time in our culture," Woody continued.

"Well, you know, I think a lot of times, too, is that's the way we cope with it. Adversity. Like that," Sequoyah said.

"I don't know how many funerals I've been to. There's laughter," Woody said.

"Yeah."

"No disrespect to the deceased," Woody said.

"After the funeral services they'll all be gathered around, they'll be telling jokes and stuff," Sammy added. "But not out of disrespect for the dead, but because, like I said, that's maybe how we cope with adversities, is laughter. Trying to get back into the good mood."

"Good standing," Woody added.

"Mmhm," I said.

"Because I think we understand the dead and departed, they're taken care of, you know?" Woody said.

"Yeah," Sammy agreed.

"And so, in actuality, they're essentially better off than we are. Because we have to face the daily grind, so might as well just laugh," Woody said and chuckled.

"A lot of times if there is crying, it's usually because we're still left behind!" Sammy said, and we all laughed. "They're in a better place, you know?"

"'Hey, he owed me a hundred bucks!'" Woody said, and we cracked up.

"If you don't deal with that grief it causes a lot of trouble," I said.

"Oh yeah," Sammy agreed.

"If you hang around us for very long, you'll find we like laughing," Sequoyah said. "You'll find us laughing, even at the most serious things. You'll hear laughter at a funeral. Because I believe the American Indian has found that out, that laughter is a medicine. And when you're sick, try laughing. It'll make you feel better."

"That's like what we say," Sammy said, "if you want us to feel sorry for you don't come to us, 'cause we won't." Everyone laughed. "We like to laugh and joke around, and, a lot of times when we do laugh and joke around it's about us! Our personal experiences and stuff that happened to us that we like to laugh about and we joke around about."

"'Cause it's happened to us," Hastings added.

"Well, there was an experience that I thought for sure I'm going to get a little sympathy on, but, Nooo," Sequoyah said after a moment. "I almost got shot a couple years ago. By accident; nobody was actually trying to shoot me."

"You sure?" Sammy said.

"Maybe not. I don't know," Sequoyah said, and we all laughed. "But I was telling Sammy and everybody else and, of course, there was no sympathy at all. But that's the way it is, though." We all cracked up again.

"One example is when Woody got hit by a car," Sammy said. "He got run over by a car. And the first thing we thought was, 'He was looking for snakes.'"

"Yeah. And he was," Hastings said.

"Yeah! And that's what he was doing. But, when we went up there we felt bad and we hoped we didn't lose him, and we all had concerns. We rushed up to the hospital to check on him. Well when we found out he was doing alright and doing good, then, here comes the jokes," said Sammy.

"We were all in the emergency room joking about it, even Woody himself laying there on the bed joking about it," Sequoyah said.

"Yeah!" said Sammy. "He's over there hurt and shaking with pain, he said, 'Sequoyah, you come here.' Sequoyah said, 'What? What?' He said, 'I want you and Sammy to go back up there and get that snake.'" Everyone burst out laughing again. "And he's laying there and we said, 'Hey, we're not doing that. We'll be laying right beside you.'"

WHERE TWO DUMMIES MET
By Sammy Still

I do cultural appearances at schools, colleges, and organizations when called upon. One day a teacher from a rural school called me and asked if I would come down to their school and do a blowgun seminar during their Native American Heritage Day. I told her I would be glad to and scheduled the event. I had mentioned to a couple of coworkers about my upcoming arrangement and they had mentioned to me that they were scheduled to do a basketweaving workshop that same day in the afternoon, but their presentation was at a vocational school in Fayetteville, Arkansas. It was the day before my planned visit to the school and my friend called and told me that at the last moment that her and her friend could not make the afternoon presentation in Fayetteville and asked if I could cover for them and present their workshop as well the next day. I told them I could; my appearance was in the morning and Fayetteville wasn't that far from where the school was located.

That evening I drove down to visit my mother to see how she was doing, and during our visit I mentioned to her about the seminars I had planned the next day. She asked if it would be okay for her to travel with me to the schools. She just wanted to get out of the house and go for a drive. I told her that would be great. I love visiting my mother and thought the trip would do her some good. Get her out and get some fresh air.

Well, I picked her up early the next morning and we drove to the rural school. The school administration and teacher met us when we arrived and guided us to the gymnasium where the events were to take place. I was on the agenda for 10 a.m. to perform my blow-gun seminar. The time came, I did my presentation, and after I told the students and teachers that I had to apologize but that I had another event I had to attend that afternoon and had to leave. So my mother and I left the school on our way to Fayetteville, not knowing exactly where the vocational school was located but I had the directions written down.

As we arrived to the outskirts of Fayetteville it was about 12 noon. I didn't need to be there until 1 p.m. I asked my mother if she was hungry and we stopped at a drive-in to get a bite to eat. As we ate, I looked over the written directions, trying to figure out the location of the vocational school. It had the location of "Old Farmington Road." We finished and drove on into the suburb of Fayetteville. While driving down the four-lane to Fayetteville, I notice a street sign that read "Old Farmington Rd." The sign turned toward a side street. I yelled out to my mom, "There's the street I'm supposed to turn onto! We passed it!"

Well, without thinking I do this u-turn on the four-lane. As I turn around, I look straight ahead and see this police vehicle sitting in a bank parking lot facing the oncoming traffic. I tell my mom, "OH NO! I just got caught doing an illegal u-Turn on the four-lane and this cop saw me." I can see his stern stare burning through me and I'm thinking to myself, "Oh man, he caught me red handed!" I can see myself standing behind jail bars with my mother beside me. Anyway, I tell my mother, "We're already caught so we might as well drive next to him and get my ticket, and maybe he'll give me directions to where this vocational school is located." Hoping anyway, as we drive up next to him, my mother yells out, "Wait, wait! I don't have my seat belt on!" So she grabs her seat belt and snaps it in place and I think to myself, "Oh great, here's another ticket!"

Well, I pull up next to the police car. His vehicle is facing traffic and so when I pull up, my driver's window and his driver's window are next to each other. I don't even bother looking at this policeman; I figured he's too busy writing up my tickets. So I pick up the written directions and point to them on this piece of paper in my hands and ask him, "Sir, do you know how I can get to this vocational school? It says it's on Old Farmington Road."

Well, he doesn't acknowledge me, so I figure he's *really* into writing me those tickets or really upset with me. I ask him again if he knows how to get to this school. Still no answers. Then I begin to think, "Does this cop have a chip on his shoulder or is he just avoiding me?" My mom keeps looking straight ahead not saying nothing. This time I'm thinking maybe he didn't hear me, so I lean my head and arms out of the window next to his and ask again about the location of the school. Half my body practically leaning out the window, surely he hears me now! Well, still not a word.

Then, my mother turns and looks at the cop, then looks my way and without hesitation says, "Hey, do you know you're talking to a dummy?" I turn and look and to my amazement, it *is* a dummy sitting in this police car. I turn and in the side rearview mirror I see people gathered inside the lobby of this bank behind us and they are all laughing and pointing in our direction. My face turns beet red and is burning with embarrassment. I back out and drive out the parking lot, my mother laughing. I'm thinking, "How awful, all those people are probably thinking to themselves, 'Look at that dummy talking to a dummy!'" I'm thinking, "How disgraceful." Anyway, we drive to where I saw the street sign that said "Old Farmington Rd." and when we turn off on this road it's not even the road; someone had turned the street sign facing it the wrong way. All this time we were on Old Farmington Road going into Fayetteville. Anyway, we found the vocational school, did our presentation and left for home. On our way back home, we passed the location of the dummy cop and my mom said to me, "You want to stop by and say bye to your friend?" I just tell her to hush and let's just go home. She laughs all the way home.

WOLF WEARS SHOES
Told by Sequoyah Guess

This story is one that
    I had forgotten for a long time.
And one day, an elder and I were heading to Tulsa and
    I don't know what triggered it
    but I started remembering
    this story
    while we was going down the road.
And I remember laughing to myself and I often wonder
    if the elder thought I was going crazy
    because there I was just starting to laugh.
But, I was telling this story in Oklahoma City one time at a Elder's
        Conference
and after I got through telling stories these two elderly ladies came
        up to me
and one had kind of a tear in her eye
and she told me
that she hadn't heard this story since she was a little girl.
And so, to her and to other elders
I dedicate this story
because this is one of those stories that was almost lost.
I call it, "Wolf Wears Shoes."

Well, one day, Rabbit and Squirrel, they were
    talking with each other and, you know,
    just passing the time away by a river,
    just minding their own business.
And up from the river here comes Beaver and he was all excited,
        waving his arms and everything else, and trying to get Rabbit
        and Squirrel's attention, and he was saying,
    "Hey you guys! Hey you guys!
    I found something down by the river!

Come and look! Come and look!"
And old Rabbit and Squirrel, they just kind of looked at each other
    and waited until Beaver got up to 'em.
And then Rabbit said, "What's going on?"
And old Beaver said, "Well, you know, there's something down
        there by the river
    I ain't never seen anything like that before."
And old Squirrel said, "You know, I, uh, you know . . . Rabbit
        probably knows what it is." And so they all agreed
that they would go down by the river
and check it out.
Well, just when they were heading to the river,
        here comes Wolf.
Now, back then, Wolf didn't always want to eat everybody.
And the main reason is because he acted like he knew
everything.
Now, I know that most people know somebody like that.
Somebody that thinks they know
everything.
Well, that's the way Wolf was.
And so he caught those little animals and he said, "Hey fellas,
        what's going on?"
And old Rabbit said, "Well, old Beaver found something down
        there by the river
    and we're gonna go check it out."
And old Wolf said, "I'll go with you, I'll probably know what it is."
And so they all went down to the river and Beaver led 'em over to
        a little place where the grass was kind of high and he said,
        "There it is."
And so Wolf started looking at it and he started going around it
    and sniffing at it and everything else.
After a little bit he set back and he was uh, kind of, uh, just, uh,
    scratching his chin and everything else.
And, after a little bit, he said, uh,
    "Yeaah, I know what this is. This is what humans call 'shooes.'"
And the other animals, they said, "Shooes?!"
And Wolf said, "Yeah, 'shooes.' See, humans, they have
    tender feet, so they have to
    wear these shooes because, you know,

when they walk on the ground,
    if they don't wear these shooes,
    they hurt their feet.
But if they wear these shooes their feet don't hurt. So these are
        'shooes.'"
And old Rabbit, boy, he was sitting back there and he thought to
        himself,
    "Oh, man, he don't know what this is. But I do."
Now, Rabbit knew
    exactly what this was
    that was hidden in the grass.
It was a trap!
And he knew because he had been
    almost
    caught in traps before.
And so Rabbit started thinking to himself, "I want to teach old
        Wolf a lesson. Somebody's got to.
    He can't always go around acting like he knows everything."
And so Rabbit said, "Well, Wolf, how do humans wear these
        shoes?"
And so Wolf said, "Well, they wear them like this."
And he walked up to that trap and he stuck his foot in and that
        thing went "Krnnng!"
And it got his foot, and, man, it hurt,
    and his ears just stuck out and he said,
"This is how they wear 'em."
And old Rabbit thought to himself, "Oh, he still hasn't learned his
        lesson."
And so he told Wolf, he said, "Well, Wolf, you know you got another
        foot there so let's
    see if we can
    find another shoe."
And so Wolf said,
"Okay."
And so they started to take off but when they took off that trap was
        hooked on to a tree by a chain. And so old Beaver had to go
        over there and gnaw around it until the tree fell
down and they got the chain free and they took off.

Well they went on down the river and pretty soon old Beaver said,
    "Here's another one! Here's another one!"
And old Rabbit said,
    "Put it on! Put it on!"
And old Wolf walked up to it and said,
    "Okay."
So he stuck his foot in there and that thing went "Krnnng!"
Boy, that hurt soo much.
And he said,
"This is how they wear 'em."
And old Rabbit thought to himself,
    "Man, he still hasn't learned his lesson."
And so he said, "Wolf, you have two more feet back there so let's
        see if we can find
    two more shoes."
And old Wolf said,
    "Okay."
And so they started to take off and again old Beaver had to gnaw
        down a tree so he could get free. So they were walking down
        the river and each step old Wolf took,
    man, it was hurting him now, and he was going,
    "ow-ow," "ow-ow," "ow-ow."
Well, after a little bit they came up on another one and old Squirrel
        said,
    "Well, there's another one! There's another one!"
And old Rabbit said,
    "Put it on! Put it on!"
And old Wolf said,
    "Okay."
So he backed up to that trap and he stuck his foot in and it went
        "Krnnng!"
Boy, it hurt so much his
    ears stuck straight out
    his eyes were bulging out
    his tail was straight out and
    he thought his hair would fall off it hurt so baad!
And he said,
"This is how they wear 'em."

And old Rabbit thought to himself,
    "He still hasn't learned his lesson."
So he said, "Well, Wolf, you got one more foot there. Let's see if we
       can find one more
    shoe."
And so Wolf said,
    "Okay."
And so they started walking down. Of course, Beaver had to set
       him free again.
So they was walking down the river and each step, you know,
    Wolf was just dying because those things hurt and
    he was going "ow-ow-owh," "ow-ow-owh," "ow-ow-owh."
Well, after a little bit old Wolf heard the words he was just
    afraid he was going to hear.
And old Rabbit said, "Here's another one! Here's another one!"
And all the animals, they said, "Put it on! Put it on!"
And so Wolf said,
      "Okay."
And so he backed up to that trap and he started to put his foot in . . .
    right at the last moment he jumped away and he started crying,
    "Take 'em off! Take 'em off! They hurt! They hurt!"
And so those little animals they had to take those traps off of his
      feet.
And so Wolf set back and he was rubbing his ankles and his wrists
and after a little bit he said,
    "You know, I've heard some humans say that
    shoes can be too small for their feet and it hurts them.
    Those shoes were probably too small for me,
    that's why they hurt my feet so baad."
And old Rabbit fell over, knowing that Wolf still hadn't learned his
      lesson.
And so that's why,
even to this day,
the Wolf is all alone.
Because everybody is sick and tired of him pretending he knows
everything.
At least that's what Gramma said.

ᏩᎭᏯ ᏥᏚᎳᏑᏝᏅ
WAHAYA, TSIDULASUTLANV
WOLF, WHEN HE WORE SHOES

ᏏᏉᏯ ᎤᏃᎮᏢᏅ
Sigwoya unohetlvnv
Sequoyah, what he told

ᎢᎸᎯᏳ ᏥᎨᏒ ᏂᎦᏓ ᎢᎾᎨ ᎠᏁᎯ ᏣᎳᎩ ᏣᏂᏬᏂᏍᎦ. ᎤᏪᏴ ᎾᎥ ᏥᏍᏚ ᎠᎴ ᏌᎶᎵ ᏓᎾᏠᏃᎮᏍᎦ.
Ilvhiyu tsigesv nigada inage anehi tsalagi tsaniwonisga. Uweya nav tsisdu ale saloli danatlonohesga.
Forever, that was, all of them, forest, dwellers, Cherokee, they spoke it. A river, near, rabbit, and squirrel, were talking.

ᎤᎾᏛ ᎤᏪᏴ ᏗᏝ ᏗᎠᎢᏒ ᏙᏯ. Ꮒ! Ꮒ! ᎠᏗᎮ ᏙᏯ.
Unadv uweya ditla diaisv doya. Ni! Ni! adihe doya.
There, the river, in that direction, was coming, beaver. Look! Look! was saying, beaver.

ᏙᎤᏍᏗ, ᏙᏯ? ᎤᏛᏁ ᏥᏍᏚ.
Dousdi, doya? Udvne tsisdu.
What is it, Beaver? said, rabbit.

ᎤᎾᏛ ᏗᏂᏙᎦ ᏥᏍᏚ ᎠᎴ ᏌᎶᎵ ᏭᎷᏤ ᏙᏯ.
Unadv dinidoga tsisdu ale saloli wulutse doya.
There, where they stood, rabbit, and, squirrel, arrived, beaver.

ᎫᎱᏍᏗ ᏥᏩᏔ ᎤᏪᏯ ᎾᎥ, ᎤᏛᏁ ᏙᏯ. Ꮭ ᎢᎸᎯᏳ ᎠᎩᎪᏛᎲ ᏍᎩᎾ ᏥᏥᏩᏔ. ᏂᎯ ᎠᎵᏭ ᏱᏣᎾᏔ ᏙᎤᏍᏗ ᎨᏒ.
Guhusdi tsiwata uweya nav, udvne doya. Tla ilvhiyu agigotvhv sgina tsitsiwata. Nihi aliwu yitsanata dousdi gesv.
Something, I have found, river, near, said, beaver. No, ever, have seen before, that, what I found. You, might (by chance), might know, what, it is.

ᎰᏩ, ᎤᏛᏂ ᏥᏍᏚ. ᎢᏕᎾ.
Howa, udvni tsisdu. Idena.
Alright, said, rabbit. Let's go.

ᎤᏪᏴ ᎾᎥ ᏩᎾᎢᏒ, ᏩᎭᏯ ᎾᎥ ᎤᎦᏌᏗᏝ.
Uweya nav wanaisv, wahaya nav ugasaditla.
River, near, they were walking, wolf, near, appeared suddenly.

Wolf's shoes

ᏝᏛ ᏯᏂᏍᎦᎮ ᏩᎭᏯ ᎠᏎᏍᎩᎾ ᏙᏳ ᎤᏦᏎᏗ ᏣᏁᎵᏍᎦ ᏍᎩᎾ ᏩᎭᏯ. ᏂᎦᏓᎮᎾ ᎤᏩᎾᏕ ᎡᎵᏍᎨ ᏩᎭᏯ.
Tladv yanisgahe wahaya asesgina doyu utsosedi tsanelisga sgina wahaya. Nigadahena uwanade elisge wahaya.
Weren't, not afraid, wolf, but, very, annoying, they thought, that, wolf. Everything, they knew, they thought, wolf.

ᎣᏏᏲ ᎤᏛᎮ ᏩᎭᏯ. ᎭᏢ ᎢᏤᎦ?
Osiyo udvhe wahaya. Hatlv itsega?
Hello, said, wolf. Where, everyone going?

ᏙᏯ ᎫᎲᏍᏓ ᎠᏩᏔ ᏧᏪᎠ ᎾᎠ, ᎤᏛᏁ ᏥᏍᏚ.
Doya guhusda awata tsuwea naa, udvne tsisdu.
Beaver, something, found, at the river, near, said, rabbit.

Ꮭ ᏳᏩᎾᏔ ᏙᎤᏍᏓ ᎨᏒ, ᎤᏛᏁ ᏌᎶᎵ.
Tla yuwanata dousda gesv, udvne saloli.
No, doesn't know, what, it is, said, squirrel.

ᎠᏯᏛ ᎠᎵᏭ ᏯᏆᎾᏔ, ᎤᏛᏁ ᏩᎭᏯ. ᏗᎨᏏ.
Ayadv aliwu yagwanata, udvne wahaya. Digesi.
I, very possible, I will know, said, wolf. I will go.

ᏂᎦᏛ ᎤᏁᏅᏎ ᏧᏪᏯ ᏗᏟ.
Nigadv unenvse tsuweya ditli.
All of them, they went, where the river is, in that direction.

ᏭᏂᎷᏤᏃ, ᎠᎭᏂ, ᎤᏛᏁ ᏙᏯ. ᏙᎤᏍᏗ?
Wunilutseno, ahani, udvne doya. Dousdi?
When they arrived there, Here, said, beaver. What is it?

ᎤᏏᏛ ᎢᎾ ᎤᏛᏒ ᎨᏒ ᎦᏅᎦᏟ ᏭᎶᏎ ᏩᎭᏯ. ᎤᏩᏛᎮ ᏍᎩᎾ ᎠᏗᏍᎬ ᏙᏯ.
Uhnadv ina utvsv gesv ganvgatli wulose wahaya. Uwadvhe sgina adisgv doya.
There, height, grown, was, grass, s/he/it went, wolf. S/he/it found, that, what s/he/it is talking about, beaver.

ᏃᏭᏛ ᎤᎴᏅᎮ ᎠᏒᎬ ᏩᎭᏯ. ᏞᎩᏃ ᎤᏓᏍᏛᏝᏁ.
Nowudv ulenvhe asvgv wahaya. Tlegino udasdvtlane.
Now, s/he/it began, smelling, wolf. Soon, s/he/it sat down.

ᎠᏆᏔᏃ ᏙᎤᏍᏗ ᎨᏒ ᎯᎠ, ᎤᏛᏁ ᏩᎭᏯ. ᎠᏂᏴᏫᏯᏃ ᎠᎳᏑᎶ ᏓᏃᏎᎰ.
Agwatano dousdi gesv hia, udvne wahaya. Aniyvwiyano alasulo danoseho.

I know, what, it is, this, said, wolf. To the people, shoe, they call
   them.

DWᎨG Dᏼ? ᎤᎨᎣᎯᎥᎵ DhᎯ.
Alasulo agi? Unadvne aniso.
Shoe, it is? they said, the others.

DWᎨGT. ᏒhWᏏᏐ ᏂᏗᏙWᏗᏝ ᎢᏒhWᎨᏝ DhᏴᎾᏮ.
Alasuloi. Dunilasidena dunestaneho idunilasutla aniyvwiya.
A shoe. Their feet, they hurt, they don't wear shoes, the people.

D4ᏙᏓYZ, ᏂᏗᎠᏗ ᎤᎨGᎾᏛ DᏝᏙᎠᎠᏙE GᏗᏳᏮ. ᏏᏙᎣ DWᎨG ᏭᏢ4 ᏗD.
Asesgino, tsisdu uwanate alisgosgv wahaya. Gesdv alasulo yigese
   hia.
However, rabbit, knew, s/he/it was lying, wolf. Wasn't, a shoe, it
   was, this.

ᏂᏗᎠᏗᎣ ᏉᎢ ᎤᎨGᎾᏚ ᏉᎤᏙᎠᏢR.
Tsisdudv doyu uwanade dousdigesv.
The rabbit, very, knew, what it was.

DRᎣᎣ Ꮰ4.
Asvdvdv gese.
A trap, it was.

ᏚᏢᎦᎯᎾ, ᎤᎣᎤᏢ4 ᏂᏗᎠᏗ. ᏏᏙᎣ hᏚᏝ GGᎾW GᏗᏳᏮ.
Detsiyeyona, uwelise tsisdu. Gesdv nigada yuwanata wahaya.
I'm going to teach him, thought, rabbit. Doesn't, all, s/he/it know
   it, wolf.

ᏱVᏜ ᎾᎤᎦᎯᏗᏝ ᎤᏝᏗᏕWᎨᎤᎾ DhᏴᎾᏮ? ᎤᎨᎥᎵ ᏂᏗᎠᏗ.
Gadohv nanvdvneho yidadulasutlona aniyvwiya? Udvne tsisdu.
What, do what they do, when they put on shoes, the people? said
   rabbit.

ᏗDᎣ ᎾᎤᎦᎯᏗᏝ, ᎤᎨᎥᎵ GᏗᏳᏮ.
Hiadv nanvdvneho, udvne wahaya.
This, do what they do, said wolf.

ᎤᎾᎣ DRᎣ ᏗᏐᎾᎥ ᏗᏝ ᎾG4 GᏗᏳᏮ.
Unadv asvdv diganav ditla wulose wahaya.
There, the trap, where it lay, in that direction, s/he/it went, wolf.

ᏎᏝ ᏀᎤᎥᏦᏁᎥF, ᎣᎥᏦᏁᏗ.

Hida nanvdvneho, udvne.

This, do what they do, s/he/it said.

ᎣᎥᏀᏦ DᏒᏦᎥ ᏗᏚᎾᎥ ᎤᏩᏝᏋᏫᏁ.

Unadv asvdv diganav wulasitane.

There, the trap, where it lay, stepped in it.

ᎬᏩ9!! ᏔᏬᏗᏖᏬᎤ ᎣᎤᏃᏖᎤ. ᏙᎤ ᎣᏩᏒᏬᏦᏞᏗᏁ ᏇᏬᏙᎤ.

Gvwe!! Istiyawu unolvse. Doyu uwesdanelv wahaya.

Kaweh!! As hard as it could, it sounded. Very, it hurt her/him/it,
wolf.

ᏎDᏦᎥ ᏀᎤᎥᏦᏁᎥF ᏎᎾᎫᏔᏋᏞᎾ, ᎣᎥᏦᏁᏗ ᏇᏬᏙᎤ ᎠᏑᏓ ᎾᎫᎰᏬᎥE.

Hiadv nanvdvneho yinadulasutlana, udvne wahaya hale
natlohisgv.

This, do what they do, when they put on shoes, said, wolf, almost,
crying.

ᎠᏬ! ᎣᏒᏙᏞ4 ᏂᏬᎤᏗ. ᏞᏏ ᏫᎾᏚᎱᏉᎥᎤᏗ.

Ha! Uwelise tsisdu. Tlasi yadetlogwasga.

Ha! S/he/it thought, rabbit. Not yet, not learning.

ᏂᏀ, ᏇᏬᏙᎤ! ᎣᎥᏦᏁᏗ ᏂᏬᎤᏗ. ᎾᎾᏌ ᏋᏔ ᏣᏝᏌᏍᏕᎾ?

Howa, wahaya! Udvne tsisdu. Nanahv soi tsalasidena?

Alright, wolf! s/he/it said, rabbit. What about that, other, your
foot?

ᏫᏗᏫᏬᎷᏍ ᏋᏔ DᏪᏋᎶ. ᏔᏣᏫᏃ DᎬᏫᏗᏞ ᏚᏪᏫᏬᎥE ᏎᏚᏪᏪᏋᎶᏗ.

Widiyaluga soi alasulo. Itsulano agvyaditla detsalasgv
yidetsalasulohi.

Let's go hunt for, other, a shoe. So both, your feet, front, will have
shoes.

ᏂᏀ, ᎣᎥᏦᏁᏗ ᏇᏬᏙᎤ. 4ᏚᏟ ᎾᏒᏙᏫ.

Howa, udvne wahaya. Segatsv nuwetse.

Okay, said, wolf. Barely, speaking.

D4ᏬᎤᎩᏃ, ᏙᏫ ᎣᏓᏇᏗᏫᏗ ᏶4 ᏗᏞᏚ. ᎣᎥᏋᎾ ᎾᏔᏞᏓ ᏒᎥᏛᏓ.

Asesgino, doya uleyvhisdi gese ditlaga. Unahena wigudale svdvda.

As it was, beaver, had to fall, it was, tree. It was there, hooked on,
trap.

ᎤᏍᎦᏛᏙᎾᏙ, ᎤᏂᎾᏅᎩᏒᎢ ᏧᏪᏯ ᏗᏞ.

Usgwadonano, uninanvgisv tsuweya ditla.

And when s/he/it finished, they went, toward the river, in that
    direction.

ᎦᎾᎢᏒᏃ ᏕᎢ ᎠᏒᏛᏗ ᎤᏩᏕᎥ ᏙᏯ.

Wanaisvno soi asvdvdi uwatvhe doya.

As they walked along, another, a trap, s/he/it found, beaver.

ᎠᎭᎾ ᏕᎢ! ᎠᎭᎾ ᏕᎢ! ᎤᏛᏁ ᏙᏯ.

Ahana soi! Ahana soi! Udvne doya.

Here is, another! Here is, another! s/he/it said, beaver.

ᎭᎳᏍᎤᏢᎩ! ᎭᎳᏍᎤᏢᎩ! ᎤᏛᏁ ᏥᏍᏚ.

Halasutlvgi! Halasutlvgi! Udvne tsisdu.

Put the shoe on! Put the shoe on! s/he/it said, rabbit.

ᎦᎭᏯᏃZ, ᎰᎹ, ᎤᏛᏁ ᏎᎦᏣᏒ ᎦᏬᏂᏍᎦ.

Wahayano, Howa, udvne segatsv gawonisga.

The wolf now, Alright, s/he/it said, barely, speaking.

ᏒᏛᏓ ᏧᏥᏯ ᎳᎾᏎ ᎦᎭᏯ ᎠᎴ ᎳᏩᏏᏁ.

Svdvda ditsiya wulose wahaya ale wulasine.

The trap, where it lay, s/he/it went, wolf, and, stepped in it.

ᏍᏓᏯ ᎤᏃᎯᎸᏎ ᎾᏒᏛᏓ.

Stayo unohilvse nasvdvda.

Hard, made a sound, the trap.

ᏅᎾᏃ ᎦᎭᏯ ᎦᏂᏓᏛ ᎠᎴ ᏗᎦᎴᎾ ᏗᏍᏛᎦᏴᎮᏗ ᏄᏢᏍᏔᏁ.

Nanano wahaya ganidadv ale digalena disdvgayvhedi nutlvstane.

Then, wolf, s/he/its tail, and, s/he/its ears, became stale (brittle),
    almost.

ᎯᎠᏛ ᎾᏅᏛᏁᎰ ᏱᎾᏚᎳᏍᎤᏔᎾ, ᎤᏛᏁ ᎦᎭᏯ ᎮᏟ ᏄᏟᎰᎢᏍᎬ.

Hiadv nanvdvneho yinadulasutlana, udvne wahaya hetle
    natlohisgv.

This, do what they do, when they put on shoes, said, wolf, almost,
    crying.

ᏙᎯᏳᎮᏃ ᏚᏪᏍᏔᏁᎮ ᏚᎳᏏᏕᎾ Ꮎ ᎦᎭᏯ.

Dohiyuheno duwestanehe dulasidena na wahaya.

Very, were hurting, s/he/its feet, that, wolf.

ᎠᎸ! ᎥᏬ Ꮣ ᏗᎬᏍᏗ ᏣᏍᎤᎢᎦᏍᏫ, ᎤᏪᎵᏏᏅ Ꮎ ᏥᏍᏚᏏ.

Ha! Doka tla guhusdi yadetlokawasgi, uwelise na tsisdu.

Ha! Very, no, something, learning, s/he/it thought, that, rabbit.

ᎧᎹ! ᏸᏛ ᏥᎵ ᏕᏂᏅᏌᏓ, ᎤᏛᏁ ᏥᏍᏚᏏ. ᏥᏙᎩᏯᎷᎦ ᏥᎵ ᎢᎦ ᏗᎳᏑᎶᎢ.

Kama! Sidv tali deninvsada, udvne tsisdu. Tsidogiyaluga tali iga dilasuloi.

Now! Still, two, you have feet, said, rabbit. Let's hunt, two, the sum, shoes.

ᏩᎭᏯᏃᏤ, ᎰᏩ, ᎤᏛᎮ ᏎᎦᏨ.

Wahayano, Howa, udvhe segatsv.

Wolf now, Alright, s/he/it said, barely.

ᏙᏯᏛ ᎤᏍᎪᎵᏍᏗ ᎥᎨᏒ ᏗᏞᎦ ᎠᏒᏛᏗ ᏫᎫᏓᎸ.

Doyadv usgolisdi vgesv ditlaga asvdvdi wigudalv.

The beaver, had to gnaw, it turned out to be, tree, the trap, hooked on to.

ᏙᏳ ᎠᎩᏟᏱᎣᎨ ᎬᎢᏒ ᏩᎭᏯ ᎠᎴ ᎤᎵᏰᏗᎮ.

Doyu agitliyoge waisv wahaya ale uliyedihe.

Very, in agony, went along, wolf, and, murmured incoherently (moaned).

ᏃᎤᏛ ᏌᎶᎵ ᎤᎪᎮ ᏐᎢ ᎠᎳᏑᎶ. ᎭᎳᏑᏢᎩ! ᎭᎳᏑᏢᎩ! ᎤᏃᏎᎴ ᏩᎭᏯ.

Nowudv saloli ugohe soi alasulo. Halasutlvgi! Halasutlvgi! Unosele wahaya.

Now, squirrel, saw, another, shoe. Put the shoe on! Put the shoe on! they told wolf.

ᎰᏩ, ᎤᏛᏁ ᏩᎭᏯ.

Howa, udvne wahaya.

Alright, s/he/it said, wolf.

ᏒᏛᏓ ᏗᏥᏯ ᎤᏏᏅᏎ, ᎤᏔᏍᏖᏎ ᏓᏁᏗᏝ ᎦᏅᏒᏓ.

Svdvda ditsiya wusinvse, wutastese snaditla ganvsvda.

The trap, where it lay, backed up to, stepped on it, behind, s/he/its foot.

ᎢᏍᏔᏬᏛ ᎤᏃᏴᏍᏕ ᎠᏒᏛᏗ.

Istawudv unoyvsde asvdvdi.

Very hard, sounded out, the trap.

ᎯᎠᏛ ᏃᏂᎥᏛᏁᎰ ᏗᏄᏓᏩᏔᏍᏬ, ᎤᏛᏁ ᏩᎭᏯ VᎦ ᎠᎩᏟᏯᎦ ZᏀ.

Hiadv nanvdvneho yinadulasutlana, udvne wahaya doyu agitliyoga
nowa.

This, do what they do, when they put on shoes, said, wolf, very,
agony, now.

ᏝᏛᏍᏛ ᏣᏕᏟᎦᏩᏍᎦ, ᎤᏪᎵᏎ ᏥᏍᏚ.

Tladvsi yadetlogawasga, uwelise tsisdu.

Still not yet, learning, s/he/it thought, rabbit.

ᏏᏛ ᏌᏇ ᎠᏫᎳᏛ, ᎠᎪᏎᎴ ᏩᎭᏯ. ᏌᏇ ᏥᏗᏩᏗ ᎠᏩᏎᎶᎢ.

Sidv sagwu hilasvda, agosele wahaya. Sagwu tsidiwadi alasuloi.

Still, one, have a foot, s/he/it told her/him/it, wolf, One, let's find,
shoe.

ᎰᏩ, ᎤᏛᏁ ᏩᎭᏯ.

Howa, udvne wahaya.

Alright, s/he/it said, wolf.

ᏙᏯᏃ ᎤᏎᏴᏎ ᏗᏠᎦ ᎠᏍᎥᏛ ᏫᎫᏓᎸ.

Doyano uleyvse ditlaga asvdv wigudalv.

Now beaver, cut down, tree, the trap, was tied to.

ᏩᏁᎢᏍᏛ ᏥᏍᏚ, ᎠᎭᏂ ᏐᎢ! ᎠᎭᏂ ᏐᎢ! ᎤᏛᎮ.

Wanaisvdv tsisdu, Ahani soi! Ahani soi! Udvhe.

As they walked, rabbit, Here's another! Here's another! s/he/it
said.

ᎭᎳᏑᏢᎩ! ᎭᎳᏑᏢᎩ! ᎤᏃᏎᎴ ᏩᎭᏯ.

Halasutlvgi! Halasutlvgi! Unosele wahaya.

Put the shoe on! Put the shoe on! they told wolf.

ᎰᏩ, ᎤᏛᎮ ᏩᎭᏯ. ᏎᎦᏨ ᎦᏬᏂᏍᎹᎢᏗ ZᏀ.

Howa, udvhe wahaya. Segatsv gawonisgvi nowa.

Alright, s/he/it said, wolf. Barely, s/he/it was speaking, now.

ᏙᏴᏛᏃ ᏚᏪᏍᏔᏁᎮ ᏧᎳᏏᏕᎾ ᏩᎭᏯ.

Doyvdvno duwestanehe tsulasidena wahaya.

Very much, they were hurting, her/his/its feet, wolf.

ᎾᎠ ᏭᎷᏤ ᎠᏍᎥᏛ ᏗᏥᏯ. ᎤᏏᎾᏛᏎ.

Naa wulutse asvdv ditsiya. Usinadvse.

Near, arrived, trap, where it lay. Backed up to it.

ᎤᏟᏍᏓ ᏥᏚᏝᏗᏗᏅᏎ! ᏗᏂᏍᎬᎾᏕᏏ! ᏗᏂᏍᎬᎾᏕᏏ! ᎤᏪᏢᎮ ᏩᎭᏯ.
Utlisda tsidutladidinvse! Dinisgvnadesi! Dinisgvnadesi! Uwetlvhe wahaya.
Quickly, s/he/it jumped away! Take them off! Take them off! screamed wolf.

ᎠᏪᏍᏔᏁᎯ! ᎠᏪᏍᏔᏁᎯ!
Awestanehi! Awestanehi!
I'm in pain! I'm in pain!

ᎠᏂᏐᏃ ᏅᎦ ᏗᏂᏅᏌᏓ ᏂᏚᏅᏔᏁᎴ.
Anisono nvga dininvsada nidunvtanele.
The others, four, footed, took them off of her/him/it.

ᏭᏂᏍᏆᏓᏃ ᎤᎳᏍᏛᏟᏁ ᏩᎭᏯ.
Wunisgwadano ulasdvtline wahaya.
When they were done, s/he/it sat down, wolf.

ᎢᎦᏛ ᎠᏂᏴᏫᏯ ᏧᎾᏍᏗᎩᏓ ᏚᎾᎳᏑᏠ ᏓᎾᏗᏍᎪ ᎠᎴ ᏚᏂᏪᏍᏔᏁᎰ.
Igadv aniyvwiya tsunasdigida dunalasutlo danadisgo ale duniwestaneho.
Some, people, too small, put on shoes, they say, and, hurts them.

ᏍᎩᏃᏳᏍᏗ Ꮎ ᏥᏓᏇᏍᏓᏁᎮ ᏗᎳᏑᎶ, ᏧᎾᏍᏗᎩᏃ ᎨᏎ.
Sginoyusdi na tsidagwesdanehe dilasulo, tsunasdigino gese.
That's why, those, they hurt me, shoes, were too small, they were.

ᎤᎾᏛ ᏚᏗᏨ ᏥᏍᏚ ᎤᏩᎾᏛ Ꮭ ᎫᎱᏍᏗ ᏳᏗᏠᏆᏍᏔᏁ ᏩᎭᏯ.
Unadv duditsv tsisdu uwanadv tla guhusdi yuditlogwastane wahaya.
Right there, fell down, rabbit, knowing, no, something, didn't learn, wolf.

ᏅᏍᎩᎮᎾᏳᏍᏗ ᎤᏩᏌ ᏤᏙᎰ ᏩᎭᏯ.
Nvsgihenayusdi uwasa tsedoho wahaya.
That's the reason, alone, walks around, wolf.

ᏏᎮᎾ ᏂᎦᏓ ᎤᏩᎾᏙ ᎤᏤᎸᏍᎰ ᏩᎭᏯ.
Sihena nigada uwanado utselvsho wahaya.
Still yet, all, s/he/it knows, pretends, wolf.

"How and Why" Stories

If you ever visit a bookstore and look for books on Cherokee stories, you'll find most of them in the children's section. Now, I like children's books, and my children do as well. But it frustrates me when Cherokee stories, like other Native American oral traditional stories, are categorized as somehow childish or simple by default. That's far from the truth.

The Liars' Club is known for telling "how and why" stories. As they travel they often tell stories at schools and other places where the majority of their audience is children. "How and why" stories are teaching tools used to educate children. These stories tell about how our world was made and how animals came to be the way they are today. On the surface, they seem to be about the physical world. But kids aren't fooled. If you listen closely, you'll see that these "how and why" stories are about how our thoughts and actions transform ourselves and the world.

Hastings said that animal stories are some of the first stories children are told. Over thousands of years, they were created through observing the natural world and its processes. These stories teach morals, or how to behave. They teach about the right way to act toward one another. They teach about the proper and improper relationships between humans, animals, plants, and all other forms of life.

Even though we grow and mature, we keep asking of the world and of ourselves "How?" and "Why?" We require explanation, and stories keep providing the answers. "How and why" stories are some of the simplest and most complex stories. While we may understand their morals, or lessons, it is much more difficult to live according to their teachings.

WHY THE MOLE LIVES UNDERGROUND
By Hastings Shade

You hardly ever hear a story about the Mole, which is called *tinequa*, or big lice. This is the only one I have ever heard.

One time, when all the animals, birds, insects, and reptiles were trying to get the fire for the Cherokees, the Mole had his turn at trying to get the fire also. When it came his turn to try, the ones that guarded the fire were beginning to find out someone was trying to get some of their fire so they were on their guard.

The Mole said, "I can get the fire. I'll dig past the fire and get some of it and I will bring it back underground. If I come out on the other side of the fire they won't be looking for anyone on that side."

So he started digging. (Back then he didn't dig as fast as he does nowadays.) He started toward the fire. As he was digging, Mole started to get tired and he thought he had gone far enough and he began digging upward. He thought he was past the fire. When he came out Mole was right under the fire and it scorched his eyes when he stuck his head out. It burned his eyes and he failed to get the fire.

To this day the Mole can't stand bright lights and the ashes turned his coat to the grey color that it is today. He can't see. This is why he lives underground where it's dark.

The Creator felt sorry for him and gave Mole strong, short arms and big paws with strong claws so now he can dig fast and can come out anywhere he wants to. He can also sense things around him underground so he doesn't have to come out of the ground. These are all gifts from the Creator for trying to help.

WHY THE MOCKINGBIRD SINGS
By Hastings Shade

This is a story told by the elders.

One day Mockingbird, *tsusga digisgi*, or head eater, was listening to the other birds sing as they flew around in the trees. He tried his voice and it didn't sound very good. He found one of the small birds and asked him to listen to his voice. He tried to sing and it didn't sound right. So he asked the little bird to look into his mouth and throat and see if he could see anything that might be causing his voice to sound like it did.

Mockingbird opened his mouth and the little bird looked into his mouth and down his throat. Mockingbird was getting tired of holding his mouth open and he closed his mouth and bit the little bird's head off. Immediately when he tried to sing he had the little bird's voice. This gave him an idea! He began to ask all the birds he seen to look down his throat.

When they would, he would bite their heads off and swallow them and he would have their voice. He did this for a while and he had swallowed several of the birds' heads and had their voices. He would sing using the voices he had stolen.

One day the Creator came to him and asked him where he had gotten the voices that he was using. He told the Creator when one of the birds would look down his throat he would bite their head off and swallow it. That's how he got the voices he was using. He said his voice wasn't very good, anyway, so he was just using theirs.

The Creator told him from this day forward whenever he would open his mouth to sing, he could not quit until he had used every voice he had stolen. This is why you hear Mockingbird sing all night long. This is how many voices he had taken. His punishment is that he can't rest until he has used every voice he has.

It is not good to take something that is not yours even if you think what you have is not as good as someone else's. Our punishment could be severe.

THE BLUE RACER AND THE FIRE
By Hastings Shade

Just like the animals, even the reptiles tried to get the fire. When it became time for the Blue Racer, or *ulitiidi*, (which means "trying to get away") to try, he, like all the rest that had tried, went to where the fire was.

He climbed the tree and looked into the opening to try to determine where the fire was and which way would be the best way to get to it. When he looked into the opening the fire started burning real hot and this startled him and he lost his hold he had on the tree and he fell into the fire.

It began to burn him and he started to crawl this way and that away, any way to get out of the fire. If you see him crawl you can see he no longer crawl straight. He throw himself this way and that way. To this day he is still trying to get out of the fire.

The fire burnt his skin so the Creator said, "From this day on, you will lose your skin several time a year." This is to keep him comfortable.

The Black Snake, *galegi* (the climber), like the Raccoon, the smoke turned him black except for his belly. To this day his belly is still white, but the rest of him is black.

HOW THE RACCOON GOT HIS MASK AND RINGED TAIL
By Hastings Shade

All the animals tried to get the fire for the people, even the Raccoon, *kvtli*, tried. When it became his turn to try to get the fire, he went to the tree where the fire was. There was a hole about halfway up the tree, and he climbed to where the hole was and looked into the tree.

About that time the fire flared up and the smoke covered his face and turned it black. He pulled his head out of the hole and began to wipe his eyes. As he did this he worked the black soot into his fur. Then he shook his head. When he done this, most of the soot came off of his head except for where he had rubbed his eyes. That part stayed, and this is why he has a mask on to this day and his fur has dark spots and streaks on it.

If you have ever been around Raccoon he doesn't give up very easy. He turned around and stuck his tail into the hole. He thought he might be able to get some of the fire onto his tail and he could get the fire this way.

As he stuck his tail into the hole in the tree the fire flared up again. When he felt the heat, he pulled his tail out as fast as he could but he wasn't fast enough. The fire had burnt black circles around his tail.

Today, when you see him you can see he still has a mask on and you can see the rings around his tail. He is also called the Ring-tailed Raccoon. He got these things by trying to help the people get the fire.

WHY THE CROW IS BLACK
By Hastings Shade

Many, many years ago, all the animals, birds, insects, and other creatures were all white. Everything that you see that has different colors got this way by trying to get the fire for the Cherokee.

The Crow is no exception. He was so white he looked like a pearl, and as he flew around the sun would shine off of his feathers and you could see all the colors of the rainbow in them. Crow knew this and he would fly so all the others could see the colors.

As each one tried and failed to get the fire for the Cherokees, it finally came time for the Crow to try. He went to where the fire was and he looked down into the tree. He could see the fire. The Crow is not like the Eagle or the Hawk; he couldn't grasp anything in his claws so he had to carry the fire with his beak.

So, he found a stick and laid it into the fire. As the stick caught on fire, he grabbed it and took off with it. While he flew along, the smoke and the soot off of the burning stick got on his feathers and turned them black. Smoke got in his eyes and he dropped the burning stick. So he had failed.

After the Indians got the fire, the Crow went to the Creator and asked Him if He would turn him back to his original color, which was white. The Creator told him He couldn't because that was his reward for trying to help the Cherokees.

The Creator told the Crow this: "Because you tried to help the Cherokees, I will give you the colors back that you had."

So the Creator gave him his colors back. To this day, if you see a black crow feather and turn it just right so the sun shines on it, you can still see the colors of the rainbow in it.

The Creator will always take care of you if you try to do what is best for everyone.

HOW THE WHITE MAN WAS MADE
Told by Hastings Shade

Just like, the other night I was watching the news about the weather. Wind storms and tornados coming through here.

And they tell the story from a long time ago about how the white man was made from the foam of the water. That's how he was made.

We were formed from the earth, or dirt, as we call it. But, it says wind was pushing this foam around one day all over the water, you know?

Once it finally pushed it up against the bank. And when it got to the bank it touched something solid and became man.

Immediately when he became man he wanted to own the land because he thought the wind pushed him around. So, since then, when the white man sees land he wants to own it.

The first thing he does is put up "KEEP OUT" signs and fences. He doesn't want anyone else on the land that he has and he's afraid he might have to go back to the water again.

But, you know, we can never own anything. One of these days it will belong to somebody else or it will fall down. It's never mine. I can use it while I'm here.

But I was listening to the weather and it said the wind velocity, wind direction, wind rotation, all that.

And I thought: "The wind is still pushing them."

They kept saying if high winds are coming toward you get out of the way. But we as Indians, when the wind comes toward us we move it. We tell it to go. We don't run from it. We respect it, but we move it. So it don't push us around. It pushes the non-Indian around. If you ever listen to the weather, you'll hear wind velocity, wind rotation, wind direction, all that. Wind gusts. But we as Native Americans, we talk to it. We don't run from it, we talk to it.

WHY CEDAR IS USED FOR PURIFICATION
By Hastings Shade

One day the Great Spirit came and said, "I need someone to help watch over Mother Earth." He was talking to the trees.

All the trees said, "We can do it!"

The Great Spirit said, "I will be back in seven days and check on you all." And he left.

The mighty oak said, "I am the strongest; surely he will pick me."

The other trees said, "I have many eyes (meaning leaves), he will pick me."

But as the nights went by, the trees couldn't stay awake. One by one they went to sleep. When the Great Spirit returned, the only ones he found awake were the Evergreen trees: the firs, pines, spruce, and cedar.

He looked at them and he picked the cedar because it had so many eyes. But he told the others, "Because you didn't go to sleep, you will also keep your eyes, so you can help the cedar keep watch. But all the others—you will lose your eyes because you went to sleep."

That is why the trees lose their leaves in the winter.

This is why the Cherokees use the cedar for purification.

When they burn the cedar, the Great Spirit can smell the odor and know the cedar is keeping watch.

FIRE, WIND, EARTH, WATER
By Hastings Shade

Respect these four things. These same four things that you depend on to live—Fire, Wind, Earth, and Water—can also take your life in an instant.

Each one of these four things can take the breath of life away from you at anytime.

So we need to treat each one with respect.

Tradition Bearers and Professional Storytellers

The Liars' Club members often perform for no pay; getting paid is not a requirement for them to go and visit a school or attend an event. Their main goal is to share tradition, and they find offensive the idea of putting money or profit first.

Hastings and I talked about the differences between the Liars' Club and professional storytellers—some of whom are Cherokee—who travel around telling stories for pay. The Liars' Club often spots these folks in their audience and then later hears they've added the stories the Liars' Club tells to their own repertoire.

"Is that right?" I said.

"Most of 'em do. Yeah."

"From stories you told?" I asked.

"Some stories they heard. I don't tell them, 'cause I know what they're gonna do with 'em."

"So they're kind of professional storytellers?"

"Yeah, well . . . pretty much."

"And not knowledge keepers?"

"No. Uh-unh. Their forte is, 'I can tell you a story for X amount of dollars,'" Hastings said.

"Okay. And I think that's important to say in this book. There's a difference between what you traditionalists and knowledge keepers are doing with the Liars' Club versus those people who tell stories as their vocation."

"We share without pay. We'll accept it, you know. Like I said, we won't turn it down. But we ain't gonna say, 'Well, I'll do this for four hundred, five hundred, a thousand dollars.' You know, 'I'll come up there and you pay me.'"

"Then you turn your knowledge into a commodity."

"Yeah. Then you start selling it and that's no good," said Hastings. "That's how come we always change our stories whenever we go out somewhere, you know? We tell 'em pretty much like we got 'em. But there's differences we add in. That way we know who's got our stories. Or who took 'em."

"I was thinking about that last night as I was driving home after dropping Sequoyah off. I thought, I want to say in the book, 'By the time you read this, the stories have already changed,'" I said.

"Yeah."

"You know? And they're moving on. They're growing, living things."

"Yeah," Hastings said quickly and nodded.

"So don't think this is the Cherokee tradition written in stone."

"Yeah. It's not in stone. I mean, there's nothing that we do is written in stone. I mean, you know a lot of people, they want science or scientific fact. But *we* know it as the truth, and that's because of how it's told. Like I've said, the stories don't change in the Cherokee language. The story never changes, even those from way back that I hear today. Even though one person lives here, another person lives two hundred miles away. There's no difference in the story."

Ulvsgedi (The Wondrous)

Huhu

There's lots of stories about transforming ourselves, right?" I asked Hastings. Our conversation had turned to stories of *ulvsgedi*, or of things which inspire wonder. More often than not, when we'd get together for a storytelling there was a point in the gathering when we'd begin to discuss the way in which spirit and world interconnect within a Cherokee worldview. These are stories of the wondrous, of those experiences that are uncanny and often inexplicable except to those with deeper knowledge of Cherokee medicine and traditional beliefs.

"Yeah."

"All tribes have stories about humans transforming into animals . . ."

"Yeah. Yeah," he said. "See, we changed into animals. That's how we got around. They changed into birds. They changed into wolves. Anything that's fast, you know. That's how they got around. See, there's a parallel world. We speak of parallel worlds. We're here, the parallel world is here," Hastings said, and gestured to two sides. "Within that step, just like the step here. The parallel world is a step here," he said, and gestured again to the side. "Within our path. That's how close we are to this spiritual world."

"Right," I said.

"We could be here, or there, you know? So, right now we're here, but we could be there just that quick. That's what's wrong with our kids nowadays. They have to rely on drugs to make 'em figure out who they are. Because we have not taught them who they are. If they *knew* who they are they'd travel in a straight line. Since they don't know who they are they go back and forth, they kind of weave."

"Mmhm."

"In this world, out of this world. Every now and then they'll get on the Indian way . . . but they're in this no-place and then they're in this different culture."

"Right."

"'Cause they don't know where this place is. They just think it feels good. It feels good for a moment. And then they realize, hey, they're back here in the everyday world. And then the Indian world is not quite—you know, they don't know quite who they are, and then they get over here in the non-Indian world, but they don't belong here either. So they just go back and forth," Hastings said, moving his hands from side to side.

"Mmhm," I said.

"We need to get 'em on this straight path. So they'll know who they are. That's how come they do a lot of drugs. That's just to make 'em feel good for a little while. 'Cause that drug is not something that makes you feel good, it's something that just grabs you. And once it grabs you it ain't gonna turn loose. You might want to take it off of you, but it's not gone. It's always going to be there. It just takes that one time."

"Yeah. Like most people I've got relatives . . . ," I said.

"I do, too," Hastings said.

"The thing is, you know, in my experience . . . ," I said. "I'm still figuring it out, but life's more beautiful and amazing and mysterious just straight up sober as you can get!"

"Yeah. Yeah. Well, there's so many bad things in your just natural life, it's like, 'Why do you want to add this extra to it?' It's hard enough without adding that."

"It's hard enough just living the life you live," Sammy said. "Don't try to throw a wrench into it." We all laughed knowingly.

"Well, they might have hit a hard spot," Hastings considered. "Only thing they know is to get into this drug that alters that. They feel good for a little while, but when they come back it's still there, you know? This hard part ain't going away, but they've gone away. But they come right back to it."

"See, the TV does that, too. Or computers. Games," I said.

"Yeah," Hastings said.

"But what makes stories different is that telling and listening to stories make you feel," I said.

"Yeah."

"You can feel alive when you listen to stories."

"Yeah."

"And you're in a group and you're . . ."

"Yeah."

"You're present with each other," I said.

"Yeah."

"With TV or the computer, you're not. It's just sound and image."

"Yeah. An image. It's something that's way over here," Hastings said, gesturing to one side. "You know? I mean, you see it, yeah. I can see a little bit of it."

"But you can turn away; you've got no responsibility to it."

"Yeah."

"Or it to you!"

The Rainbow Is a Pathway

"But, you know," Hastings said, "the travel mode . . . we were talking about this the other night. In one of my classes. The rainbow that we see in the sky after it rains. That was one of the pathways that the people traveled. But they didn't travel in this form. They traveled in . . . The Creator gave us the ability to do things that people can't *imagine*. And that's how we got around. That's how we traveled. People say, 'Y'all didn't do that.' I said, 'He gave us that ability.' He gave us the ability to change into . . . things. He gave us the ability to control some of the elements. Which, if you read the Bible, him and his sons is the only one's that's capable of doing that. So who are we? If we can do it, then who are we?

"Because the Creator says . . . Christ, when he looked at the sea and made it calm. Peter actually, if he'd have had that faith, he could have walked on water. Which somebody said he took two or three steps. But he looked down and seen the water. And there went his faith. I've seen . . . not in *this* form, again . . . but I've seen things go across the water. And when they come up on the other side, it was a man. I seen man on this side, go across, and man on the other side. So we had that ability to . . . travel. That arc. That rainbow. People says, 'You can't travel it. You *can't* touch it.' *We* can't . . . in this form. But, a different form, a different *spirit*. The spirit that the elders say never dies, that's what travels that. Because if you talk to an elder, the spirit will never leave. Only the form that you see here is going to be buried. The human, the solid form, is what we put in the ground when we bury somebody. The *spirit*, that gray spirit, is always going to be around. And, if you'll look, if you lost a loved one or something, you can actually see 'em."

"They're gray?" I asked.

"Yeah. And, once you focus on it, it may not be them. But at that moment in time that's who it is. You can't focus, but you know they're there."

"You can feel someone's presence."

"You don't have time to focus, you just take what's there. 'Cause once you focus then it becomes what it is. It's that little moment in time that the spirit says it's here. 'Look at me.' And when you look and try to . . . it's gone. But it's there. I mean, they're there. I mean, they'll always be there.

"That's why, around a mound, I won't get on it. Because you don't know what you're going to pick up. I hate to see people that dig into 'em. I know archaeologists love it. 'Cause I had one tell me one time, I forget what it was, a bowl or something. He said he took it home with him and the next day he took it back. He says, 'I couldn't sleep that night.' I said, 'Well, you took something home with you that you wasn't supposed to take home.'"

Getting Around

"Those trade networks went everywhere, you know," I said, referring to the ancient trade networks that crisscrossed North America. "People forget about that, but copper and . . ."

"Well it's just like this mound down here at Spiro. It's Caddo. I mean they traded up and down the Rio Grande," Hastings said.

"They had to have," Woody added.

"They said they've been trying to figure out Aztec mythology and iconography," I said. "They found a lot of similarities with the Hopi and the Pueblos. They know that the Santa Fe Trail goes all the way up to Colorado. That went all the way back to Mexico City. And there had to be trails across the southern Plains, those trade networks."

"You know, somebody said, 'How'd they get around?' Well, they *knew* how to get around," Hastings said. "I mean, I remember this when I was young. One of my cousins got real sick. And it's four miles to town from where I live. Four miles exact, I don't care how you walked. Straight through it's four miles. And they told him he needs some medicine. He said, 'Alright.' And, you know, being young, I thought to myself, 'It's going to take him two hours, three or four hours.' I knew that much. We used to walk and we'd leave early in the morning and get back eleven or twelve o'clock, you know? And I was sitting there and we was eating. Matter of fact we was getting ready to eat when he left. We was finishing up and he was back. Which was probably an hour, forty-five minutes. And he had the medicine. Nobody ever questioned how he'd done it or what. They just said to start giving him the medicine."

"I heard people used to sing, runners used to sing songs that could make them . . . take giant leaps," I said.

"Yeah. Yeah," Hasting nodded. "My grandpa, you could see him coming, you'd look again and he'd be gone. You'd walk by and he'd be standing there laughing at you; he'd be right next to you standing behind a little tree about that big. And he'd say, 'Ah, you didn't see me, did you?'" Hastings said and laughed. "But he would, he'd hide from you. And he'd tell us when we could go down to the creek and when we couldn't go. He'd say, 'Nah, guess you better not today. Not a good time to go.'"

"Why was that?" I asked.

"Someone might get hurt or something might happen."

"Little person might be there or something," Woody said.

"And he would just know?" I asked.

"He would just know," Hastings said. "He would know. We'd say, 'Well, we're going to the creek.' Like, we'd talk about it the night before, four or five boys say, 'We're going to go fishin.' Or go gigging. He'd walk off, you know, and he'd come back and say, 'Tomorrow's not a good day. I'd wait another day.' One time we went and the game warden was going up and down the creek almost all day. We had to run up and down the creek," Hastings paused and laughed. "And Grandpa got mad. When we got back we told him and he got mad at us." Hastings laughed again. "'I told you all not to go.' He seen something happening, you know? So after that we didn't question him. When he said 'Don't go' we didn't go. A lot of times we don't pay attention to what's been told to us. We'd want to go gigging at night, and he'd say, 'Yeah, this is a good night for it.' A lot of times he'd go with us. He'd just sit by the fire. I think he was just down there watching us, watching over us. A lot of times he'd say '*Jotlestawu.*' 'Don't go tonight.' He told my cousins that one night and they went and got caught. Fined 'em $150 apiece."

After a few moments, Sequoyah said, "And again, just like Sammy said last night, these are the kind of stories that we don't share with everybody because they won't believe it."

THE OLD WOMAN
Told by Sequoyah Guess

Gramma would always call me over
to her house at night and tell me these scary stories.
And this is one that she told me that happened to her when she was
    a little girl.
I think she said she was about eleven, twelve, thirteen years old at
    the time.
Anyway, this is what she said happened.

She said there was this old woman that she liked a lot.
And that old woman liked her.
But she was about the only one that did like this old woman
because everybody else was scared of her.
Everybody thought that she was a ravenmocker,
because nobody knew exactly how old she was.

Now ravenmockers,
what they will do is,
well what they are are mean medicine people.
And what they'll do is they can turn into different things.
They can turn into ravens
or balls of fire
or just about anything they want.
But what they will do is come and sneak in on you
when you're sick or dying.
And they will eat your heart or your liver.
And when you die, the life that you were
supposed to live is added on to them.
And so they get to live a long, long time.
So that's why people thought this old woman was a ravenmocker.
Because nobody knew exactly how old she was,
and she was really, really old.

Well one day, Gramma heard the news that this old woman was
     dying.
  But they were having a hard time finding somebody
  to go stay with her and take care of her.
Because back then, when somebody was sick or dying,
they wouldn't send 'em off to a hospice or nursing home
or something like that.
What they would do is a member of the family
would go and stay with 'em.
Until they got better or passed on.

But this old woman,
nobody wanted to stay with her.
So finally Gramma told everybody,
    "I'll go stay with her. I'm not afraid of her."
And so they took her down there, this little girl.
Ten-, eleven-, twelve-, thirteen-year-old girl.
They took her down there to stay with this old woman who was
     dying.
Well as soon as they took her there,
the person who had been staying there before
come running out and said,
"Get me out of here! I want out of here now!"

And so they left and Gramma was there at the old woman's house,
  all by herself,
  just like that.

Gramma said she went into the house
and she started cleaning everything up, you know.
Cleaned the house.
She'd go in there and check on the old woman.
Now that old woman was lying in her bedroom on a bed.
And that house that she lived in was a real, little bitty old house.
It just had three rooms.
A bedroom, a living room, and a kitchen.
They had an outhouse, to go use the restroom.
Well, Gramma, you know, she didn't have much to do except to sit
    around.
So, when the evening came she fixed herself something to eat.
But she noticed that that old woman hardly ever moved.
And she said that evening when she went in to check on her,
  she couldn't even tell if the old woman was still alive or not.
She said she stood at the doorway really looking hard,
and finally she noticed that the old woman's chest was rising and
    falling,
telling Gramma that the old woman was still breathing.
And so she went on and ate and everything else.
And when it started really getting dark,
    Gramma lit this kerosene lamp
    and she put it in that old woman's bedroom,
    and turned the flame way down
    until there was just a soft glow in that old woman's bedroom.

Well Gramma went back into the living room and she started . . .
they had a little cot, a little bed there in the living room for
whoever staying there to sleep on.
Well Gramma started fixing that up
and while she was fixing it up she had this bright idea.
If she moved the cot up a little bit,
when she laid down all she would have to do is just
turn her head and she would be able to see
that old woman laying there in her bed in the next room.
And so, that's what Gramma did.

She pulled the cot up and finally when she got ready to go to bed,
she laid down and her idea worked.
All she had to do was just turn her head
and she could see that old woman laying in her bed
through the bedroom door.

Well Gramma said that she had a hard time going to sleep.
Because all those stories that they told
about this old woman started coming back to her.
About how she was a ravenmocker.
About how she was a mean medicine person.
How she could turn into a raven and a ball of fire.
A dog, a cat, or maybe even somebody you know.
    She could do all these things
    and she would come in and eat your heart and your liver.
And, you know, she could cast spells on people.
And so, all these stories started coming back to her.

Gramma said she didn't know how long she laid there.
But she finally went to sleep.
    But way, way late at night,
    something woke her.

She says she was laying there
    and she woke up.
    And the first thing that she noticed
    was she couldn't move.
    She couldn't move her legs.
    She couldn't move her arms.
    She couldn't even open her eyes.
    Most of all,
    she couldn't scream.
And she said she was laying there, and while she was laying there,
she started hearing somebody breathing
right next to her ear.
Huh-hunh. Huh-huhn.
And she could feel that breath
going over her neck.

Well, Gramma said that she did all she could
to try to move but she couldn't move at all.

She was trying to scream and she couldn't scream.
She was trying to open her eyes and she couldn't open her eyes.
Until finally, she remembered somebody telling her
that if she ever found herself in that way
where she couldn't move or scream or open her eyes,
all she'd have to do is just move something
like her pinky or toe or anything,
and she would be able to move after that.
And so she started concentrating,
she started thinking about just moving her pinky.
And while she was doing that,
she said she heard that breathing go from her ear
    up until it was right in front of her face.
And she said she knew somebody was looking at her,
real close, because she could still hear that breathing.
Huh-huhn. Huh-huhn.
    And it was going over her face.
    And she said that breath was *sour*.
    It was so sour it made her sick.
She knew somebody was right above her looking down at her.

Well, Gramma she kept trying to move her pinky
and she kept trying and trying until,
finally, she was able just to move it just a little bit.
And in that second, a scream came out of her mouth
and her eyes opened and there it was,
right above her looking down at her.
    It was that old woman's head.
And just like that, it flew back across the room.
And Gramma said out of the corner of her eye
she noticed while that head was above her,
she saw that old woman's neck stretched
all the way across the room on the floor
like a snake
and attached to her body in the next room.
And when her head flew back,
that neck snapped back like a rubber band.

Well, Gramma said she jumped up
and she was screaming and everything else.

She didn't know what to do.
She finally, finally calmed down enough to sit down.
And then she said she realized
    that she was gonna have to check
    on that old woman
    in the next room.
She said it took all the strength that she had in her heart
    to get up
    and walk
    over to the bedroom
    to check on that old woman.
Gramma said she stood at the door and looked at that old woman
in the glow of that lantern.

She said she couldn't see the rise and fall of that old woman's
        chest.
    So she got a little bit closer.
    She still couldn't see it.
    She got a little bit closer.
    She still couldn't see it.
    She got closer,
    and closer,
    and closer.
    Until she was standing
    right next to the bed.
And she said she couldn't see that woman breathing,
so she leaned over
    and listened
    for a heartbeat.
And Gramma said there was none.
    That old woman
    was dead.
And Gramma said,
    "Ahh!"

She said she ran out of there real quick,
but she knew she had nowhere to go.
So she had to stay in that old house
with that dead woman in the next room all night long.
And she said while she was in that house

something was crawling over the roof and knocking on the
    windows
and knocking on the doors and rattling the doorknobs, and
    everything else.
All night long that happened.
She said, as soon as the sun came up
she ran out of that house and she ran to the nearest neighbor's
who lived like a mile away.
And she told him, "Hey, I think the old woman's dead. Go get a
    doctor!"
And so they went out and got a doctor.
And they brought him in and that doctor checked on that old
    woman.
And he said, yes, the old woman was dead.
But then he said, but she didn't die of old age or whatever she was
    dying from.
    The doctor said that that old woman
    died
    of a broken neck.

Now back where I come from,
there's a small community
where every once in a while this story comes up
about how this woman
broke her neck
lying in bed.
Nobody knows what happened.
And Gramma said that she never told anybody what happened that
    night
until she told me.
    And now,
    I've told you.

THE OWL
Told by Sequoyah Guess

I'm gonna tell you another story that actually happened to me.
This one, well, it's not really scary
but it might be a little bit weird.
This happened not really all that long ago.

Maybe about ten years ago.
So, anyway.

I have this good friend, his name is Sam.
And, uh, he's a storyteller, too.
And a lot of times, not all the time but a lot of times,
he will have what he calls "storytelling night."
Out by his house.
What he'll do is he'll start a fire and everything else
and we'll have a campfire
and everybody will bring something to eat and everything else.
And, uh, sometimes we have the only rule is
you have to tell a story or say something in order to be able to eat.
And so, like I said, either on Fridays or Saturdays we'll do that.

Well, this one day he came up to me and he said,
"Hey, we're gonna have storytelling tonight. Come on over."
And I said, "Sure."
And he said, "It's gonna be right after work."
And so right after work at five o'clock I went over to his house.
He lived right outside of town.
And, uh, so I went over there and I was the first one there.
Well his wife and two daughters,
Dama and Tonya and Tiffany, they were still there.
And, uh, his wife, Sam's wife, said,
"Well you boys get the fire going.
Me and the girls are gonna go to the store
and get some chili and weenies and other things." And so they
        left.
And so me and Sam, we started gathering up firewood
and we got the fire going and everything else.
Well we were sitting there and we decided to go ahead and start.

Now, the sun had just gone down.
You know when the sun is gone but it's still light.
    It was about that time.

Well me and Sam, we were sitting on each side of the fire.
He was facing toward his house and I had my back to the house.
And, uh, he was telling me a story.
And, uh, I was listening and he finally finished and it was my turn

to tell him one. So I started telling him a story, and right in
  the middle of my story,
I noticed he wasn't looking at me anymore,
but he was looking past me.
And he said, "What is that?"
And I said, "What?"
And he said, "That up there."
He pointed behind me.

Now, behind his house there's a row of trees
that led to a small wooded area.
So I turned around and looked in the direction that he was
  pointing.
And way up there at the very top of the tree line,
there was one tree that I guess was dead because it didn't have no
  leaves on it. There were just bare branches sticking
way up further than the other trees that had leaves.
And right on top of that tree
there was a big owl sitting up there.
And, uh, that thing looked to be about
three feet tall.
It was huge.
And I said, "Looks like an owl."
And Sam said, "An owl! That big!"
And I said, "Yeah . . ."
But something registered in my mind about this owl.
I remembered Gramma telling me if you see an owl that big,
it might be a somebody.
And I noticed also, too, that it was sitting
on a limb that couldn't possibly hold it up
because that limb was probably about the size of my pinky.
But that owl was like three feet tall,
so it had to weigh something and that little limb couldn't hold that
  owl up.
And so, I remembered what Gramma said about it might not be a
  real owl,
but a somebody or a something.
And she said, if you see something like that, you ask it who it is.
And so I hollered up at it and said, "*Kanehe*?"

Which in our language is, "Who are you?"
And that owl looked down at us,
at me and Sam,
    and it shook its head.
    Like it didn't want to answer.

Well, you've heard of people's hair standing up when they get
        scared?
I know how that feels now.
Because the hair on the back of my neck stood up when it did
        that.
Well when it did that I remembered something else Gramma
        told me.
She said when you see something like that and you're kind of sure
that it's not a real thing but it might be a booger or a *sgili,*
which is a ghost or spirit, in our language,
if you're kind of sure that's what it is,
you take a piece of cloth and you tie it in a knot.
And she told me that tying that cloth in a knot
symbolizes that you're choking the thing.
And so I looked around and I was wearing a sweatshirt
that had a drawstring around the waist; I didn't have no sleeves.
So I had nothing on my person to tie into a knot.
But I looked over at Sam and he was wearing this huge t-shirt.
And so I told him, "Grab your shirttail, twist it and tie it in a knot."
And so he started doing that.
And so while he was doing that I was checking on the owl
to see if it was still there.
And I would look back to see how far Sam was on tying the knot.
And about the same time as Sam tightened the knot in his shirttail,
I looked up at the owl
and probably the same time that that knot tightened,
that owl jumped up from that tree
and shook all over like it had been shot or something.
And it took off real fast.
It just flew away real fast.

Well Sam and I, we sat there and just kind of looked at each other
        across the fire. And we were quiet for a long time.

After a while, we both said,
    "Cool."
We had a cool story to tell, now.
And it actually happened.
And so when the rest of the guys came later on that evening,
we told 'em about the owl that we had seen and what happened.
And, unfortunately, that's not the end of the story.

Exactly a week later, and almost to the same hour
when we saw that owl,
a good friend of ours got killed in a car wreck.
Now, among Keetoowahs and Cherokees,
and probably other tribes,
    the owl is a messenger.
And usually, the message that it has
is that there is going to be a death.
Not all the time,
    but usually.
Now, it's lessons like those and teachings like those
that still stay with us who we think are modern Indians.
But we still hold our traditions, our customs, and our teachings,
close to our hearts.

THE OWL AT THE WINDOW

By Hastings Shade

Not too long ago, about the time they started to build new Indian homes, there was a family that qualified for a new home. The new home was to be built about a half a mile from their old house. Once the new home was completed and the family had moved in, the two boys of the family would sometimes go back to the old homeplace to stay all night.

One night they had planned to spend the night at the old place and invited their cousin to go with them. They had bought some bread and wieners so they could snack that night. But as they were walking toward the old place that evening they had to pass by their uncle's place. As they walked by he told them, "I wouldn't go there tonight if I were you boys. It's not a good night to be there." The kids listened to him but went on anyway.

As it began to get dark they had brought a radio and they turned it on and the oldest boy had brought a .22 rifle and five shells with him. As it got darker, they heard an owl outside. Their father had put hail screens on the window because it was stronger than regular screen wire and the squares in it were bigger but not big enough to let flies in. The owl got closer to the house and got louder. The boys turned up the radio.

Soon the owl was right outside the window and they could hear it over the radio even though the radio was turned up as loud as it would go. Finally, one of the boys said, "I'm going to run it off." So he went out but once he got outside he found he couldn't run the night bird off. He went back in the old house and told the older boy he couldn't run the owl off.

"I'll go out there and shoot it," the older boy said. He picked up the gun and walked out. As he was stepping out the door he loaded the rifle with a shell. When he got out there, the owl was sitting on one of the low limbs of the tree that stood in the yard. He took aim and pulled the trigger but the firing pin only made a snapping sound. The oldest boy thought the .22 bullet was no good so he took out another shell and loaded the rifle again. It did the same thing. He tried all five shells and they all wouldn't fire so he felt around on the ground and found a piece of wood lying near his feet. He picked it up and threw it at the owl. With that, the owl finally flew off. The boy walked back into the old house and told the other two boys, "Well, I ran him off."

Just about that time they heard something hit the screen and they looked and saw talons hanging on the screen. One of the boys grabbed something and threw it at the window. When the object bounced off the screen the owl flew off. The boys turned and started to get ready to lay down. Suddenly, they heard the noise at the window once again and when they looked they saw fingers sticking through the screen where the talons were before.

They ran out of the house, leaving everything there. As they were running back home they had to pass by their uncle's house and he was sitting on his porch, laughing at them as they ran by.

The next day, about noon time, the boys gathered up their courage and went back after their stuff. When the oldest one picked up his .22 rifle, he said he was going to try the shells again. When he did, they all went off as he tried each one. They all stared at each other as one of the boys asked if any of the other two had noticed something strange about one of the fingers that had been sticking through the screen the night before.

"One of the fingers was half gone," one of them said, and they remembered one of the fingers on their uncle's hand had been cut off. Half of it was missing!

Did their uncle try to scare them? Who knows. But they never went back to stay all night again.

CHEROKEES AND THE OWL
By Hastings Shade

Many people are afraid of owls. Some claim they bring bad luck, others say they bring death. But you have to remember an owl is only a bird, except . . .

This story is about a Cherokee family and an owl. The Cherokee family lived in a log cabin that others in the family had helped them build. The father of the family had been ill for a while. Some days he would feel better, other days worse. His oldest daughter, Anawegi, helped her mother take care of her younger brothers and sisters. Being the oldest, her father had taught her how to hunt. When he started getting sick she done the hunting to help feed the family.

On the days her father felt worse, she had noticed that an owl had been close to their house on those nights. She mentioned this to her mother. She had heard the elders say that the *aniskili*, the ones that could turn themselves into other things, would come around and bother the ones that were sick and weak. Her mother said, "We will just have to watch and make sure we run it off."

When the Owl would come around, Anawegi would try to run it off. Sometimes it would leave, other times it would fly a short ways and hoot again. It done this for a while.

One evening, Anawegi was fixing supper and made some soup for her father. Her mother went into the bedroom where her father was laying and told him, "Sit up. Anawegi has made you some soup." As Anawegi walked into the bedroom with the soup, her father began to sit up. And as he sat up he looked towards the window and said, "*Ni!*" "Look!" Anawegi looked towards the window and saw an owl sitting in the window. She looked for something to throw at the Owl and it flew into the bedroom and circled the bed where her father was. As it done this, her father grabbed his chest and slumped over, and the Owl flew out the window. Anawegi noticed as the Owl flew by her it had two light-colored stripes on its head. When she turned back to look at her father she heard her mother say, "He's dead." And her mother started to cry.

Four days later they buried her father near the house, which was the custom back in the old days.

As time went on, the memories of her father got easier for Anawegi. Now her and her mother and her younger brothers and sisters faced hard times. Anawegi was the hunter again and even rabbits were hard to find. Each day she had to go farther and farther into the woods to hunt and she stayed out longer and longer. Sometimes it would be dark when she got back. Her mother got on to her: "It's not good to stay out too long at night. The Owl might get you." She remembered the Owl that was there the night her father died, the one with the two stripes on its head. She thought, "I wish I could get my hands on that Owl."

The Owl in the form of a bird watched her as she hunted in the woods. While in this form he could communicate with the other birds and animals. He said to the possum, "She is pretty." The possum didn't answer; he just hung there by his tail as possums do. But as the Owl turned his head the possum seen the two stripes on his head. The Owl said, "I have to have her."

The Owl at one time was human, but something that he was working with didn't turn out right. He had hurt himself and had turned into an owl.

One evening as the two women were gathering wood for the night, a young man walked into the yard. "*Osiyo tohitsu? Adawosgi dawadoa.*" "Hello, how are you? My name is Swimmer." In his hand he had a bow and some arrows. There was something strange about the bow and arrows, something the girl had not seen before. They had the flint points and feathers, and she thought, "Maybe it's the feathers." He had a piece of cloth wrapped around his head.

The girl and her mother both answered almost at the same time. "*Siyo.*" "Hello."

The girl asked, "*Tsalisdayvnvtsv?*" "Have you eaten?"

The young man answered "*Tla.*" "No."

The girl said, "All we have is soup. You are welcome to it, but there is hardly any meat in it. I haven't killed anything in two days."

The young man said, "If you don't mind, I'll bring you something in the morning."

Before the girl could answer, her mother said, "*Vv.*" "Okay."

The young man turned and started down the path, and the women started to pick up wood again. They both stood up and looked down the path, but the young man was gone. "Where did he go?" asked the mother, "We should still be able to see him."

Early the next morning just before daylight, there was a knock on the door. When the mother answered the door there stood the young man with two rabbits. "These were all I could get," he said. "I'll get more next time."

The mother said, "This is plenty. *Wado.* Thank you. Stay and eat with us."

He answered, "Maybe next time," and he left. The young girl cleaned the rabbits and they had a good meal, the first one in quite a while.

That evening the young man was back again. "I'll bring you something else tomorrow," he said and left.

Just before daylight the next morning he was back. This time he had a turkey. He done this for some time and the girl didn't have to hunt anymore.

One day the girl told her mother, "He's good looking." The mother said, "A good hunter, too." She said, "I was wondering . . . does he hunt at night?" The girl said, "No one hunts at night. He probably kills it during the day and brings it over early the next morning."

One evening he came over and this time he sat down, "*Dagia-wega.* I'm tired," he said.

The mother said, "Why don't you stay all night?" We have a pallet we could lay on the floor. You could sleep there.

"That's alright," said the young man. "I'll sleep outside. I'm used to it."

They all went to bed. Sometime during the night, the young girl thought she heard something. She got up and looked out the window. The young man was gone. Off in the distance she heard an owl, and it seemed like she had heard this one before.

The next morning they looked for him and he was gone. That evening he was back. "I had to leave last night and I didn't want to wake anyone," he said.

As time went on, he became bolder and bolder and the young girl began to like him more and more. When he wasn't at the house he would sit in the trees around the house and watch the young girl. He had told the possum before he wanted her. He began to hunt bigger animals. He killed a very big deer and hung it up to cure so he could take the young girl and her family some meat.

One evening when he brought the family something to eat, he asked the girl's mother if he could marry her. If the girl had an uncle he would have asked the uncle and the uncle would have asked the mother. Her not having an uncle, he asked the mother, which is the custom.

There is no elaborate wedding ceremony; a gift of venison from the man to the girl's parents or parent, a gift of ears of corn to the man from the girl, and the wedding is complete. The gift of venison means that the man would provide the girl all the things that she needs and the gift of corn means the girl will take care of the man and raise their children.

So the marriage was set, the exchange of gifts made, and the ceremony was complete. The only thing he didn't tell the girl was who or what he was.

One night as he came into the house, the cloth that he always wore on his head got hung on a piece of wood and came off. When it did, it revealed the two stripes on his head. The girl knew who he was. She rushed towards him to hit him, and one of the arrows that he always carried with him pierced her stomach. As she fell back she said, "You killed my father!" He said, "No, I was only the messenger sent to tell you it was your father's time to die." She said, "I'm glad it wasn't you that killed him."

As she was dying she began to turn into an owl. The arrows the young man carried with him were given to him by a medicine man. He was told to be very careful with them, but he wasn't. He had cut himself with one of them also. This was how he had become Owl.

Sometimes we don't do as we are told. Sometimes we are not careful with things that we have been given to take care of.

So at night, sometimes you will hear more than one owl. Don't be afraid. They are only the messengers trying to tell us something. We have to learn how to listen to nature again like our elders did.

The young man or Owl did get the girl. From that day on he has never changed into a human form again.

Talking to the Elements

The Liars' Club and I talked often about traditional notions of the relationships between humans, animals, plants, and the elements. The Cherokee worldview holds that the universe is alive. And you can communicate with anything that is living. All you need to do is talk to it and listen to its response. The response may not be in your language, but if you listen hard enough you may come to understand its meaning.

"I've heard stories of how you can talk to a tornado?" I said.

"It's alive. It's a living thing, you know," Hastings said. "So, anything alive you can talk to. Just like our plants, whenever we go get medicine, we don't just go get it and use it. We talk to it and tell it what it's for. Because if you don't then it's no good."

"My dad did that one time," Woody said. "It was a wall of clouds coming in. You could see the swirling. Didn't see so much the front of it but it was going to happen any minute now. He got his axe, said a few things, and chopped it right there on the wooden block. Split it."

"We were playing music one night over at Roy's. There was a storm line, I mean, from the state of Kansas almost down to Texas. Roy's wife was non-Indian, and she was running around saying, 'What are we going to do?! What are we going to do?!' And we were sitting there playing and I told Roy, 'Don't worry about it.' And pretty soon it got to Wagoner and just come apart." Hastings laughed.

"I did it one time," Woody offered. "I didn't know what dad was saying but I just said a prayer and did the same thing he did and it worked. And I had a cousin of mine and his friends with me. They couldn't believe it!"

"Do you point it at the direction you want to split it?" I asked.

"Uh-hunh. A turtle shell, terrapin's shell. A lot of our Native people put a turtle shell facing southwest," Hastings said.

"What does that do?" I asked.

"It separates it. Slows it down. It will rain; we want it to rain. We don't want the violent part of it. We want the soothing part of it. There are so many variations of stories you can talk about as far as the weather. Even the fire that's racing out in California. A long time ago they used to talk to the fire and tell it how to burn. Anymore, the fire is mad because it doesn't have anybody to talk to. It's mad and it will burn anything in its way. A long time ago they used to set a fire and it would crawl. It didn't leap. It just *crawl*. It was a gentle fire. This is a mad fire that they're dealing with. The fire was gentle back then. But now it's mad. It's not a gentle fire anymore; it's a vengeful fire for what's happening."

"And they try to suppress it for so long," I said.

"Yeah," said Hastings. "You got to let fire do its thing every now and then. Even way back in our culture if we didn't burn certain areas we didn't have food. Like the piñon."

"They say that the early European explorers, whenever they would come to an Indian community, there was always smoke from fires. Fires were a constant," I said.

"Yeah. You see, when Europeans first see us dancing around fire they thought we was worshipping Satan because that's their concept. To us, the fire is a direct gift from the Creator. There was no meanness about it. As far as I know, none of our tribes thought that when they die they were going to be tormented in Hell for eternity. Ours, an elder would say, 'When I leave this earth here I'll go to a better place where I can rest.' They weren't going to be tormented for the rest of their lives. They were going to go rest. There's an old saying that 'When my mother earth holds me again then I'm going to rest again.' A long time ago we wrapped our dead in blankets and skins and put them into Mother Earth and Mother Earth did hold them. Anymore . . ." Hastings said.

"'Into the bosom of Mother Earth,' I was told," Woody said. "'Into the bosom of Mother again.' As we were born we were wrapped in clothing in mother's bosom and as we die we're wrapped. That's what I was told."

"Anymore, though, we put them in a box and there's a rock around it," Hastings said. "We don't feel Mother Earth. But a long time ago we'd dig a hole and Mother Earth would wrap us and hold us again. But that concept is gone. And again, it was the disease the Europeans brought us. It was the smallpox and all that they didn't want in the ground because they said it would stay for a long time before Mother Earth absorbed it. Anymore now they put us in a box and embalm us . . ."

"'Preserved,'" I said and laughed. "And people are scared of that, I think. I hear a lot of people want to be cremated."

"Because of that," Woody agreed. "I want to be cremated and scattered on the water."

"I want to be back in Mother Earth again," Hastings said. "See, I can actually be buried right in this yard. Again, I have to get permission from the state."

"I'd like to be taken back to the Smokies and put straight into the ground. But it's against the law," I said.

"Yeah, it's against the law. You got to have that box and rock around you," Hastings said. After a moment, he continued, "You know, Indian tradition or Indian beliefs is totally different from the world's. Any Native person is different. We consider. Even in Iraq, lots of our Indian boys say the Iraqis took us in. They said you were one of us, and they went by the color."

CONTROLLING THE ELEMENTS
Told by Hastings Shade

One time my aunt and her husband were visiting us. Back then, when someone would visit they would stay several days. Dad and I had to get some wood and my aunt's husband went with us. My aunt's husband's name in Cherokee was Dinilewisda, meaning "Stop."

Back then we only had a wagon and team of horses. We were getting some dead wood for the cookstove and it began to cloud up. We could see it lightning off in the distance. Dad said we better hurry or we were going to get wet. By then, the clouds were right over us and it was lightning.

As we got into the wagon to leave, the old man said, "There's nothing to be afraid of. The lightning won't hurt you." Dad said, "Up here on this hill lightning strikes pretty often." The old man just laughed.

As we started off the hill I looked at the old man and he was saying something, mumbling something, and about that time I seen him point his finger at a tree and at that moment a lightning bolt came and struck the tree he had pointed at and it wasn't very far from where we were coming off the hill. The horses kind of spooked and Dad had to hang on to the reins.

I watched him do this again and the same thing happened. He would point at a tree and the lightning would strike. He done this several times as we came of off the hill. Soon I began to notice a black ring around his mouth and eyes and I also noticed that the lightning strikes were getting closer and closer to us. I was really glad to see the house. As we went in the house, the lightning struck close to the house and my aunt really got on to him for putting us in danger. She told him you are only supposed to do that when you are by yourself. She said the lightning almost got the best of him for showing off.

THE HORSE THAT WOULDN'T LEAVE THE BARN

By Hastings Shade

We had an old mare that we called Usdi, which means "little" or "tiny," that was so gentle everyone wanted to ride her, but you could only ride her during the day. You tried to ride her at night she wouldn't leave the barn, I don't care how much you prodded her.

Half of her tail was gone, so every chance we got during the summer when she was around the barn we would go out there and swat the horse flies off of her. Her tail was so short she couldn't shoo them away. One day we asked Grandma why Usdi had such a short tail. She told us this story.

Our uncle got Usdi when she was just a colt, that was why he gave her that name. He raised her, and when she got old enough, broke her to ride.

When our uncle was young he used to go everywhere, and after he broke Usdi to ride, he rode her everywhere he went. Back then they used to have pie suppers and dances at peoples' homes around here.

One evening he said he was going to a dance across the creek which we called the Hinton Community. If you went around the road it was about three miles, if you went straight through the woods, as we used to say, it was less than two miles. So it was a lot shorter distance.

As he was getting ready to leave, our Great Grandpa told him, "Maybe you shouldn't go anywhere tonight. It is not a good time to be out." Our uncle went anyway.

When the dance was over about midnight, he started back home. Instead of going around the road the long way, he decided to take the shortcut through the woods.

Along this way was an old wagon road. People used it sometimes during the day. It was real rough. Very few used it at night for the reason some had said something would get in the wagon or on your horse and by the time you got through there your horses would give out.

As our uncle was riding along he heard something running through the woods. It sounded real heavy. It passed him and his horse and sounded like it stopped on the road in front of them. His horse stopped and wouldn't move. His horse wouldn't go any farther as he tried to make her move.

Soon, whatever it was started towards them. Still he couldn't see anything. He knew it was coming by the way his horse was acting. The horse moved to one side of the road as if to let it by. Our uncle sensed the horse wanted to run, so he grabbed the saddle horn. As he did this whatever it was started towards the horse. The horse jumped forwards almost throwing our uncle off. As he struggled to get back into the saddle, he sensed something on the horse in back of him. The horse jumped again, this time our uncle was ready. Whatever was on the horse slipped off.

Whatever was back there was holding onto the horse. The horse could hardly move, like something was holding it back. Soon it felt like whatever it was let go and the horse took off real fast like she couldn't wait to get away from there.

The horse ran all the way to the barn. When she stopped, our uncle jerked the saddle and bridle off and she went into the barn. When he walked into the house our Great Grandpa was still up. All he said was, "It was not a good night to be out."

The next day our uncle went out to feed the horses and he noticed that half of Usdi's tail was gone. When he looked closer it looked like it was already healed up, no sign of blood anywhere.

From that day on you couldn't get Usdi to leave the barn at night. During the day she would go anywhere, but when it started getting late she wanted to get back to the barn. When she got ready to go you had better be on her or she left without you!

Two or three days later they went back to the old road to see if they could find anything. They never found nothing. Usdi wouldn't go down that road even during the day.

You can still see a faint sign of the old road to this day. I often wonder if something is still there, waiting for a ride.

CHANGELINGS: THE SMALL DOG
By Hastings Shade

The elders told stories like this about how some of the old ones could change into different things. There are many stories like this one, but many people do not believe you when you tell them something like this. Is it because they grew up not hearing things like this or is it because they don't want to hear things like this? I wonder. But I was always told it is not good to let just anything get close to your family.

One time there was a family that lived near an elder I knew. There was three or four children ages six to twelve years old that lived there. One day, this small dog came around late one evening and started playing with the children out in the yard and their father ask them, "Where did you all get the dog?" The children said, "We don't know where it came from. It just showed up and started playing with us. Can we keep it?" Their father said, "We have to find out if anyone owns it first. If it belongs to someone we have to take it back. We will see, if it's still here in the morning."

The next morning the dog was gone, but it came back that evening just before dark. It done this a couple more times and they began to ask their neighbors if anyone had a small dog. No one had even seen one around there. So the father said, "If it will stay you can keep it." It made the children feel good. But every morning it would be gone, only to return in the evening. This went on for a couple weeks and one evening the dog started to chase the chickens around the yard. The father said, "If it's going to do that then the dog will have to go."

The children didn't want to see the dog go so they would get on to it whenever it started to chase the chickens. Whenever they got on to it the dog would act like it was crying, and this bothered the father. So he tried to catch the dog, but it wouldn't let him get close to it. He got one of the children to catch it and put a rope around its neck and he took the dog into the house. The dog started to gnaw on the rope. The father didn't want to let the dog get away, so he went outside and got some bailing wire and put this around the dog's neck and tied it to the bed. And they all laid down and went to sleep.

Just before daylight the dog started barking and howling and the father woke up. As he went to check on the dog, the dog spoke to him. It said, "Turn me loose before it gets daylight." The father had heard about how some people could change into different things and he wouldn't turn it loose. He wanted to find out what it was.

When it got daylight there was an old lady sitting there, one of their neighbors. He never said a word to her when he turned her loose. He just knew who she was.

Seven days later the old lady died. They say if you recognize whoever it is that changes into something, they will die within seven days.

One of the elders also told him that she was trying to get one of the children. These kinds of people usually pick the weakest one. They usually know which it is. This is how they prolong their lives by living off of the young.

DOCTORED DOGS

By Hastings Shade

This is a story about my grandpa's mom and dad, my great grandma and great grandpa. This happened in the 1870s and was told to me by my grandpa. Back then many families relied on their dogs for food and protection so they took good care of them.

Great Grandpa had a pair of mixed-breed hounds and they were good-size dogs who were able to take care of themselves. He had had them doctored. They would doctor the dogs by taking the small wing bone from a Great Horned Owl. This bone is located on the second joint of the wing, or at the elbow. The bone sticks out and is about a half inch long. They would take this bone from the left wing of the owl and make a small slit in the dog's left shoulder and insert the bone in this slit and sew it back up. After the dog was doctored like this nothing could get away from the dog if he ever caught it. I mean nothing, real or unreal, natural or supernatural.

After they had the dogs doctored, they would keep them tied up during the daytime and they would turn them loose at night if they felt they had a need to untie them. When you do dogs like this they get real mean. And back then the neighbors were sometimes at least a mile apart or farther, and you never knew when someone would come to visit. It wasn't good to leave them untied.

One evening as they sat down for supper they heard this woman crying outside the living room window and they got up to see what had happened. They thought someone had died or had an accident. As they stepped outside, the crying was farther down the trail around the bend in the trail, so they went back into the house and got ready to finish their supper. Just as they sat down they heard the crying again outside the window and Grandpa said, "This woman better be there this time." Again when they got outside the crying was down the trail again and Grandpa got ready to turn the dogs loose. They were already barking and trying to get loose.

Grandma said, "Maybe we are making a mistake; we can't hear good anyway. Maybe that's where she has been crying all this time and we think it's right outside the house." Grandpa said, "Well I'll let her go this time and I'll go see if I can find her and see what's wrong." He went back inside the house and got his hat and jacket and went down the trail. The crying had stopped. When he got to where he thought she should be he didn't find anything. And he went back to the house. When he got back to the house he said, "Maybe she got alright. I didn't find her or anything. Or I didn't go far enough down the trail. Anyway, I didn't hear or see anything. Maybe we will hear something."

They finished their supper and went on to bed and nothing else happened that night and they didn't hear anything the next day about anything happening to anyone.

The next evening as they sat down to eat supper again they heard the woman crying outside the window again. When Grandpa got up, he said, "Well let's find out who it is." He went straight to where the dogs were tied up and turned the dogs loose. By then the woman was crying down the trail again and the dogs took off down the trail and caught whoever that was. They could hear her hollering and screaming as the dogs got hold of her. Pretty soon she quit hollering and the dogs came back. He left the dogs loose the rest of the night, just in case it came back again.

The next day about noon one of their neighbors came by and told them they had found the old lady that lived about two miles from them at her house in real bad shape. She looked like she had been bitten by some dogs. Four days later she died. Great Grandpa never said anything about what had happened. The only thing he said was, "It's not good to mess around someone's house, not unless you really need something. If you mess around someone's house looking for trouble or trying to cause trouble, you might just find it."

Mooney's Swimmer Manuscript

"You get into that Swimmer manuscript, that Swimmer manuscript isn't *complete*," Hastings said. We were discussing ethnologist James Mooney's *Swimmer Manuscript: Cherokee Sacred Formulas and Medicinal Pre-*

scriptions (1932). "I mean, it's a medicine book," Hastings continued, "but nobody ever writes their complete manuscripts down. What they do is write bits and pieces so that they can remember."

"It could never be complete," I said. "I mean, you couldn't make a book big enough to contain Cherokee medicine."

"No. The scary thing about the formulas is, if they're true you got to watch it," Hastings continued.

"Mmhm," Sequoyah said. We had discussed how one needs to speak fluent Cherokee for the medicine formulas to work.

"That's the scary part. I mean, there's things in that book that even I wouldn't read. I look at it, part of it, and I'll just put it back. I got two books still in wrappers at the house," Hastings said and laughed. "The big Mooney book. Somebody said, 'Here's a book.' And out of respect I said, 'Okay.' 'Cause I hate to say, 'Well I got two or three.' 'Cause I can always give it to somebody who would want to read it. I got one. There's certain things I like to look at. Some of the stories. But I heard these stories before I ever knew who Mooney was. That's the thing about it, you know. Somebody said, 'You get this from Mooney?' I said, 'I didn't even know who Mooney was.'"

"And the funny thing about it, when you read the stories in Mooney, there's always something different in his book than the way, like, my gramma taught me," Sequoyah said. "And I think, 'Well that's where they changed it at, 'cause I didn't hear it that way.' Or, maybe in the end the other person won, but in my story the other . . . Well, case in point . . . I'm not sure, but I think, is the Fox and Crawdad racing in the Mooney book?"

"Mmhm," Hastings said.

"In there, does the Fox eat the Crawdad?" Sequoyah asked. "In my version the Fox eats the Crawdad, but I remember reading one where he didn't eat the Crawdad. In the version that Gramma told me the Fox ate the Crawdad. But there's a lot of stories that end different than what I've heard in the Mooney book, and that gave me the belief, 'These Cherokees that told him these stories, they messed them up for him.' But, just like Hastings always said, and I believe it, I'd rather believe what my elders tell me than something I read in a book."

"Mmhm," Hastings said.

"'Cause the stuff that you read in the book, it's not going to be all right, because, even today, even when we do our presentations, we don't give the *whole* truth," Sequoyah said. "Even when they ask about the medicine and beliefs and stuff like that, we'll tell 'em just so much. But we won't give 'em the whole thing. 'Cause there are going to be people out there that's going to try to make money off it."

"We can't. I mean, culturally, we're bound to share only so much," Hastings said.

Constellations

In considering the Cherokee spirit world, I thought it would be important to include contemporary examples of some of the stories that Mooney recorded on the Qualla Boundary when he visited there in 1886. So, as we sat in the chapel one afternoon, I asked Hastings about the story of Kanati, the First Man, and Selu, or Corn Woman.

"So, Kanati . . . there's no translation for it anymore? But Selu . . . ," I said.

"Yeah, Selu. That is corn, but that Kanati . . . to me, *kanadi*, that's as close as you can get to it. The Lucky One. Or the Smart One, if you want to take it a different step further. *Kanad*, you know," Hastings said.

"The 'd' instead of the 't' in the syllabary," Woody added.

"But it's often translated as 'First Hunter,'" I said.

"The First Hunter?" Hastings asked me.

"Yeah, that's what it seems to be translated as," I said. "But that's different, it doesn't mean hunter."

"A *kanadi* means a . . . smart. It could be a hunter. It could be a Smart Hunter. But it also means 'lucky,'" Hastings said.

"'Lucky Hunter,' maybe?" I asked.

"Lucky at whatever," Hastings corrected me.

"Just lucky!"

"Well I guess if you look at it in terms of how it was in the 1700s maybe," Woody said. "When you have your man go out and come back and bring a bunch of game, somebody would say, probably, in essence . . ."

"Yeah. *Kanadi*," Hastings said.

"He's lucky. Or, 'Man, he's smart! He knows where to go or how to hunt,'" said Woody.

"Or a good hunter, a *kanad*," Hastings said.

"Hunter's probably a given," I said. "You probably wouldn't have to repeat that, right?"

"So," Woody said. "You know, just like, from what I'm learning in class in theology is, the new King James version is totally . . . not totally, but there's a lot of difference from the original Hebrew and Aramaic languages, as it's been translated through the years. The meanings of, like, our Cherokee words has changed to a point where, like what we're talking about right now. The King James Bible has been, what, translated eight times? To make it get to where it's going . . . So I got to thinking, like, 'Wow, our Cherokee Bible's probably really kind of further removed from the original intent and words.' So, that's a project I want to get into later. Or as soon as I can. I've got to learn Greek and Hebrew first."

"Good luck," Hastings said.

"That's what everybody says: 'Good luck.'"

"Had hard enough time learning English," Hastings said and laughed.

"I can hardly read Cherokee yet," Woody said. "How am I gonna do Greek? But, you know, it's prayer. It's something that God says, 'You ought to check it out.'" He laughed.

"Are there Cherokee stories about the stars? About the constellations?" I asked after a moment.

"Yeah, like the Bear," Hastings said. "Like the Bear constellation. That's where that word *jogo* comes from. That's where they talk about the story of the boys. One of 'em, all he liked to do was dance. Not regular dance, but a stomp dance. Every time he walked out that's all he did was dance. Then you don't tell him, he'd quit on you. And soon as he got a chance he'd start dancing again. Pretty soon he had a circle with him, you know, dancing. And they kept saying, 'You know, you need to quit. You don't do that all the time, just at certain times.' But every chance he got he would start dancing. And *jogon* the clan itself. So one day, there was several of 'em dancing and they went out there and they got on to him. But they just kept dancing. Kept saying, 'No, you all quit.' Pretty soon they looked, and they began to rise. Just went on up and became Ursa, the Bear constellation. Nadiwidi-losd, they say . . . There's no English translation of Ani Jogon. There's no English word for that. So I don't know what it is. But that's what they were called. Just like the Ani Giskin. They talked about this last joint, where your skull sits on your backbone. The last joint there's a ball, I guess, if you've ever seen a skull. But that's that joint, Ani Giskin. The Nape of the Neck Clan. But any time you have a illness, that's what the elders first doctored. 'Cause that's where most of your ailments come from. That's their connecting point to everything else. Like strokes, that's where it starts," Hastings continued. "And that's gone, that Nape of the Neck Clan's gone."

"So were they the ones that doctored the nape of the neck?" I asked.

"Yeah, they were the ones that knew that. There are some that still know it, but that clan is gone."

"Mm."

"Uh, the other clan that's gone is the Nuyuksuht. The Rattlesnake Clan. See, we know what those are. But that Ani Jogon, there's no know English word for them. 'Cause we don't know . . . we could sit here all day long and not figure out what . . .'Cause I've tried!" Hastings said.

"It just almost sounds like . . . because I'm studying theology, the Enoch, he went on up, he didn't die," Woody said.

"Yeah."

"It just almost kind of reminded me of that. That he was taken up, you know, and he's up there in the heavens. With the Creator."

"There's only two that mentions Enoch and . . . who's the other one?" Hastings asked.

"Elijah," said Woody.

"Elijah."

"In my studies, when I'm thinking and reading about Old Testament, I just see a lot of things Native. Cherokee, in particular. I just feel a connection between the Old Testament and us," Woody said and laughed.

"Where you going to school at?" Hastings asked.

"OBU. Oklahoma Baptist University," Woody answered.

"OBU?"

"In Miami. Just started last spring. So. But it's just like, boy, there's definitely a connection here. And like you said the nape of the neck, it just almost to me feels like they're not here, but they're going to come back."

"Yeah," Hastings said.

"They're kind of angelic," Woody said.

"Yeah."

"God's people. They left us for a reason."

"Yeah."

"Because I think because of our, how men and how our people are, the healing has left, but his mercy, there's still a few who can do that," Woody said.

"Yeah. Yeah, because, you know, it says 'I'll leave you comfort,'" Hastings said.

"Mmhm," Woody said and nodded. "Even the Exodus from Moses is like us leaving the old country."

"Yeah. So there's a lot of parallels in the Bible," Hastings agreed.

"For a European term, 'Native Americans' were heathen and godless; they were totally wrong," Woody said and laughed.

"Well, those are tribal peoples in the Bible," I added.

"Yeah. You know they call us 'savages,'" Hastings said. "That term's always been used for Indians. 'Indian savages,' you know? But, it's a known fact that some of our U.S. presidents, senators, you know, they paid a bounty for scalps. The younger the scalp the more money was paid. So who's a savage?"

Monsters

Hastings, Woody, Sequoyah, and I were in the chapel at the Cherokee Heritage Center talking about a Cherokee conception of monsters. I had always understood a monster to be an abomination—an awful mix of things that shouldn't be mixed. Frankenstein was a monster because he was a patchwork of dead human body parts brought back to life. The Minotaur was a monster because he was part human and part bull. In each case, the unification of things that should not be mixed had a bad result. We began speaking about monsters because monsters are a central part of Cherokee mythology.

"But, you know, the monsters like Spearfinger and Stonecoat and even Uk'tan and all those," Sequoyah said. "These are *real things*. I mean, the people that don't have Native blood, they think, 'Well, those are neat stories. Neat characters. But they could never be . . .' But those are *real* things; they *do* exist. They did exist. And, nowadays, they have other names for 'em."

"Cancer. Murder. Rape. You know?" Woody said.

"Yeah," Sequoyah looked at Woody and nodded.

"Like to me, the stories of old, to me transcends into cancer, murder, thievery . . . greediness. Alcoholism. Drug abuse," Woody said.

"Mmhm," Hastings said. "Well, to give you an example, they talk about the great falcon. Tlanuwa. The big one. And Siniqua is the Pteradactyl. They were big enough to carry kids off. The falcon was not killed. The old people said, 'It's going to come back one of these days.' But they didn't say what form it was gonna come back in."

"I think that's something that maybe we need to make clear in this book is that things transform," I said.

"Yeah," Hastings said. "'One of these days it's going to come back.' But it doesn't say it's going to be in that form. 'Cause we would have recognized it right now if it come back in that form. 'Cause if it's big enough to carry off a child it's gotta be pretty good size. But, we have little things that can carry off a child, too. Not literally pick it up, but it can take it away from us real quick. Our drugs. The alcohol."

"Promiscuity among teenagers," Woody added.

"So, the stories talk about real things, like that are actual things, but then they're also symbolic of other things?" I asked.

"Yeah. Yeah," Hastings said.

"Like some of the dreams I received, in my life," Woody said. "There's a lot of symbolism in my dreams that's come to pass. But it's up to me to recognize it or not, you know?"

"See these are things we deal with when we go to schools, when we're teaching, like even telling stories, you know?" After a moment, Hastings continued. "We have to . . . kind of include, not directly, but kind of watch for things. Just like the story of the rattlesnake and the boy. The rattlesnake said, 'No I won't bite you.' But the boy recognized him as a snake. 'Yeah, but you're a snake.' 'No, I won't bite you. Just take me down there and turn me loose and I'll be alright.' Begged him to take him off this mountain, but when he got down there and put him down he bit him. The boy threw him down. 'You said you wouldn't bite me.' Said, 'Yeah, but you also knew I was a snake when you picked me up.'"

"Mmhm," Woody said. "Which could be drugs or alcohol."

"Yeah."

"And that's a story I include when I do my snake presentation," Woody continued. "'You wouldn't stick your arm in this aquarium full of poisonous snakes, would you?' 'Oh no!' 'Then why would you drink alcohol? Or do drugs? You're doing the same thing with your whole body!' Parallelism."

"Right," I said.

"See, whenever we go to a school this is part of our teachings. 'Cause they have to *hear* it. We have to kind of describe it to 'em in such a way that they don't want to *try* it. 'Cause a lot of 'em are *daring*. Kids are *daring* anymore; well, we was, too," Hastings said and laughed.

"Yeah. They're more bold," said Woody.

"Yeah. They're bold. So we kind of teach it like, just like Wood said, 'You wouldn't want to put your hand where all these snakes are.' 'No!' 'Well why would you want to take this pill? You don't know what it's going to do to you. Or drink this alcohol.' So our teaching, it covers all that."

Utluga (Spearfinger)

As I listened to the Liars' Club talk about monsters, my thoughts went to Stonecoat and Spearfinger, whom I'd read about in Mooney. Stonecoat was supposed to be covered in skin like stone. It was impervious to attack with conventional weapons and could only be killed with fire. Spearfinger was known by her awl-like finger she used to tear out the livers and hearts of hunters she would relentlessly track down by their scent. But, like all things in the Cherokee world, these monsters had a side to them that was beneficial to the people. Spearfinger was finally captured, and as she burned in a fire she sang medicine songs that the people learned and used. We still have these songs today.

Hastings, Sequoyah, Woody, and I gathered and talked about these monsters, old and new.

"That Spearfinger, the lady that we talked about," Hastings said. "To use a modern word, 'witch,' you know. Back then, I guess you would call her like a conjurer. She was a mean one. And that's the one that went around and she would use that spearfinger to get into your liver. And the heart. And they knew this, you know. They was wanting to get rid of her. 'Cause she was the only one that knew these things. She's the only one that had that learning. They wanted to get rid of her so they went to a medicine man. He said, 'Take seven women that are on their monthly cycle. And as she comes by, they would weaken her.' Time she got to the seventh they bound her and threw her into a pit that was fire. And how we learned these things is, as she was dying, she was saying these chants. And I don't know whether that was a good thing or not, because she threw everything out and we learned. I don't know whether it would have been best just to let her die with it or what, you know? So that's Spearfinger. That was her that would go around to the sick people and use that finger to dig into their livers and their hearts and stuff. That's how she prolonged her life. At one time she was the only one that knew this, until they captured her and threw her into that fire. And then, as she was dying, she began to say these chants. And people began to listen."

"But, another part of it, what she would do is she would see kids playing," Sequoyah said. "And, she would disguise herself as an old woman. A kind-looking old woman. And she would sit there and watch them play for a little bit. Then she'd call one of the kids over and say, 'Here, let me fix your hair.' Or, 'Let me comb your hair.' But while she was doing that, while she had them distracted doing whatever she was doing with their hair, she would take that finger and cut that liver. So she was a mean, deceptive being."

After a moment, Woody said, "Which kind of, then again, parallelism to the Bible is, the witch getting thrown into the pit, just like it is said in the Bible that Satan will be thrown in the pit. But before that, you know, he'll be bound for a thousand years and he'll be released again for a short time. And that just kind of reminds me of the chants that she was saying. That he's still here, but then he'll meet his ultimate. And as far as the old witch, combing her hair, I've seen my daughters do that to each other. Braid them. Boy, they get relaxed. And then, next thing you know . . . she's deceitful," Woody continued. "This is the deceit that is perpetrated. What Satan does—the Devil, whatever you call him—is to get you in a relaxed state and the next thing you know, wham! You're either ensnared or something."

"Mmhm. Are those stories like that, like Stonecoat and Spearfinger, are they told today?" I asked.

"Not as much. They were actually told kind of individually to certain ones. Not told to a group," Hastings said.

"To teach someone?"

"Yeah, to teach just certain ones that had to be taught that. Not as a family unit. The young ones, they wouldn't tell you one of those. More as you got into maturity age."

"Adulthood. Yeah," Woody said.

"It was more of a . . . like the little ones won't watch war movies," Hastings said.

"And then when they get a little older, then they get . . . ," I said.

"The elders would watch you. They'd read you," Hastings said. "And they'd know who they can tell these to, and who they can't. Who would kind of learn it as a teaching tool and who would actually understand its deeper perspective and its fear. I mean, there's a point to be scared; there's a point to be cautious. So, not scared, but cautious."

"Mm. To be *aware*," Woody said.

"To be aware," Hastings echoed.

"Of the real nature of other individuals in a village, the community— maybe sometimes even your own home," Woody said. "There is a darkened nature about some things and some people. But through these stories, using witch and all these others . . . Spearfinger, you know, it could be attached to that person or another person. I've heard that story."

An Uk'tan

I picked up Sequoyah on a Saturday afternoon before a storytelling and we drove around his neck of the woods in Kansas, Oklahoma, and headed northwest up to Kenwood. Along the way we took some pictures at Spring Creek and stopped and got some pictures of the spot where Woody was hit while trying to catch the copperhead—the Four Corners of Kenwood.

Funny thing is, there are no corners directly around where he got hit, just straight pavement. But it was a crossroads, nevertheless.

Sequoyah and I drove into Kenwood and he showed me an old Cherokee Baptist church downtown where his father preached. While we were looking around, a friendly gentleman came out and offered to show us around the complex. We were shown the new worship center, complete with a videotaping platform at the back. It was a good-sized church. The little old church was very small in comparison to the concrete brick structure they now have. The old church is now used as a meeting area.

As we drove south toward Tahlequah to meet up with the others at the storytelling, Sequoyah told me the story of the Uk'tan that was seen by his father and several other men on the creek near the church.

"Well, my dad was there, but this is what Gramma told me," Sequoyah began. "She said they were having a quarterly meeting. And when they have a quarterly meeting on Sundays, in the afternoon they have a Lord's Supper and they have a potluck dinner. And so, everybody had ate and everything, but nobody really wanted to go home, so everybody was standing around talking and stuff.

"And, pretty soon they started hearing this sound. It was like a bull crying, way off. And it kept slowly getting closer and closer. And, there's a creek that runs near that church. But it doesn't flow all the time. But this time there was water there. I guess it had been raining quite a bit. So, anyway, that sound of the bull kept getting closer and closer. Then, some of the men thought, you know, it's probably a cow or a bull looking for its mate. And then, pretty soon, it just kept on making that noise. You know, that bawling and mooing, and just crying.

"Then, some of the men started thinking, 'Maybe it's a cow or a bull stuck in the mud,' 'cause there was a mud bog going down there. And so they decided to go out there and help it out. And so, a bunch of men went out there to go pull the bull out. It wasn't too much longer after that that they all came back. And they told everybody it hadn't been a bull at all.

"Now, this is what they said. They said they got down to the creek and they could hear the sound of the bull getting closer and closer. And, it was coming around a bend, and before it came around the bend they could see something like a light or like something was glowing that was coming around. And when it finally came around the bend where they could see it, they said it wasn't a cow or a bull. It was big old snake swimming in the water.

Uk'tan

"And they said that glowing was coming from its head. And when they looked closer, they noticed that there was this horn in the middle of its forehead. And that's what was glowing. And as it got closer and closer, they noticed that that was what was making that bull sound. The mooing or the bawling of the bull. It was coming from this snake. They said it swam right past them. And on the opposite side of the creek there was like a small bluff there, and just at water level there was a hole that went into that bluff. And they said that's where that snake went into.

"Now this was a pretty large snake. It wasn't just some little bitty ordinary water snake. This was a pretty large snake, they said. But that snake went into that hole and they said they could hear it crying as it went into the earth. It just kept getting fainter and fainter until finally it just faded away. So, anyway, that's what these men saw.

"But, I don't remember if Gramma said it was seven days or seven weeks, might even been seven years, but she said that within a period of seven something, all the men that had seen that snake had died. And so, I don't know if it was because they saw it or if that's what the Uk'tan was telling them. Because, historically, and culturally, and traditionally, when you see an Uk'tan or somebody sees an Uk'tan, you're not supposed to tell anybody for, like, seven years that you seen it. But these men had gone right back and told 'em.

"But, here's another thing. When people see an Uk'tan, it announces that there's going to be some kind of great event that's going to happen to the people, to the Cherokee or Keetoowah people. And it wasn't too long after these people saw this Uk'tan near the church that the Cherokee Nation started up again. It was like a few years later. I think they saw the Uk'tan in the late 60s. Probably '69 or something like that. And Cherokee Nation started back up, when, '72? '73? So, I believe that's what it was announcing to the world that was gonna happen. But, like I said, every time somebody sees an Uk'tan it announces that something big is going to happen.

"The first time it was seen, according to Gramma, there was these two boys. They liked to go fishing. The boys were friends, and their parents told them both, 'Don't go fishing in this one place in the river. You just don't go down there, no matter how good the fishing is down there.' But those boys knew that the men of the village where they lived usually went down to that one spot in the river to go fish. And, typical boys, they decided one day, 'Well let's go where everybody else goes fishing, because they always catch the biggest fish there and a lot of fish there. So let's go there and fish.'

And so they went and got a boat and they headed out for that one part of the river. And they were sitting out there in that part of the river and they were really catching a lot of fish, a lot of big fish. But, as they were sitting there in the boat fishing, these two boys, they heard this sound like a cow. Like a bull. I guess back then it would have been a bison. They kept hearing that as it kept getting closer and closer. Then pretty soon they started hearing this splashing sound like there was something really huge splashing out of the water. Now, all this was happening around a corner in the river, around the bend. And so the boys decided. Their curiosity got the better of them and they decided to go see what this was.

"And so, when they got closer to the being, these huge waves were coming towards them so they fought against the waves, rowing the boat closer to the bend. And when they got to the bend they could hear something mooing really loud. And the splashes were getting louder. And the waves were getting bigger. But, finally, those boys worked their way around the bend. And they said what they saw was a big old snake that was kind of like splashing around in the water. It would go in and then it would come back up, then it would go back in. And that's what was making that mooing sound, that cow sound. Again, they said it was a snake that had horns. The waves that the creature was making was so big that it knocked those boys out of their boat. And they hurried up and swam to shore. And it scared them so bad that they ran back to their village and they told their parents what they had saw. And, of course, they got into trouble because they were told not to go there. But, it wasn't too long after that, after those two boys had seen that big snake with the horns, Gramma said, it wasn't too long after that European contact was made."

"Mm."

"And so this happened hundreds of years ago. That was the first time the Uk'tan was ever seen," Sequoyah said.

"What about when the Uk'tan fought with . . ."

"Thunder and Lightning?"

"Mmhm."

"The Red Man?"

"Is that the same or different kind of Uk'tan?" I asked.

"It's the same; there isn't just one Uk'tan. Originally, the Uk'tan was a human being, a man. And, uh, I believe it was the Little People that turned him into an Uk'tan. They turned one man into an Uk'tan and another man into a rattlesnake. Their mission was supposed to be, I believe, was to kill the moon. They were sent by the sun. From what I remember, that story is the sun was jealous of the moon. 'Cause one day the moon said, 'You know, I love those people on earth, they look at me and they just look at me with love. So I just love them so much.' And the sun got made 'cause he said, 'Well, when they look at me they make all these funny faces. The squint and everything else. I don't like it.' And so the sun got jealous because they looked at the moon with love and adoring eyes. And the sun asked the Little People to help him out. He wanted to get rid of the moon. And so, they got this man, talked him into letting them turn him into a rattlesnake. And so, the plan was, when the moon came out that evening to travel across the sky, the rattlesnake was supposed to jump up and bite him. But it just so happened, the moon didn't come out that night. And the rattlesnake got tired of waiting on it so he just went away. Of course, the sun got mad because this rattlesnake hadn't done what he was supposed to do. So he asked the Little People again to help him out. And so the Little People talked another man into letting them turn him into this creature that we call the Uk'tan. The Uk'tan, or 'The Eye.' An Uk'tan's supposed to look like a big old snake. And it has horns. Now, depending on who's telling this story, some people say it has horns like antlers, like a deer. And other people say it has horns much like a cow, like a bull. Of course, they all agree that the Uk'tan has one single horn in the middle of its forehead. And this horn is supposed to be a crystal. A crystal horn. Now, down the middle of that crystal there's supposed to be a blood-red streak, running straight down the middle of it. And it's supposed to be the most desired piece of artifact that medicine people would like to have. Because it has great medicine. Apparently, the last known horn that was had was a medicine man back in the old country had one. But, I forget if he moved here to Indian Territory and gave it to somebody, or they gave it to somebody and they moved here to Indian Territory. But it wound up here in Indian Territory."

"Hm."

"And, uh, they were under instructions where they were supposed to keep it hidden. And, uh, they were supposed to keep it in a sack and they were supposed to feed it blood every so often. And if it didn't get blood every so often it would come out and go hunt on its own. And so, the man who had it here in Oklahoma, he hid it in a cave and whenever he needed help from that crystal horn he would go to that cave and get whatever help he wanted. And he would always bring a blood offering to it.

"Well, of course, you know, the man died and . . . the horn, not getting any blood from this man, came out a few times and went out and got blood on its own. But, after a while, it became dormant. It went to sleep. And nobody knows where that cave is. And, supposedly, that crystal horn is there to this day. Still in that cave. Sleeping. Waiting for somebody to find it. But anyway, that's what an Uk'tan looks like. So. It's a snake with horns and then it has the crystal horn. And some people say that it kind of looks like a bull. Its head does."

"And its scales . . ."

"Yeah, there's scales. I believe there's seven rings near its neck. And some people say it has feathers behind its head. And some people even said that the Uk'tan can fly. I remember hearing some stories that the Uk'tan can fly. I don't know how true that is. There's only one way to kill an Uk'tan, and I believe you're supposed to shoot an arrow in its belly around either the third or the fourth ring of the Uk'tan. But only if you're lucky to get that close, because to smell an Uk'tan it will make you deathly sick. To see an Uk'tan, of course, is almost certain death. And as far as I know, there's only one person that has been able to kill an Uk'tan, and he wasn't even a Keetoowah or Cherokee. He was a Shawnee medicine man. And I forget exactly how he done it, but this Shawnee medicine man was the only person that killed an Uk'tan.

"But, the last time I heard anybody seen one was back in 1998, and it was seen by a couple of boys that were fishing on the Illinois River. And they saw a log come floating down. It was kind of across the river and it was floating down, going with the flow. And they didn't really pay much attention to it. But that log went so far, and then it turned around and started coming back up against the flow of the river. Coming toward them. And they said they could see what they thought was branches sticking out at the front of the log that was coming toward them. Then they realized it was horns sticking out of the water. And those boys left and went home and told their mom and dad and they all went back to the river but there was nothing there. I believe the Uk'tan was heralding the last fullblood, cultural, traditional person to hold an office at Cherokee Nation. And that was Deputy Chief Hastings Shade. And so, that's what I think this Uk'tan was telling everybody. Because, like I said, every time somebody sees an Uk'tan something big happens. Something enormous happens. Great. And it doesn't necessarily have to be a good thing. But they're telling something, these Uk'tans. And, I believe other tribes have their version of the Uk'tans, too. These creatures are still around."

Our Own Council House

At our final meeting to go over the manuscript, Sammy, Sequoyah, Woody, and I reflected on the book we'd created with Hastings. At the time we began recording the stories, the creation of a book was a distant goal. Now, a few short years later, we had gotten word from the University of North Carolina Press that they wanted to publish *Cherokee Stories of the Turtle Island Liars' Club*.

"It's kind of overwhelming," Woody said. "Like, 'Wow, this is really going to happen.'"

"It really is exciting," I said. "And so, it is going to happen. But the challenge is, I feel a tremendous weight of responsibility." I laughed. I'd been thinking about how folks would react to the book. I knew there were some who would like it and some who would not; that's the nature of things. The book had come together as a collaboration, not just with the Liars' Club but also through the counsel I had found with family, friends, and colleagues. All of these voices became part of the story. "But I've worked with you all, and we shaped it," I said. "I just feel like, if I stick to the integrity of what I've been taught . . ."

"Well, you know, everyone's here for a purpose," Woody said.

"Mmhm," Sequoyah agreed.

"Everyone has gotten together under the auspices of God, knowing today, yesterday, but also the future." Woody paused a moment, then said, "Just a thought came to mind, like, when you said . . . I consider you, and I know Sequoyah and Sammy do, consider you a member of the Liars' Club, if he hasn't told you."

"No," I said. I'd never thought of myself in that way, and I was taken aback.

"You just mentioned your contribution. You have your talent and you're placed here by the Creator to be a part of the group. So, it just kind of flashed in my mind. It's kind of like when I told Sequoyah, 'I'm not a storyteller! You guys are the storytellers!' Yet they keep saying, 'You're a storyteller, too!' But I just have different kinds of stories."

"I'm a story lover!" I said and laughed. But I also have my stories, as we all do.

"That's interesting what you just said that Chris is a member," Sequoyah said. "Uh, I just never thought of it that way I guess." He laughed. "But you *are*. I just never thought of it that way."

"He just got his foot in the door; he's not standing there," Woody joked. "More than that, you know. You're *opening* the door. You're . . . I guess in our own way, we are our own council house. Every one of us are. You know? In our own spirits and soul."

"Mmhm."

"But, you know, you're being used by the Creator to help open the door to the council house, for others to see and to . . . unfortunately, we won't be around forever, but the books will and the words, you know?"

"Yeah," Sequoyah said.

"So that's the opening of the door."

Afterword Standing in the Middle

I arrived late into Cherokee, North Carolina, and took a hotel room along the Oconaluftee River across from the Museum of the Cherokee Indian. It was early September 2010, and Sequoyah and Woody would be representing the Liars' Club this weekend at the Southeastern Tribes Festival hosted by the museum and the Eastern Band of Cherokee Indians. They'd called me from the road earlier and were now somewhere in Tennessee. I looked forward to catching up with them and talking with them about how the book was coming together. I had stories to share of my life in Victoria, British Columbia, where I'd moved my family recently to teach indigenous literature at the University of Victoria. I was sure they'd have stories to share as well.

I spent the evening alone in Cherokee, and after visiting the casino I headed back to the motel and sat in a rocker watching the gently flowing Oconaluftee. Though I've lived in the Smoky Mountains for only a year of my life, they remain a homeland for me. They are the original Cherokee homelands, the place we settled after our long migration from the island surrounded by water one could not drink. This is the land Cherokees commonly refer to as the "old country," and it remains central to Cherokee peoplehood. I remember the elation I felt when I first visited the Smokies with my brother, Sean, many years ago. High up on the Appalachian Trail, it suddenly dawned on me that as far as I could see, this was our land, not another people's. Everywhere else I'd lived in America had been on another Native people's homeland. Here, I was free to imagine my connection to this place. And this, I experienced, was what it truly meant to be home. I grew healthy during my time in the mountains. I quit smoking and began running. Our daughter, Azalea, was born near the banks of the New River.

Driving up from Atlanta earlier in the evening, my anticipation for home grew. There were friends to see and new people to meet. And I'd have time to reconnect with the mountains and rivers. But though I was excited for the weekend in Cherokee, the strip malls, gas stations, and exclusive resorts I passed, all modern trappings of American life, filled me with sadness and anger for this corruption of our Cherokee homeland. How many lives were lost in the struggle to settle this place? These were the things I thought about as I rocked late into the evening having a conversation with Long Man, the river.

The next morning Sequoyah and I sat on a bench in Cherokee and I shared with him my thoughts of the night before. He said he felt something similar whenever he goes back to the old country. It's a bittersweet homecoming, one involving the simultaneous recognition of change, separation, and continuity with a land, a history, and a people.

Later in the day, one would not register such somber thoughts in the presentation of the Turtle Island Liars' Club. I sat with the audience in the outdoor amphitheatre and watched my friends and elders entertain and educate us with stories—today, of the humorous type. There were no stories of the wondrous, or of our origins as a people. Instead, the Liars' Club kept it light for this audience of fellow southeastern Native and non-Native folks alike. And as they took turns telling lies and introducing one another, I realized again how much of a privilege it has been for me to spend these years working with and learning from the Liars' Club. These folks at the festival were only offered a glimpse of the club, just enough to pique their interest in Cherokee oral tradition. The book we'd created would represent the *sgadug* that truly is the Turtle Island Liars' Club. And if the stories are read and considered, they may open a door for readers who are simply curious about Cherokee tradition or who are seeking knowledge of what Hastings called the middle way.

Like any *sgadug*—any living community—the Liars' Club has changed over time. As we discussed the manuscript, Sammy, Sequoyah, Woody, and I would often remark how we could remember the times we were reading about. Life builds story, and in our time working on this book we became part of each other's lives, each other's story. We looked back fondly at our time with Hastings and how he anchored the group. Recently, Woody told me that Hastings was the glue that held them all together. Since his passing the friends see each other less and less, and only time will tell what the future holds for the Liars' Club.

But in the time we have together on this middle world, may we remember and share the teachings and stories we've learned from our elders and from each other. May we welcome each other in, seek balance, and continually renew the relationships that shape us. May we care for one another, as an elder once told me, like a mother loves her child.

GV

ZᏭᎣ

Acknowledgments

The members of the Turtle Island Liars' Club would like to thank their families, friends, elders, and members of the Cherokee community for their love, wisdom, strength, and guidance. Over nearly twenty years, the club has been supported by many organizations and has had the opportunity to share its members' knowledge with schools, groups, and audiences across the continent. They wish to thank those who supported them and attended their storytellings and events, especially the younger people, whom they hope will carry the stories and teachings forward. Finally, they wish to thank Creator for the blessings they've received throughout their lives.

In addition, I would like to recognize the many people and organizations that enabled me to write *Cherokee Stories of the Turtle Island Liars' Club*. Fernando Guzman of the University of Denver Center for Multicultural Excellence provided funds for travel from Denver to Oklahoma. I want to thank Dr. Guzman and the CME for the generous funding of my work. The University of Denver Department of English and Division of Arts, Humanities, and Social Sciences also were instrumental in providing the time and funding necessary for me to research and write. I would like to thank Ann Dobyns, Clark Davis, and Dean Anne McCall in particular for their assistance.

A key moment in the creation of *Cherokee Stories of the Turtle Island Liars' Club* came on an early spring afternoon in 2009 when I received a call from James F. Brooks, Director of the School for Advanced Research in Santa Fe, New Mexico, who on behalf of SAR offered me the Katrin H. Lamon Fellowship for 2009–10. I composed the first full draft of this manuscript during the nine months I spent in residency at SAR, and I am certain that without the Lamon Fellowship this book would still be in its early stages. I want to thank the SAR staff members for their help with my work, and especially James F. Brooks, John Kantner, Linda Cordell, Cynthia Chavez Lamar, Rebecca Allahyari, and Nancy Owen Lewis for cultivating such a vibrant intellectual and artistic community. I feel extremely fortunate to have shared nine months of camaraderie, friendship, and discussion with all the SAR fellows of 2009–10, but in particular with Sherry Farrell Racette, James A. Trostle, Lynn M. Morgan, Charles L. Briggs, and Clara Mantini-Briggs. Each of these friends helped me develop as a thinker and a writer, and I'll be forever grateful for our time together.

While in Santa Fe I became friends with Cherokee Nation artist America Meredith. Over lunch we'd have far-ranging conversations about the book and all things Cherokee. I want to thank her for illustrating the book with her beautiful art.

I also want to thank the staff of the University of North Carolina Press for their dedication to making this an exemplary book. From idea to text, Mark Simpson-Vos and UNC Press have ushered this project to completion with professionalism and aplomb. A crucial part of that process was finding excellent readers of the manuscript. I want to thank the readers for their useful feedback and suggestions. The book is much stronger for their care and expertise.

My friend and mentor, Craig Werner, of the University of Wisconsin Department of Afro-American Studies, was an ever-present source of wise guidance throughout the writing of this book. He read each draft of the manuscript, and when the book became too close for my eyes to see, he'd help me see it again. Thank you, Craig.

All of my family, but especially my wife, Melissa, my children, Markus and Azalea, and my brother, Sean, have come to know the words of the Liars' Club. My children have grown up listening to their stories. For the love and joy you all have brought to this journey with me, I want to say GV and that I love you.

Finally, I would like to thank the members of the Turtle Island Liars' Club, and especially Hastings Shade, Sammy Still, Sequoyah Guess, and Woody Hansen for entrusting me with their words and teachings. It has been a tremendous honor and pleasure to create this book with them. It is a greater honor to call them my teachers, friends, and elders.

GV

Works Cited

Acoose, Janice, Craig S. Womack, Daniel Heath Justice, Christopher B. Teuton, et al., eds. *Reasoning Together: The Native Critics Collective*. Norman: University of Oklahoma Press, 2008.

Basso, Keith. *Wisdom Sits in Places: Landscape and Language Among the Western Apache*. Albuquerque: University of New Mexico Press, 1996.

Duncan, Barbara R., ed. *Living Stories of the Cherokee*. Chapel Hill: University of North Carolina Press, 1998.

Evers, Larry, and Felipe S. Molina. *Yaqui Deer Songs, Maso Bwikam: A Native American Poetry*. Tucson: University of Arizona Press, 1987.

Guess, Sequoyah. Interview with Chris Teuton. "Scary Stories: An Interview with Traditional Keetoowah/Cherokee Storyteller, Novelist, and Filmmaker Mr. Sequoyah Guess." *Mississippi Quarterly* 60, no. 1 (2006–7): 151–77.

Hurston, Zora Neale. *Mules and Men*. Philadelphia: Lippincott Publishers, 1935.

Kilpatrick, Jack F. and Anna G. *Friends of Thunder: Folktales of the Oklahoma Cherokees*. Norman: University of Oklahoma Press, 1964.

Momaday, N. Scott. *The Way to Rainy Mountain*. Albuquerque: University of New Mexico Press, 1969.

Mooney, James. *Myths of the Cherokee*. New York: Dover, 1900.

———. *The Swimmer Manuscript: Cherokee Sacred Formulas and Medicinal Prescriptions*. Edited by Frans M. Olbrechts. Washington: Government Printing Office, 1932.

Teuton, Christopher B. *Deep Waters: The Textual Continuum in American Indian Literature*. Lincoln: University of Nebraska Press, 2010.